Renaissance Drama and Contemporary Literary Theory

From the same publisher:

Shakespeare and the Loss of Eden	*Catherine Belsey*
A Shakespeare Reader	*R. D. Brown and D. Johnson*
How to Study a Renaissance Play	*Chris Coles*
Six Renaissance Tragedies	*Colin Gibson*
Shakespeare: Texts and Contexts	*Kiernan Ryan*
Webster and Ford	*Rowland Wymer*

Renaissance Drama and Contemporary Literary Theory

Andy Mousley

First published 2000 by
MACMILLAN PRESS LTD
Houndmills, Basingstoke, Hampshire RG21 6XS
and London
Companies and representatives
throughout the world

ISBN 0–333–69458–9 hardcover
ISBN 0–333–69459–7 paperback

A catalogue record for this book is available
from the British Library.

This book is printed on paper suitable for recycling and made from fully managed and sustained forest sources.

10   9   8   7   6   5   4   3   2   1
09 08 07 06 05 04 03 02 01 00

Printed in Hong Kong

Published in the United States of America by
ST. MARTIN'S PRESS, INC.
Scholarly and Reference Division,
175 Fifth Avenue, New York, N.Y. 10010
ISBN 0–312–23173–3 (cloth)
ISBN 0–312–23174–1 (paper)

For Debbie and Dan and my parents

Contents

Acknowledgements

I would like to thank Makiko Minow-Pinkney and Janet Lewison for their comments on draft chapters and for talking through with me some of the subjects discussed in the book. John Peacocke has also been badly exploited as a sounding board. A long-standing source of both tangible and intangible inspiration has been Bernard Sharratt and the books of Bernard Sharratt. Thanks, also, to Margaret Bartley for her unwavering support and to Bolton Institute for granting me study leave. The gratitude that comes with bottles of Cava and much love is to Debbie, who has helped me in all ways. The gratitude that comes with summer games is to the incommensurable Dan.

By thanking these people, I don't mean to incriminate them: the book's foibles are mine.

Introduction

The aims of this introduction are to identify the differences that modern literary theory has made to literary studies, and to explore the continuities which also exist between old and new critical approaches. Having offered an overview of literary theory's challenges, shortcomings and complex relationship with its main predecessor, humanism, the rest of the book will be devoted to examining specific theories in detail, tracing their similarities and dissimilarities, and putting them into practice.

LOVE *OR* THEORY?

To be paid to read, teach and write about literature might be thought a labour of love. People still speak, after all, of having a 'love' of literature, a passion for reading, as though the relationship that can form between a reader and a text is every bit as intense and meaningful as an actual relationship. The feminist critic Hélène Cixous believes that literary criticism should originate in love:

> Everything begins with love. If we work on a text we don't love, we are automatically at the wrong distance. This happens in many institutions where, in general, one works on a text as if it were an object, using theoretical instruments. It's perfectly possible to make a machine out of the text, to treat it like a machine and be treated by it like a machine. The contemporary tendency has been to find theoretical instruments, a reading technique which has bridled the text, mastered it like a wild horse with saddle and bridle, enslaving it. I am wary of formalist approaches, those which cut up structure, which impose their systematic grid.[1]

Cixous places before us a fairly stark choice: between love and theory, between intimate and impersonal ways of reading. We shall need to think carefully about Cixous's characterisation of theoretically informed reading as loveless and mechanistic, but

1

before doing so, I want to explore further the idea of reading with love, and locate it as an example of a humanist approach to literature. Humanism is the label that is often stuck on the kinds of literary criticism which were practised before the advent of modern literary theory, whereas anti-humanism is often tagged to modern theoretical approaches – witness Cixous's own image of theoretical 'instruments' clinically dissecting an object thereby rendered inanimate.[2] The labels contain some truth, but they are misleading in the way that labels often are. Not all theory is loveless. Not all theory is anti-humanist. Humanism and anti-humanism can mean different things. Anti-humanism is not necessarily a 'bad thing'. Humanism is not necessarily a 'good thing'. So let us begin by looking at some of the several things that reading with love, or reading from a humanist perspective, can mean.

HUMANIST LITERARY CRITICISMS

Cixous says that the text will treat us as we treat it: 'It's perfectly possible to make a machine out of the text, to treat it like a machine and be treated by it like a machine.' The corollary of this is that if we love the text, the text will love us back. Using the language of love that Cixous prefers to the language of machines, we might think of the literary text, not as 'object' of analysis, but as a kind of love letter, addressed to us, which draws us in by speaking intimately to us. A somewhat troubling example of someone reading in this way occurs in Shakespeare's *Twelfth Night*. The killjoy servant Malvolio is tricked into thinking that his mistress Olivia is in love with him through the ploy of a forged love poem and letter. The scene in which the deceived Malvolio reads the poem and letter is overlooked by his deceivers:

Malvolio. [*Reads*]
"I may command where I adore,
    But silence, like a Lucrece knife,
With bloodless stroke my heart doth gore.
    M. O. A. I. doth sway my life."
Fabian. A fustian riddle.
Toby. Excellent wench, say I.
Malvolio. "M. O. A. I. doth sway my life." Nay but first, let me see, let me see, let me see.

Fabian. What dish o' poison has she dressed him!
Toby. And with what wing the staniel checks at it!
Malvolio. "I may command where I adore." Why, she may command me: I serve her; she is my lady. Why, this is evident to any formal capacity. There is no obstruction in this. And the end; what should that alphabetical position portend? If I could make that resemble something in me! Softly, "M. O. A. I.".[3]

The amorous text calls to Malvolio, almost but not quite spelling out his name. In the context of a love poem, the written marks 'M. O. A. I.' are not coldly anonymous marks which he can take or leave. They are not designed to breed indifference. They are a hook, intended to involve. The letter is for him – or so it seems.

The phrase used by Malvolio – 'If I could make that resemble something in me!' – can serve as an aphorism for one way of thinking about a humanist conception of literature. From a humanist perspective, we might be thought of as reading, like Malvolio, to find ourselves lovingly mirrored in the text. The text is from this perspective an act of confirmation, it consolidates a sense of who we are. The pleasure of literature is thus the pleasure of *identification*. Identification depends upon a recognition of what is already supposed to exist, of what we already intuitively or subconsciously know (about ourselves, about the world, about others), but which the literary text makes explicit. Love, like reading, can make us captive, and perhaps part of being a captive audience or reader is based upon the idea that what we are seeing or reading is profoundly and intensely true to experience. The text, it seems, strikes a chord. We cannot help but be affected by a text, and get on intimate terms with it, because it speaks to us about who we are.

Humanist critics have often emphasised the notion that great literature communicates human truths. F. R. Leavis, for example, whose writing is often taken to exemplify an influential strand of twentieth-century humanist literary criticism, values literature for the human 'life' that it embodies. The 'impact' of T. S. Eliot's 'genius', according to Leavis, is its 'disturbing force' which makes it 'therefore capable of ministering to life'.[4] Another such humanist appeal to literature as the place where we recognise ourselves is the claim, made by Helen Gardner, a contemporary of Leavis, that 'Certain books, and certain ideas which we meet with in our reading, move us deeply and become part of our way of thinking because they make us conscious of the meaning of our own experience and reveal us to ourselves.'[5] It would not be difficult to find further examples, dating from various times before the advent of modern literary theory, of this type of humanist literary criticism, such is the influence which it has had on literary studies.

However, humanism is not monolithic. Identification with human life as we already think we know it is one way of thinking about humanist literary criticism. Another is to think about the text as a journey of exploration which takes us, not to the same places – the places we already know – but to new ones. Would our interest in the text, or love object, to revert back to the Cixous vocabulary, be sustained if the text was without an element of mystery? Malvolio *thinks* he can find himself in the love letter he reads, but he is not absolutely sure that his name is intended. The letter is a tease, inviting identification but also postponing it. So he ponders the letter, repeating its phrases, wondering whether he has read it aright. The letters 'M, O, A, I' form a secret hieroglyph, or 'simulation', as Malvolio himself calls them (II.v.139), which will not quite reveal their hidden meaning. If Malvolio's narcissism, his 'self-love', as Olivia refers to it (I.v.89), tells him that he is indeed the letter's addressee, then the slight element of doubt which nags him suggests that there might be something else that the letter is saying, something frustratingly but also enticingly beyond Malvolio.

Literature, according to a second humanist perspective, can enlarge and expand our consciousness, and take us out of ourselves (or further into them) on a journey of discovery. The discovery metaphor is used to describe the role of criticism in the following comment of A. E. Dyson:

> The critical forum is a place of vigorous conflict and disagreement, but there is nothing in this to cause dismay. What is attested is the complexity of human experience and the richness of literature, not any chaos or relativity of taste. A critic is better seen, no doubt, as an explorer than an 'authority', but explorers ought to be, and usually are, well equipped. The effect of good criticism is to convince us of what C. S. Lewis called 'the enormous extension of our being which we owe to authors'.[6]

Literature is still thought about in humanist terms, but the emphasis is now less on what we already know than upon the unknown depths and possibilities of the human. Humanist literary criticism can thus involve identification ('that's me!', 'that's the way the world is!') and/or exploration ('"the enormous extension of our being"', in C. S. Lewis's phrase). If reading as a humanist means reading with love, then various amorous scenarios may be said to be involved: the captive reader/lover who hangs on the text's/love object's each and every word and takes them to be profoundly 'true'; the reader/lover who is taken on a voyage of *discovery* by the text/love object and so further enamoured/captivated by that aspect of the love object/text which is enticingly 'other'. And so on.

The point of likening reading to loving is to emphasise the way that literature, within a humanist context, is supposed to *matter* to us in such a way as to become the site of intense emotional and psychological investment. It is difficult to ignore a love letter, especially when the love object – as has often been the case with literature – is placed on a pedestal: Dyson's words are written in reverence of the work of art; one of Leavis's phrases is 'intensely admire' – '*Salutation* . . . [is] a poem I intensely admire.'[7] Such reverence and admiration are based upon the supposed power of revelation of the work of art, and speak to the way literature has taken over from religion as a source of supposedly timeless truths, which guide and nurture. The word 'canon' was formerly a religious word, one use of which was to designate a list of authorised sacred texts. Transferred to a secular context, a literary 'canon' refers to a valued body of writing which, like a sacred text, is deemed to be permanently meaningful.[8] Given the continuing relevance of the great work of art, how can one fail to be deeply affected by it? How can one *not* be on intimate, loving terms with words which spell out our names?

I have spent some time reconstructing humanism for several reasons: first, because, in books of this kind, humanism is often treated quickly and/or dismissively and/or as an homogeneous concept; second, because the full impact of modern literary theory can only fully be appreciated via comparison with what came before it; and third, to indicate how humanist assumptions still inform the way people read and, to anticipate a later phase of my argument, still inform *some* versions of modern literary theory.

HUMANISM *VERSUS* ANTI-HUMANISM

What, then, is the difference which modern literary theory has made? The opposition to which Cixous appeals, between reading lovingly and reading theoretically, offers a way of articulating the difference in fairly strong, unequivocal terms. It will be useful to do this initially, because an exaggerated case is a clarified case and because modern literary theory and humanism *have* often been clear antagonists. However, the account will gradually be toned down and complexities dealt with.

Theory, as characterised by Cixous, may be thought of as intruding, like the father in psychoanalytic theory (see Chapter 4), upon the scene of intimate humanist communion between text and reader and issuing a series of anti-humanist commandments. If modern literary theory could be broken down into axioms then these might be them:

1. *Be suspicious of identification,* for identification seduces us into passive and uncritical acceptance of the way people supposedly are or the way the world supposedly is. One should instead question the identifications which a text is proffering by asking: what am I being asked to identify with, on what terms, and on behalf of what agenda? What am I, as a reader, being asked to feel and think? How is this text manipulating me? How is it *constructing* ideas about what it means to be a man or a woman?

2. *Do not treat language as transparent.* Language should not be treated as though it provided a transparent 'window' through which we are given an unobstructed view of human or other kinds of reality. Language should instead be closely interrogated for the assumptions about the world which are presented – as assumptions usually are – as 'true'. Consider again the metaphor – of exploration – which Dyson uses to describe the role of the critic: 'A critic is better seen . . . as an explorer than as an "authority", but explorers ought to be, and usually are, well equipped.' Is this not a rather colonialist metaphor which casts critics and writers alike in the role of heroic and independent pioneers who are seemingly unencumbered by social and historical determinations?

3. *Decentre the self,* for what is the 'self' that is so central to humanist discourses other than the product of history, language

and unconscious forces? Theory has regularly invoked the mighty triptych of Marx, Saussure and Freud to undermine the concept of the self as a free, autonomous and rational agent, thereby deflecting attention away from the self and on to historical and social determinations (Marx), language (Saussure), and unconscious forces (Freud).

4. *Purge your critical vocabulary of humanist terms.* Words and phrases such as 'life', 'ministering to life', 'first-hand experience', 'human being', 'enormous extension of our being', 'consciousness', 'genius', 'individual', 'insight into human nature' and 'intuition' have by and large been dropped by modern theoretical approaches in favour of 'structure', 'system', 'systems of meaning', 'linguistic and social codes', 'social and linguistic construction of identity', 'discourse' and 'inscription'. The precise nature of the shift in vocabulary which has taken place is exemplified in the displacement of the humanist word 'influence' by the post-humanist, theoretical term 'intertextuality'. Their meaning is comparable, 'intertextuality' referring to the way in which no text exists in isolation of other texts, but where 'influence' is suggestive of interpersonal or quasi-interpersonal contact between people, intertextuality rewrites influence as an impersonally linguistic or textual phenomenon which happens independently of human agents.[9]

These, then, are some of the founding axioms of modern literary theory. Cixous is thus in many ways correct: theory *is* loveless, depersonalising and anti-humanist, in that it breaks up that cosily intimate bond between admiring reader and admired text, and asks us to ask questions. It is reductive, however, to characterise the anti-humanism of theory in an entirely negative way (in the way that Cixous tends to, for example), for the anti-humanism of theory may be seen as its intellectual strength. In the place of identification, it puts critical consciousness. In the place of subjective involvement, it asks us to look beyond the individual to the determination of subjects by language, history and the unconscious. In the place of passive acceptance and/or reverential awe ('how true', 'that's so true to life'), it puts an active, questioning scepticism ('with what am I being asked to identify?', 'by what means is the text attempting to make me complicit with it?'). And in the place of subjective impressionism and intuition ('the writer seems to capture perfectly the natural rhythm of rural life'), it puts more precise as well as *attainable* technical and intellectual resources (the signifier and signified of linguistic theory, for example – see Chapter 1).

Modern literary theory *is* alienating, but alienation is no bad thing if it means becoming estranged from ways of thinking that have become so habitual that we no longer truly 'think' about them. The anti-humanism of modern literary theory can therefore be understood in positive as well as negative ways. Positively, theory encourages critical consciousness, scepticism, and technical/ professional expertise. Negatively, theory heralds the further professionalisation, now in a bad sense, of literary studies, and the domination of the impersonal, technical and technocratic language of theory over the more idiosyncratic and intuitive skills nurtured by humanist literary criticism.[10] The choice that Cixous places before us, between love and theory, humanism and anti-humanism, is still stark (in that it is still an either/or), but I have hopefully gone some way towards redressing Cixous's prejudice against theory, by outlining the advantages and disadvantages of *both* humanist and anti-humanist approaches. There should, now, be a sense of a genuinely difficult choice.

LOVE *AND* THEORY, HUMANISM *AND* ANTI-HUMANISM

The final complication to be added to this introductory narrative is to qualify, without completely dismantling, the stark opposition between the humanism of pre-modern-theoretical criticism and the anti-humanism of modern theory. As I suggested earlier, not all literary theory is anti-humanist, impersonal and loveless. Some theories are anti-humanist in some respects but not in others, or eschew one form of humanism in favour of another. This last point seems to me to be vital, for too often humanism has been taken to mean one thing only: namely, a theology of 'man' (the gender is deliberate) as a free, sovereign, rational agent, and autonomous centre of consciousness. *This* humanism has plenty of opponents in modern literary theory and has on numerous occasions been questioned and/or pronounced dead. Witness the following examples:

In our day, and once again Nietzsche indicated the turning

point from a long way off, it is not so much the absence or the death of God that is affirmed as the end of man.[11]

So I accept the characterization of aesthete in so far as I believe the ultimate goal of the human sciences to be not to constitute, but to dissolve man.[12]

linguistics has recently provided the destruction of the Author with a valuable analytical tool by showing that the whole of the enunciation is an empty process, functioning perfectly without there being any need for it to be filled with the person of the interlocutors.[13]

Common sense proposes a *humanism* based on an *empiricist–idealist* interpretation of the world. In other words, common sense urges that 'man' is the origin and source of meaning, action, and of history (*humanism*). Our concepts and our knowledge are held to be the product of experience (*empiricism*), and this experience is produced and interpreted by the mind, reason or thought, the property of a transcendent human nature whose essence is the attribute of each individual (*idealism*). These propositions, radically called into question by the implications of post-Saussurean linguistics, constitute the basis of a practice of reading which assumes, whether explicitly or implicitly, the theory of expressive realism.[14]

Unfortunately, and as some of these examples demonstrate, because the humanism which theory attacks is often taken to represent the whole of humanism, it becomes difficult to imagine any other kind. Certain varieties of modern literary theory can nevertheless be construed as humanist despite their own use of the term as a catch-all category.

If there are thus vital differences between humanist forms of literary criticism and their modern theoretical counterparts, there are continuities as well, depending on which texts are taken to be representative and how one reads them. Although it is very difficult, in many cases, to build bridges between the old and the new, there are still many other examples where continuities exist. So what kind of humanism is it that persists into the modern theoretical regime of literary criticism?

If I think of myself, in accordance with the type of humanism which theory has often attacked, as a language-independent and society-independent free agent, then there is not much reason for me to be overly concerned about language, society or history. If my conception of who I am does not seem to depend upon linguistic and social processes, then such processes will not seem to matter much. On the one hand, there is 'me', and, on the other, there are things such as language and history in which I may have a passing academic interest but which do not much detain me. It seems to me that while a good many literary theorists decentre the self and refocus attention upon language and history, some of them leave intact the opposition between psyche and society, or subject and signifier, by treating language and society as impersonal systems which have little or nothing to do with the psyche. The kinds of literary theory (for example, structuralism, formalism, and some varieties of Marxism and poststructuralism) that do this are unremittingly anti-humanist. However, there are other – feminist, historicist, psychoanalytic, and again Marxist and poststructuralist – inflections of literary theory which decentre the self while retaining a humanist dimension. They do both of these things at once by overcoming the psyche/society opposition and *writing the psyche back into society, language and history* at the same time as *writing society, language and history back into the psyche*. The subject is thus returned to language, history and society; and language, history and society are returned to the subject. If my conception of who I am takes into account my dependence upon linguistic, social and historical processes, I am much more likely to invest these processes with psychological and emotional meaning.

Reading with love, as though texts matter to us, was one of the great strengths of humanist criticism. The humanism which has survived within literary theory retains the notion that reading catalyses an intense and meaningful relationship between text and reader but broadens it. The intense encounter between text and reader acts as a model, as it were, for the rediscovered relationship between self and language, self and society, self and history. If literature was once the privileged site of an intense experiential encounter, then within some strands of modern literary theory, language, history and society now occupy that zone of intensity where we work out what we are. Language, history and society thereby become *expressive* instead of mute, inexpressive and/or impersonally indifferent to the subject.

MODERN LITERARY THEORY AND RENAISSANCE DRAMA

But why Renaissance drama? Why apply modern literary theories, in the sustained way that this book will, to Renaissance plays? One answer would be, well, why not? Theory would surely not have had the impact that it has had unless its insights were applicable to a range of texts, genres and historical periods. However, this answer strikes me as slightly unsatisfactory, for it smacks of that negatively mechanistic approach to texts so disliked by Cixous. It makes of theories a series of templates which can be superimposed on any text regardless – to put it in humanist terms – of its living, breathing, unique qualities. 'Have theory, will travel.' Thought of in this way, as a kind of globally valid credit card or passport, theory will get you access to anything and anywhere you want. From Renaissance drama to *Beowulf* to the Koran – everything can be processed through the machine of theory.

So how can Renaissance drama become a more active partner in this potentially unequal marriage? How can the *specificity* of Renaissance drama, and the further specificities of individual Renaissance plays be taken account of? It seems to me that Renaissance drama plays its own distinctive series of variations upon the conflicts and concerns which my introduction has been outlining – so much so that is tempting to think that the Renaissance is at least *one* of their places of origin. Take, as one famous example, the example of Hamlet and Hamlet's attitude towards what he refers to as the 'customary suits' of mourning:

> 'Tis not alone my inky cloak, good mother,
> Nor customary suits of solemn black,
> Nor windy suspiration of forc'd breath,
> No, nor the fruitful river in the eye,
> Nor the dejected haviour of the visage,
> Together with all the forms, moods, shapes of grief,
> That can denote me truly. These indeed seem,
> For they are actions that a man might play,
> But I have that within which passes show,
> These but the trappings and the suits of woe.[15]

A rift is opened here between signs and psyche, public and private, external displays of grief and internal feeling. Because signs are taken by Hamlet to be *in*expressive, he turns away from them into his 'own' interior world.

Hamlet's recoil from the visible world is one of many examples in the Renaissance and Renaissance drama of the dissociation of feeling from public life. Religious reformers, for instance, made their own, different contribution to the 'silencing' of external phenomena, by downgrading the mainly Catholic doctrine of justification by works and upgrading justification by faith. Works were thereby rendered less expressive of religious belief than the faith that supposedly came from within. The story of the disappearance of psyche from society is a complex one, far more complex than the brief discussion of these two examples suggests. They nevertheless serve to make the point that modern theory does not suddenly appear from nowhere, but is implicated in various, complex histories – it is again important to emphasise the plural – such as the one I have just gestured towards. To recognise some of the ways in which the concerns of the Renaissance/Renaissance drama anticipate some of the concerns of theory makes for a more equal, mutually illuminating relationship: theory is no longer the master machine which processes and illuminates texts, for the texts themselves now cast significant light upon theory.

The way in which this book therefore understands theories and the way they interrelate has not been reached in the absence of Renaissance drama. The plays have exerted considerable influence over the way in which I think theory and apply theory to them. Instead of using them as blank slates upon which theory may write what it will, the plays have in many ways cued the kinds of theory that seem appropriate to them. Incest in *'Tis Pity She's a Whore*, for example, cued psychoanalysis; the volatility of love in *A Midsummer Night's Dream*, and of self in *Hamlet*, poststructuralism; tragedy's preoccupation with foundations, structuralism; money in *A Shoemaker's Holiday*, Marxism. In these specific, and the more general ways outlined above, the drama has driven the choice as well as the understanding of theory.

1

Semiotics

Tamburlaine; The Knight of the Burning Pestle; Othello

In David Lodge's mischievously parodic novel, *Nice Work*, Robyn Penrose, 'Temporary Lecturer in English Literature at the University of Rummidge', attempts to educate her unlikely sexual partner, Vic, into the science or art of semiotics:[1]

> Ever the teacher, Robyn is, of course, trying to make a point, to demystify 'love'.
> 'I love you,' he says, kissing her throat, stroking her breasts, tracing the curve of her hip.
> 'No, you don't, Vic.'
> 'I've been in love with you for weeks.'
> 'There's no such thing,' she says. 'It's a rhetorical device. It's a bourgeois fallacy.'
> 'Haven't you ever been in love, then?'
> 'When I was younger,' she says, 'I allowed myself to be constructed by the discourse of romantic love for a while, yes.'
> 'What the hell does that mean?'
> 'We aren't essences, Vic. We aren't unique individual essences prior to language. There is only language.'
> 'What about this?' he says, sliding his hand between her legs.[2]

Vic does not give much thought to language. He has feelings and uses language simply to express those feelings. What could be more straightforward? Why the need to draw attention to something that he uses for simple descriptive or expressive purposes? If Vic thinks too little about language, then Robyn thinks too much about it. 'Do you think we could possibly stop talking

13

now?' asks Vic, in an attempt to stop Robyn from being what her professional interest in '"semiotic materialism"' encourages her to be:[3] namely, a self-conscious language user who takes very seriously the role that language plays in *constructing* reality. 'There is only language', says Robyn, meaning that language comes before reality rather than the other way round. Language, for Robyn, is something more than a simple medium of expression for feelings which *precede* it. Romantic love is first and foremost a 'discourse' which encourages us to have certain intense feelings about another person. Whereas for Vic, the feeling comes first and the words afterwards, for Robyn, the discourse comes first and the feeling after.

Robyn's attitude to romantic or any other sort of feeling is easy to parody (especially in the context of a bedroom scene) because feelings *feel* so much a part of us that to think of them as 'constructed' from outside seems counter-intuitive. The challenge of semiotics – a challenge which makes it vulnerable to parody – is to question intuition by treating what we might commonsensically have understood to be *intrinsic* as *extrinsic*. Vic assumes that 'I love you' originates from deep within him, but Robyn thinks that 'I love you' has its origins not in the individual psyche but in the discourse of romantic love.

Parody – as this chapter will go on to explore – can introduce a healthily sceptical distance between us and ideas which we may otherwise be in danger of taking too earnestly. But parody may also prevent us from making the effort of fully engaging with its objects of ridicule. It may be that *Nice Work* offers a useful warning about the anti-humanist excesses of semiotics in particular and modern literary theory in general, but the feeling of knowing superiority that parody can fuel may make us lazily dismissive of new (or now not quite so new) ideas. This chapter will itself sometimes take a sceptical attitude towards semiotics, but it will not always remain on the outside looking in at something which, seen through the lens of parody, may *only* appear comic.

LANGUAGE AND REALITY

Feelings are not the only reality of which semiotics doubts the language-independent existence. We also refer to *things* as though the things existed independently of the *words*. But things are partly the product of words. 'Oak', for example, is a name which we have invented to differentiate a certain type of tree from other types of tree on the basis of its leaf shape, size, texture of wood, and so on. But in another world – in another language – oak trees might be differentiated on another basis (according to the types of bird which nest in them, for example), or they might not be differentiated from other trees at all. Likewise, we refer to *concepts* as though they too preceded language. The parental morality at work in 'Don't you think it was unfair to take the toy Dan was playing with?' assumes that fairness is a given, universal concept which exists beyond and above any particular cultural, linguistic or parental mediation of it.

The idea that there is a world of feelings, things or concepts beyond the world of words and *to which those words simply refer* is a feature of what has sometimes been referred to as a *realist* epistemology or *realist* way of knowing. Within such an epistemology, language is viewed as a more or less transparent medium of expression for feelings, things or ideas which exist prior to it. The relationship of language to reality could be likened to the relationship of a servant to his/her master/mistress, reality being the prior and privileged phenomenon to which language should remain ideally 'faithful'.

When words fail to perform their 'duty' as names for independently existing objects, experiences or concepts, then they are likely to be called 'creative' or 'poetic' or 'lying', on the basis that these uses of language form special cases whereby words are given licence (at least in the case of poetry and works of art) to take leave of reality. The concept of a prior reality is in this way kept intact by conceiving of art as a form of temporary escape from it. Alternatively, we may locate art *within* rather than *outside* a realist epistemology by suggesting that art gives us access to 'higher' truths and realities than the ones we normally perceive. Either way, each of these views, of the artist as licensed liar on the one hand, or as gifted soothsayer on the other, contributes to a realist epistemology which understands the role of language to be the naming of an independent and prior reality. This influential way of thinking about the relationship of language to reality has a long pedigree in the West, though it is of course important to recognise that there have been many different inflections of the notion that reality has an existence which is independent of language.

The alternative, *constructionist* view is the view of semiotics, semiotics or semiology being the study of linguistic signs which places far greater emphasis upon the role language plays in *mediating* and *constructing* reality. Semiotics, which is often thought to have been invented *ex nihilo* by Ferdinand de Saussure but which has a number of other previous incarnations (for example, in classical and Renaissance theories of rhetoric, and in Indian philosophy), substantially upgrades language and downgrades the notion of a language-independent reality. It does so by showing how words do not simply mirror already existing realities. A semiotic view of time, for example, would argue that time does not naturally divide itself into weeks and years. These are artificial rather than natural divisions. The words 'year' and 'week' mediate reality; they construct our concepts of time. Rejecting the idea that language is 'a nomenclature: a list of terms corresponding to a list of things' as well as the notion that 'ideas already exist independently of words', Saussure develops a terminology which calls into question – rather than *totally* annihilates – language's contact with the supposedly independent realities of ideas, feelings and objects.[4] So the term *signifiant*, or signifier, which refers to the sound of a word (or in written language, to the physical mark a word makes on the page), and the *signifié*, or signified, which refers to the concept habitually associated with the sound, draw attention to the way meaning is created in and through language rather than by things, feelings or ideas supposedly external to it.

There are two related aspects of Saussure's discussion of the internal dynamics of language upon which I want briefly to focus in order to specify further the nature of Saussure's empowerment of language and disempowerment of the idea of an external reality. One is relatively uncontentious, the other less so. First, and fairly uncontentiously, Saussure claims that the relationship between signifier and signified, sound and concept, is arbitrary. 'There is no internal connexion' writes Saussure, 'between the idea "sister" and the French sequence of sounds *s-ö-r* which acts as its signal. The same idea might as well be represented by any other sequence of sounds.'[5] Language is, in other words, organised noise, and it is a matter of arbitrary linguistic convention that a concept should be represented by one kind of noise rather than another. There is no good reason why some noises, such as 'dog', should have meaning, while others, such as 'grosnump',

do not. The insistence upon the arbitrariness of the signifier encourages us to see that languages possess their own intriguingly
different realities. It motivates the question: would my outlook
on life be different had I grown up using a different set of organised noises?

This question leads to the second, more contentious – and
already touched upon – feature of Saussure's theory of language,
namely the suggestion that not only is the signifier a matter of
convention, but the signified is likewise the product of linguistic
and cultural convention. That is to say, the signified or concept
does not obey any transcendent human principle or law. Concepts do not reside outside language as the mainstays and proof
of a universal human nature. Rather, concepts are produced from
within language and, as languages differ, so, too, do concepts.
To reiterate, reality does not, on this account, exist *outside* language. Language and reality are instead coterminous. To be
an English-speaking subject is to inhabit a different reality from
a French- or Hindustani-speaking subject. The absence of 'predetermined categories' leads Saussure to the conclusion that
'instead of *ideas* given in advance, are *values* emanating from a
linguistic system'.[6]

So. Language is now the master/mistress and reality is its
servant, for reality is determined/created by language.

Before drawing this section to a close, I want to consider some
of the implications, both positive and negative, of a semiotic view
of the world, and to suggest ways in which semiotic and realist
perspectives need not become polarised. Positively, semiotics lib-
erates us from all that is supposedly predetermined and fixed.
If we understand reality to be the product of changing human
conventions and sign systems, then those conventions and sign
systems may be changed once more to accommodate different
inscriptions of reality. From this perspective, the loss of predetermined categories – categories which precede language – is really
a gain. In the absence of any essential truths, we can ceaselessly
rewrite and reinvent ourselves and our realities. Thus understood, semiotics is of obvious value to political movements, such
as feminism and Marxism, which seek to change the world.

Negatively, semiotics can inspire – has inspired – a form of
pantextualism which maintains, in the often quoted phrase of
Jacques Derrida, that '*There is nothing outside of the text.*'[7] This
phrase echoes some of Saussure's own, more tentative, in my

opinion, disavowals of the existence of a reality external to language, while at the same time signalling a further move towards a complete textualisation of the real, a complete break with the stabilising influence which the world of ideas, things and feelings might once have had upon language. Sealed off from the constraints and limits implied by the existence of a pre-existing reality, language may seem disturbingly unanchored. It may also be the case that the extreme form of semiotics manifested in a rampant pantextualism is entirely appropriate to a world in which 'reality' has become increasingly virtualised through our dependence upon second-hand media representations of it. Can we really grasp the reality of war by sitting in front of a TV and watching highly mediated and often sanitised representations of it? The 'real', writes Jean Baudrillard, in partial celebration of the coming of the age of virtual realities, 'is no longer real', for contemporary reality is 'of the order of the hyperreal and of simulation'.[8] For Baudrillard, the 'real' Los Angeles is just as unreal as Disneyland:

> Enchanted Village, Magic Mountain, Marine World: Los Angeles is encircled by these 'imaginary stations' which feed reality, reality-energy, to a town whose mystery is precisely that it is nothing more than a network of endless, unreal circulation – a town of fabulous proportions . . . nothing more than an immense script and a perpetual motion picture.[9]

Emphasis upon the fabricated, textual construction of reality may not inevitably lead to Disneyland, but there is nevertheless a worrying connection between semiotics and contemporary capitalism's transformation of the world into a succession of disposable and ceaselessly mutating signs and simulations. If the world is a text which we can rewrite at will, then why shouldn't it be rewritten as a theme park?

The idea that the world is a blank slate upon which we can write what we will is one of the more disquieting aspects of a pantextualism overdosed on semiotics. As an extreme version of semiotics, pantextualism merely replaces one kind of hegemony (the hegemony of an external and unchangeable reality) with another (the hegemony of language). To counter these excesses we need to develop a more nuanced and open-minded approach which avoids the tendency of provocative insights to congeal through unthinking acceptance into formulae. The mediation of reality by language may be so thorough as to cause us to think that language *is* reality, but this should not blind us to the alternative possibility that language may sometimes be dictated to by a reality which exists apart from it. For example, the division of time through the use of the signifiers 'night' and 'day' seems to me to be much less *purely* arbitrary and conventional than divisions into weeks, months and years. This is because the linguistic differentiation between night and day appears to correspond to a difference in nature. The division into seasons is a more problematic case, for if on the one hand the division again seems to be motivated by natural differences, then on the other we could ask why we have just four as opposed to six or eight differentiating terms. Of course, global warming – 'sign' of the domination of nature by human culture, language and technology – may eradicate seasonal difference altogether. One of the reasons why pantextualists see constructed human signs and sign systems everywhere may have something to do with the ever more intensifying encroachment of the artificial into the natural.

The above examples suggest that semiotic perspectives emphasising the textual construction of reality and realist perspectives emphasising the extra-linguistic nature of the real need not – indeed should not – become totally polarised. It is possible and probably desirable to be mindful of both positions and/or to utilise insights from either one or the other depending on the nature of the intellectual task in hand. In the sections which follow, I shall try to maintain these delicate equilibria by developing a semiotic analysis of Renaissance theatre which is at the same time aware of that theatre's search for its 'real' identity.

SEMIOTICS IN SUMMARY

- As the study of signs and sign systems, semiotics poses a challenge to realist perspectives which overlook the role that language plays in shaping reality.
- Where some versions of semiotics (for example, Saussure's) call into question the existence of the *prior* reality of things and concepts, other more extreme, *pantextualist* versions (Baudrillard's, for example) more iconoclastically break the

(supposed) contact between language and a (supposedly) external reality by making of language and reality one and the same thing.

- The extremes of *pantextualism* are arguably the result of the increasing domination of nature by culture, 'first-hand' experience by 'second-hand' mediations of experience and reality by virtual reality.
- The total assimilation of reality to language may be countered by wedding semiotic to realist perspectives, thereby entertaining the possibility that language may sometimes be dictated to by external realities.

TOWARDS A SEMIOTICS OF THE RENAISSANCE THEATRE

Renaissance theatre is amenable to semiotic analysis because of its own intense preoccupation with the nature of theatrical signs: that is, with how and what theatre signifies. Unlike the signifiers 'night' and 'day' which could be said to take their bearing from nature, the theatre has no such obvious basis in either nature or metaphysics. This is especially true of the Renaissance theatre, which is a theatre in search of itself, a theatre whose complex and changeful semiotics do not easily lend themselves to one single all-encompassing categorisation. The Renaissance theatre does not have a settled *raison d'être*; it does not have a permanent physiognomy or foundation. There is no Platonic Idea of the theatre in the Renaissance. The one name or sign that the theatre may be thought of as going under is the sign of Proteus, Greek god of change and mutability.[10] This is hardly a sign which will allow us to think about the theatre as an *unchanging* concept. At the same time, I want to argue that the Renaissance theatre is itself concerned to transform its unstable and protean semiotics into 'something of great constancy . . . howsoever, strange and admirable'.[11]

The large, open-air arena playhouses of the Elizabethan period were the first commercial, purpose-built playhouses to be erected (or converted into theatres) in England.[12] Prior to 1567, the date of construction of the Red Lion, the first of these playhouses, the theatre had no fixed abode and took place mainly under the auspices of the Church or aristocracy, or on an occasional basis in market-places and inn yards. The year 1567 is thus something of a watershed, signalling as it does a moment when theatre becomes a commercial venture and occupies – at least potentially – its own autonomous or semi-autonomous space. Reinventing its religious and aristocratic heritage and unstintingly varying the metaphor of the world-as-theatre in the light of its own changing self-image, locations and clientele, the questions as to what kind of space the new theatres occupied and precisely how autonomous that space was receive very different answers in the plays of the Elizabethan and Jacobean period. Renaissance drama, in other words, stages a debate about its own identity. In semiotic terms, the Renaissance theatre is a signifier in search of a signified.

The construction of the Red Lion was succeeded by the building and/or conversion of numerous further amphitheatres such as the Theatre (1576), the Curtain (1577), the Rose (1587), the Swan (1595), the Globe (1599), the Fortune (1600) and the Hope (1614). It has become commonplace to distinguish these large 'public' theatres, in which adult acting companies would play before mixed audiences, from the smaller, more intimate and socially exclusive 'private' theatres worked by boy actors drawn from the choir and grammar schools connected to St Paul's cathedral and the Chapel Royal at Windsor.[13] The company of boy actors re-established in 1600 in the private Blackfriars playhouse *did* no doubt intensify the competition which had begun in 1576 between the public and private theatres. To demarcate too rigidly, however, between the semiotics of the private and public theatres would be to ignore some of the continuities which existed between them, as well as to overlook the contestation of the meaning of theatre which takes place often within a single play.

There are three main headings under which I shall consider the semiotics of the Renaissance theatre. These are: *the illusionist theatre of spectacle, the anti-illusionist theatre of human judgement* and *the theatre of irony and ventriloquism*.[14] These are three of the ways – there are undoubtedly more – in which I see theatre as signifying during the Renaissance. The relationship between these conceptions of theatre is complex: sometimes they work together, sometimes they part company. The following sections will explore in detail the full meanings and implications of these categories, as well as the nature of their changing relationships.

TAMBURLAINE

Christopher Marlowe's *Tamburlaine Part I* (1587) and *Tamburlaine Part II* (1588) were both first performed in the Rose public theatre which had itself only opened in 1587. *Tamburlaine* could therefore be seen as the equivalent of an inaugural speech: an early and celebratory defining statement for the third of London's new public theatres.[15] What kind of theatre is *Tamburlaine* attempting to consecrate?

Early on in *Tamburlaine Part I* the humbly born protagonist discards his shepherd's weeds and dons instead the signs and symbols of martial hero. The words which accompany the action and which are addressed to the captive but soon amorously inclined Zenocrate, are themselves a kind of inaugural statement about what it means to be an actor:

> I am a lord, for so my deeds shall prove,
> And yet a shepherd by my parentage.
> But lady, this fair face and heavenly hue
> Must grace his bed that conquers Asia,
> And means to be a terror to the world,
> Measuring the limits of his empery
> By east and west, as Phoebus doth his course.
> Lie here, ye weeds that I disdain to wear!
> This complete armour and this curtle-axe
> Are adjuncts more beseeming Tamburlaine.
> And, madam, whatsoever you esteem
> Of this success, and loss unvalued,
> Both may invest you empress of the East.
> And these, that seem but silly country swains,
> May have the leading of so great a host
> As with their weight shall make the mountains quake,
> Even as when windy exhalations,
> Fighting for passage, tilt within the earth.[16]

For a few moments Tamburlaine is caught between old and new identities; he is neither quite one thing nor the other, neither shepherd nor soldier. He is, in other words, like an actor readying himself for a role he is about to assimilate. The speech partly reinforces this sense of hiatus, for Tamburlaine is not yet the world-beater he promises to become. The sense that Tamburlaine is momentarily neither/nor or both/and defines one crucially important aspect of the semiotics of Renaissance acting. The plays of the period, particularly after *Tamburlaine*, never tire of drawing attention to the idea of the actor as a divided being, whose identity as an actor is still partly or wholly visible through the role he is adopting. Renaissance acting, to generalise for a moment, is precisely this mixture of illusionism and anti-illusionism, engagement and disengagement, pretence and the laying bare of pretence. It is a mixture which is largely appropriate to the theatrical conditions of both private and public theatres. For these were theatres in which one could see and probably talk to one's fellow spectator(s) during performances, in which the boundary between actors and audience was fluid because of the lack of proscenium arches and of darkened auditoria, and in which fixed scenery establishing once and for all the illusion of a particular location is also absent. Illusionism is thus sporadic rather than permanent; and roles can be put on and put off as a way of involving the audience in metatheatrical debate about the significance of theatre and acting.[17]

But *Tamburlaine* is not *Hamlet* or *As You Like It* or – to anticipate a later section of this chapter – *The Knight of the Burning Pestle*, plays (to name but a few) whose metatheatrical element is unavoidable. Tamburlaine's speech does not generate, as it does in any number of later plays, a discussion about theatre and/or a profusion of world-as-theatre metaphors. It would be tempting to suggest that self-consciousness and metatheatricality are the features of an ostensibly more sophisticated theatre which the later private playhouses will not exactly monopolise but will nevertheless specialise in. The corollary would then be to suggest that a play like *Tamburlaine* appeals to an unsophisticated popular taste for straightforward illusionism. However, I want to avoid making such assumptions about popular taste (the term 'popular' is itself a signifier to which a variety of signifieds can be and have been attached), by suggesting that Tamburlaine's avoidance of an overly self-conscious dramatic idiom is partly the point of the play. The moment between Tamburlaine's identities as shepherd and soldier opens a gap which is immediately closed by his embrace of the idea of an absolute self-transformation. For what Tamburlaine wants us to forget, suppress and leave behind are all of the barriers (such as a metatheatrical discourse might create) between ourselves and our desire to imagine ourselves otherwise. Tamburlaine is creating himself anew, as legend, icon, star. And the image of the theatre appropriate to such a project – an image which he anxiously tries to maintain over two plays – is of the theatre as the space of spectacular, uninhibited transformation. This, then, is the *illusionist theatre of spectacle*.

Through its central protagonist the play creates a potent image of the theatre as the site of alternative possibility and unleashed imagination. Intent upon the *achievement* of prestigious identity – 'I am a lord, for so my deeds shall prove' – Tamburlaine shows how identity is a matter of self-belief, rhetoric, imagination and strength of mind rather than inherited titles. Signs and symbols of aristocratic and other forms of identity can therefore be appropriated by the individual with the capacity to imagine himself in the role of another, and what is theatre, according to the image of it which Tamburlaine is seeking to maintain, if not the art of successful impersonation? Writing of the influence of carnival upon theatre, Michael Bristol suggests that the 'participatory masquerades [of carnival] permit people to "put on" new social roles, to borrow the clothing and the identity of someone else, and to adopt the language and manners of a different social status'.[18] *Tamburlaine* seems to fit this image of carnivalesque theatre.

Such, then, is the nature of the *illusionist theatre of spectacle* in which men and women can transform themselves by borrowing the identities of others. But what is it, precisely, that Tamburlaine is borrowing? What is the specific nature of his adopted identity? There are two related aspects of Tamburlaine's appropriated role which I want to explore: one is his borrowing of *religious iconography*, the other is his use of what might be called an aristocratic form of *publicity*. Publicity is the term Jürgen Habermas uses to describe that form of – usually aristocratic – public life dominated by the inseparability of authority from the personal charisma and aura of particular individuals. To caricature the position of the aristocratic a little, a lord is a lord not by virtue of what he *does* (mending roads, writing books, being kind to animals) but by virtue of his innate specialness. Habermas contrasts aristocratic publicity, based upon image and charisma, with the later (half-realised) ideal of public life embodied in a bourgeois public sphere based upon reason, debate and the requirement that social systems properly justify themselves.

One of the several mutations of the concept of publicity cited by Habermas is the decline of the aura and status of the 'independent feudal nobility' and the concentration of 'publicity of representation . . . at the prince's court'.[19] Such centralisation of aristocratic publicity was enabled by the monarchial use of religious iconography referred to above. Following the Reformation and its destruction of religious images as signifiers of Popish superstition, religious iconography was appropriated to secular purposes to elicit greater veneration of Elizabeth I as head of a sanctified body politic. An example cited by Leonard Tennenhouse is Elizabeth's renewal of the practice 'initiated by her father and continued by her brother which installed the royal coat of arms over the chancel arch of the churches of England'. Her 'coat of arms', continues Tennenhouse, 'thus replaced the religious images which had been condemned in the iconoclastic reform of the English Church. . . . As the church came to house the secular emblems of state, the queen's sexual body acquired the power of a religious image.'[20]

The monarchial monopolisation of aristocratic publicity achieved through the reinvention and reapplication of religious imagery was not absolute, however, for aristocratic charisma and religious veneration were appropriated to a variety of purposes. Witness Tamburlaine and the image of the theatre which Tamburlaine represents as the place where both aristocratic publicity and religious iconography can be further transformed and appropriated. Thus the lowly shepherd Tamburlaine becomes the object of religious veneration and his every body part and body movement lovingly invoked:

Of stature tall, and straightly fashioned
Like his desire, lift upwards and divine.
So large of limbs, his joints so stringly knit,
Such breadth of shoulders as might mainly bear
Old Atlas' burden. 'Twixt his manly pitch,
A pearl more worth than all the world is plac'd,
Wherein by curious sovereignty of art
Are fix'd his piercing instruments of sight,
Whose fiery circles bear encompassed
A heaven of heavenly bodies in their spheres,
That guides his steps and actions to the throne
Where honour sits invested royally.

Pale of complexion, wrought in him with passion,
Thirsting with sovereignty and love of arms,
His lofty brows in folds do figure death,
And in their smoothness amity and life.
About them hangs a knot of amber hair,
Wrapped in curls, as fierce Achilles' was,
On which the breath of heaven delights to play,
Making it dance with wanton majesty.
His arms and fingers long and sinewy,
Betokening valour and excess of strength.
In every part proportion'd like the man
Should make the world subdu'd to Tamburlaine.

(II.i.7–30)

The experience of Tamburlaine is akin to the self-cancelling experience of infatuation. Lost in admiration, Menaphon, the speaker, gives himself up to Tamburlaine, ceding all authority to this superior being who rules not by virtue of the enlightened political ideas he has about the class struggle or the advantages of living in a liberal bourgeois democracy, but by virtue of the charismatic presence which exudes from every pore of his body. On this reading, the play stages desire, not dialogue; its erotic, aestheticised politics disarm rational and any other kind of judgement. Tamburlaine is not in the play to catalyse debate about the limits of authority. Tamburlaine is to die for. As super-human demigod, he also demands immunity from ordinary human judgement and perception. If a demigod calls for mass human sacrifice then so be it, for it is not for us to reason why but to admire.

Aristocratic publicity thus combines with religious iconography to produce Tamburlaine as an object of desire and veneration capable of eradicating all existing loyalties to established figures of authority, whether secular or divine. Such is the power of theatre in the age of its partial autonomy to extend the possibilities of consecration and publicity to ordinary mortals.

So much, then, for a theatre whose semiotics can be *generally* understood in terms of illusionist spectacle whereby the actor successfully appropriates and maintains the illusion of an identity not necessarily his own, and *specifically* in terms of Tamburlaine's carnivalesque appropriation of aristocratic publicity and religious iconography. However, as I have already implied, *Tamburlaine* the play is and is not synonymous with its central character. It is and is not reducible to the protagonist who seeks to make the play and semiotics of playing entirely his own. So let me now move on to explore further that version of theatre semiotics which I referred to earlier as *the anti-illusionist theatre of human judgement*. What I shall be looking at in detail here is the way in which the play encourages scepticism, judgement and a degree of suspicion of the illusionist theatre.

Leonard Tennenhouse's discussion, in *Power on Display*, of the post-Reformation reinvention of religious iconography is a useful corrective to the view that Protestantism was a religion of the book rather than of the image. Religious imagery did not suddenly stop with the demise of Catholicism. It was reoriented. Nevertheless, such proto-Reformation texts as Erasmus's *Praise of Folly* encourage a suspicion of external religious and aristocratic images and insignia which, insofar as they lack any corresponding internal, heartfelt foundation, become empty of meaning and inspire a merely superstitious or automatic reverence.[21] Tamburlaine's insistence that he is the man he professes to be, together with his desire to match words to action – 'Then shall we fight courageously with them?/Or look you I should play the orator?' (I.ii.128–9) – betrays an anxiety about the relationship of image to reality which is exploited in a play whose imagined reality is always in excess of what can be shown on stage. Menaphon's wonder-struck speech in praise of Tamburlaine is itself uttered in the absence of Tamburlaine. Does this mean that Menaphon is worshipping an image, or, to use Jean Baudrillard's terminology, a simulacrum whose contact with reality is severed? Is *Tamburlaine* making its audience, and now readers, aware of the dangerously enchanting power of word and image to create the world *ex nihilo*? Is it encouraging us to maintain a critical distance from the illusionist theatre?

These questions create a rather different play from the one that unambiguously celebrates the power of theatre to transform. Theatre instead exposes the lie of aristocratic publicity machines, and reveals Tamburlaine to be the victim of his own hype, slave to his own created self-image. In subduing the world to his increasingly tyrannical will, Tamburlaine becomes an ever more immovable object, incapable of change and unstirred by pleas for mercy: 'my customs', Tamburlaine announces to the Virgins of Damascus, 'are as peremptory/As wrathful planets, death, or destiny' (V.i.64–5). The decimation of Damascus inevitably ensues. Once the signifier of enlarged horizons and expanded consciousness, Tamburlaine's adopted role as lord instead comes to indicate the existence of a set script from which Tamburlaine cannot depart. The illusionist theatre of spectacular transformation has changed meaning to suggest Tamburlaine's *confinement* within his adopted role. The illusionism required to re-create oneself as another now signifies myopia and closure.

For Tamburlaine's performance to work – and carry on working – the various ways in which theatre can signify have to be suppressed. Alternatives, however, keep on suggesting themselves. These alternatives contribute to another kind of theatre semiotics, based upon the apprehension of a critical distance opening up between us and Tamburlaine's *single-minded* conception of theatre. Thus while Tamburlaine continually strives, in the name of an illusionist performance and an illusionist theatre, to close the gap between himself and the illusion of who he is, we, the participants in a more sceptical, anti-illusionist theatre, become increasingly aware of that very gap. What, for example, of the shepherd's 'weeds' which Tamburlaine 'disdain[s] to wear'? For how long do these reminders of his former self '[l]ie here' on the stage? The play may not make explicit use of a metatheatrical language, but a complicating awareness of a division between Tamburlaine and his 'adjuncts' (whether these adjuncts are shepherd's weeds or soldier's armour) is nevertheless sufficiently present to cause Tamburlaine to have to prove himself to himself again and again. I am not making the élitist point that a shepherd could not possibly know how to act like a general. What I am suggesting is that in order to control his destiny Tamburlaine has to control the semiotics of theatrical representation, such that his followers on stage and potential admirers off stage will be persuaded by the power of his illusionistic performance to propel him further into the desired role and make the illusionism ever more complete. However, for theatre to signify and only to signify as the space of spectacular and successful transformation – of actor into character, shepherd into war hero, stage into battlefield (plus whatever else the play and/or Tamburlaine imagine it to be), and audience into captive audience enthralled by Tamburlaine's performance – that other, anti-illusionist aspect of the Renaissance theatre has to be contained. How can this occur, though, when Tamburlaine's self-conscious casting off of one 'costume' and enthusiastic donning of another has the effect of partly *theatricalising* identity – in the sense now of *making each and every identity visible as a role?* Theatricalised identity no longer signifies identity as a charismatic spectacle but as a mere set of clothes, a temporary improvisation, the *illusion* of which is always incomplete.[22]

The Tamburlaine show is never so thoroughly wrecked, however, as to identify the play unambiguously as satire. Satire and irony are not *sustained* in the play. *Tamburlaine* is much too interested in the magic of theatre to be *continually* puncturing its own creations. Nevertheless, the two *Tamburlaine* plays increasingly qualify admiration for their star performer, so much so, that by the end of part II, the plays look as though they might be most aptly characterised as an extended study of tyranny. The theatre of spectacle and charisma thus partly gives way to a theatre which approximates a prototype of a Habermasian bourgeois public sphere characterised by debate, critical thinking and a sceptical attitude towards arbitrary and/or charismatic authority. Such is the *anti-illusionist theatre of human judgement.*

Surprisingly perhaps, religion itself contributes to this construction of theatre as a forum for critical debate/judgement, for although religion is used by Tamburlaine and his acolytes to create Tamburlaine as an object of veneration, it is not exhausted by this function. Tamburlaine may seek to be the sole interpreter of his own actions, and signify his constancy, for example, as a god-like strength of purpose (as opposed to a chronic and unpitying inflexibility), but the play frequently suggests the existence of a broader religious framework, a larger religious sign-system than the one invented by Tamburlaine. So, for example, Tamburlaine's stubborn refusal to listen to the entreaties of the Virgins of Damascus could be taken to imply an Old Testament wrath untempered by New Testament mercy. I use the word 'imply' advisedly here, for unlike numerous other Renaissance plays (including Marlowe's own *Dr Faustus*), *Tamburlaine* does not explicitly frame the play with a religious interpretation through the use of a stage-heaven and stage-hell, or presenters who moralise the action. The morality of the play is not given in advance of an action which, in dramatising the susceptibility of morality and religion to appropriation, raises questions about their metaphysical fixedness. In semiotic terms, one could say that morality is put into linguistic/dramatic process. Moral concepts and categories do not, in other words, precede or transcend the play as indisputably timeless verities. They are themselves subject to public debate by an audience involved in a process of attempting to clarify them and so retrieve a degree of moral certainty. In semiotic/metaphysical terms, this would mean reconnecting the linguistic world made arbitrary by Tamburlaine to a transcendent moral reality. If such a metaphysical reality exists beyond the contingent reality of language, then it is for the audience to discover or recover. As Edward Burns, in another context, usefully puts it, the 'god-like practices of judgement become the responsibility of a human audience, and a notion of theatre emerges in which human self-judgement – on an individual or social level – is the main dynamic of spectatorship'.[23]

To consolidate these last points: the religious judgement of Tamburlaine invited by the play suggests the existence of timeless moral truths against which to measure Tamburlaine's transgression of them. However, religious interpretation is not obvious due to the absence of stage-heavens, stage-hells and moral commentators. Judgement is therefore subject to the kind of debate which, according to Habermas, characterises the semi-enlightened bourgeois public sphere.

It would be tempting to suggest that this notion of an anti-illusionist theatre of human judgement combines with the notion of an illusionist theatre of spectacle to serve the Renaissance theatre with its most compelling self-image. *Tamburlaine* invites identification with the spectacular and transgressive self-transformation of its protagonist at the same time as it encourages us to redraw the lines and limits of acceptability. It is both a semiotic extravaganza in which Tamburlaine delights in the power of rhetoric to bring reality into being and an anxious study of the subservience of reality to rhetoric. Located somewhere between semiotics and metaphysics – as neither a totally protean signifier nor a definitively anchored concept – the Renaissance theatre thus paradoxically finds its own approximation of a metaphysical identity by staging the loss of and/or release from metaphysical absolutes which it simultaneously suggests may be rediscovered. The Elizabethan public theatre, as *Tamburlaine* represents it, is both a theatre of spectacle and a theatre of human judgement.

As the commercial playhouses spawned more commercial playhouses, however, so the theatre further diversified its semiotics. It is upon the transformation of judgement into irony and ventriloquism which I now want to focus, and related to this, upon the way that illusionism and anti-illusionism become increasingly polarised.

THE KNIGHT OF THE BURNING PESTLE

Francis Beaumont's avant-garde *The Knight of the Burning Pestle* was probably performed in 1607 in an indoor, 'private' playhouse (the second Blackfriars theatre) by the company of boy actors which had been in operation since 1600. Simon Shepherd and Peter Womack interestingly suggest that the play constitutes an intervention in the commercial theatres' drive towards 'product identity'. It is an attempt – a failed attempt, as it happens – to mark off one type of theatre semiotics from another (private from public, fashionable from unfashionable and so on), and so to establish differentiated theatrical experiences or 'brand names':

> The play, *The Knight of the Burning Pestle*, was a failure at its first performance, but was later much more successfully revived. In other words, the movement towards product identity – especially the relationship between fashionable and unfashionable theatre – is still only in process in 1607, not yet finished. Hence there is a lot of self-consciousness about performing here rather than there, performing this way rather than that, which tells us clearly about a key element in achieving the product identity: namely, the development of a particular performance–audience relationship.[24]

The specialised theatrical product which *The Knight of the Burning Pestle* is trying out on its Blackfriars audience is most obviously manifested in its mocking negation of already existing theatre styles and semiotics. Mockery, satire, parody and pastiche characterise a play which supplies its audience with an inventory of theatrical conventions now marked as dead, passé, outmoded. As a result, the large corporate concerns of the Marlovian public theatre with anti-illusionist judgement and illusionist spectacle are transformed. In what follows, I shall be exploring in detail the ways in which public theatre spectacle is at once made safe and ridiculous, and public theatre irony and judgement are overtaken by the more *sustained* irony of the private theatre.

No sooner does the Speaker of the Prologue begin to set the scene for a play – called *The London Merchant* – which the audience assumes it will shortly be watching, than he is interrupted by two citizens – a grocer and his wife – who leap up on to the stage and begin to make demands about the kind of play they wish to see. 'I will have a grocer', says the citizen, 'and he shall do admirable things' – such as, adds the citizen's wife, 'kill a lion with a pestle'.[25] What the citizens want, in other words, is a Tamburlaine, but a Tamburlaine adapted to their own trade and class interests. The humble man able to play such a starring role is their very own apprentice, Rafe. For his audition, Rafe chooses a 'huffing' ('Induction', l. 74) speech from Shakespeare's *I Henry IV* by that Tamburlaine of English honour, Hotspur:

> *Rafe.* By Heaven, methinks it were an easy leap
>   To pluck bright honour from the pale-fac'd moon;
>   Or dive into the bottom of the sea,
>   Where never fathom line touched any ground,
>   And pluck up drowned honour from the lake of hell.
>
> ('Induction', ll. 77–81)

Rafe is accepted and the play that was to be *The London Merchant* but is now, under pressure of the citizens' demands, *The Knight of the Burning Pestle*, begins, only for the citizens to make numerous further interruptions and interventions. What are we to make of this strange and intriguing play, whose subject matter is now very obviously and self-consciously the contested semiotics of theatre?

An initial point of entry is to consider the customer power exerted by the citizens as an example of a demand for a further extension of the theatre's capacity to publicise, romanticise, and endow with charismatic aura particular individuals, groups of individuals or classes. The citizens' idea of theatre is thus in *some sort of* continuity with the Marlovian image of public theatre as charismatic spectacle. They want to see a grocer putting on a show, doing 'admirable things'.[26] The objects of veneration have changed – as paying customers, the citizens reserve the right to select their own preferred objects for veneration – but the underlying or one of the underlying principles is the same. What is not so palatable as it once might have been is the thought of any kind of irony or complicating perspective which might interfere with their total identification with the play and play's hero. The 'girds [sneers] at citizens' ('Induction', l. 8), which the original play The London Merchant is suspected of intending to make, are thus strictly outlawed. Unmitigated portrayal of the grocer-citizen as hero is what the paying citizen public want in their revised version of the play. Tamburlaine minus its ironies and questions, minus its concerns with the problems of judgement – this is what the citizens desire.

The style of acting appropriate to these demands is a seamless illusionism, a total commitment to one's role or adopted identity. I argued that in Tamburlaine a gap between the character and his 'adjuncts' is visible, despite or perhaps even because of Tamburlaine's attempt to close it. What makes Tamburlaine's virtuoso performance risky and exhilarating is the ever present danger of this gap widening. Likewise, the energetic Hotspur's total commitment to honour seems to me to be born of a fear of becoming separated from it: the thought of dishonour drives the desire to maintain honour. The case of Rafe in The Knight of the Burning Pestle is different, for there is no risk, no flirtation with the possibility of being 'found out' playing a game of pretend. From the moment, which echoes the equivalent identity-switching scene in Tamburlaine, when Rafe casts aside his 'blue apron' and determines to become a 'grocer-errant', the illusion is so complete that we are likely to call it – simply and unambiguously – self-deceit (I.250, 260). Of all the words that are available to signify the activity of play-acting – such as pretence, escape, release, transformation, dream, fantasy, alternative reality, virtual reality, imagined reality, 'real' reality, lie – it is the last term, lie, which seems most appropriate to describe Rafe's anachronistic life as a knight in a conspicuously unchivalric modern London. So utterly cocooned are Rafe and his former fellow apprentices Tim and George in their new identities that they superimpose an imagined chivalric landscape upon one so obviously quotidian as to make such imagining ridiculous rather than risky. When the Bell Inn at Waltham is (mis)taken by Rafe and his entourage as an 'ancient castle, held by the old knight/Of the most holy order of the Bell' (II.357–8), we realise that the grocers-errant are not risking anything because risk would involve some slight or subliminal awareness of a difference between their own and other perceptions of the same phenomenon. Even in a work so wholeheartedly devoted to the cause of updating chivalry as

Spenser's *The Faerie Queene*, there is a strong sense that chivalry is continually on trial as a code which has to be tested against other codes of (mis)conduct. There are no such risks and tests involved for the man/woman who is utterly seduced by his/her created persona. Rafe lives and breathes his chivalric role and is oblivious to anything outside it. Likewise, the citizens identify with 'their' Rafe, who plays the role of citizen-hero with such wholehearted commitment that they become utterly absorbed in the illusion of the play and oblivious to any distinction between play-world and the world outside the play. Thus they speak to Rafe as though Rafe the actor and Rafe who has sustained an injury in his role in the play as grocer-errant are one and the same person:

> *Wife.* Oh, husband, here's Rafe again – Stay, Rafe, let me speak with thee. How dost thou, Rafe? Art thou not shrodly hurt? The foul great lungies laid unmercifully on thee. There's some sugar-candy for thee. Proceed. Thou shalt have another bout with him.
> *Citizen.* If Rafe had him at the fencing-school, if he did not make a puppy of him, and drive him up and down the school, he should ne'er come in my shop more.
>
> (II.327–34)

This is illusionism with a vengeance, illusionism gone mad.

Thus for the citizens, who are intended to represent a type of public theatre audience, the theatre is all about identification, enchantment and the customer power which can dictate the nature and extent of the theatre's imagined realities. For those who are watching the citizens watching the play, however, the opposite principles, of disenchantment and anti-illusionism (or disillusion), mark the difference between theatre audiences and theatre styles. The offstage Blackfriars spectators are expected to see Rafe's commitment to his role as a joke and the citizens' over-involvement in the illusion of the play as an education in how *not* to watch a play. What the citizens lack is irony, and the distance which irony affords.

So when the Speaker of the Prologue suggests *The Knight of the Burning Pestle* as a title for the revised play, the citizens do not see the ironically intended, élitist humour suggested by the incongruity between the conventionally high social discourse of chivalry and the low social status of grocer and grocer's pestle. 'I'll be sworn', says the citizen's wife, 'that's as good a name as can be' ('Induction', l. 94). The citizens enthuse, while the Blackfriars audience sit in mockery of an enthusiasm which misses the irony. The citizens' bluff enthusiasm is just one of the many attitudes which the play makes available to its more knowing Blackfriars audience as attitudes to be negated through parody. The more sophisticated Blackfriars spectator will not or cannot now *be* bluffly enthusiastic. This is an attitude which character-ises the citizen, not the sophisticate, and the mark of sophistication will be to put the attitude into ironic quotation marks.

The semiotics of theatre are thus changing once more. Irony now fans out to encompass and usurp the ethical questions towards which it might once have reached. And the theatre which corresponds to this more insulated irony is a theatre of ventriloquism, a theatre which makes available to its audience a range of styles, verbal resources, attitudes and postures, none of which are to be intensely engaged with in the way that Rafe and the citizens become so utterly absorbed in the language of chivalry.

As pastiche, the play borrows both directly and indirectly from a variety of literary and dramatic sources. From *I Henry IV*, as already indicated, is borrowed the language of honour and chiv-alry. The love scene (I.1–91) between Jasper and Luce set in Waltham Forest echoes the loves scenes set in the Athenian for-est in *A Midsummer Night's Dream*. Jasper's impersonation of a ghost (V.6–28) mocks the supernatural visitations which occur in *Macbeth* and *Hamlet* as well as in numerous revenge plays. Rafe's high-flown death speeches (V.282–317; V.319–32) parody attempts in previous tragedies (such as *A Spanish Tragedy*) to salvage at the moment of death some ultimate, metaphysical truth. Rafe's optimistic speech as May-lord (IV.393–428) invokes fes-tive traditions of renewal still influential in carnivalesque drama. Citizen-hero romantic comedies, such as Thomas Dekker's *The Shoemaker's Holiday*, are additionally alluded to, as are various Spanish chivalric romances. The anti-romance, *Don Quixote* – the model for the play's own negations – is also echoed. *The Knight of the Burning Pestle* thus stockpiles conventions which, through parody and inversion, are effectively announced dead. These bygone traditions are emptied out to become shadows of their former selves. They become, that is, *mere* fictions, fictions which no longer have the power to seduce, involve, or engage, but which may nevertheless be ironically or parodically quoted as a mark of the sophisticate's freedom from passionate engagements. For what characterises most if not all of the play's borrowed discourses – of romance, chivalry, heroism, love and the supernatural – is that they require a passionate kind of commitment, or even faith, which can of course all too easily slide into the slavish devotion mocked by the play, but whose opposite has its own downside in the form of an alienated cynicism.

I want to pick out one further feature of the widening divide between detached and committed kinds of spectatorship. This is the way in which the citizens attempt to overcome various kinds of estrangement by making themselves 'at home' in the theatre, in contrast with the implied stance of the Blackfriars audience which is to accept a condition of detachment or exile.

'I'm a stranger here', says the citizen's wife in the 'Induction' (l. 51). If the citizens have, as Shepherd and Womack suggest, 'walked into the wrong theatre', because to 'see the sort of performance they wanted, they should have gone to the Red Bull at Clerkenwell',[27] then they spend their time in the Blackfriars theatre trying to make up for that mistake by rewriting the play to their taste, talking freely to the actors and audience, introducing 'their' Rafe and treating not just Rafe but all the other players as though they are or have become members of their family:

> *Wife.* But here comes Master Humphrey and his love again now, George.
> *Cit.* Ay, cony, peace.
>
> (IV.127–9)

> *Wife.* Come hither, Master Humphrey. Has he hurt you? Now beshrew his fingers for't! Here, sweetheart, here's some green ginger for thee. – Now, beshrew my heart, but 'a has peppernel in's head, as big as a pullet's egg! – Alas, sweet lamb, how thy temples beat!
>
> (II.255–9)

If seventeenth-century London, due to its population growth, was becoming increasingly anonymous and heterogeneous, and if the playhouses themselves sometimes reflected that anonymity and heterogeneity in the way that, say, a particular theatre and theatre product might be (or might become) an alien experience for some of its clientele (such as going to an away football match), then the citizens at the Blackfriars overcompensate by over-identifying. Whatever is strange is thus domesticated. Consequently, the amused *detachment* which parody and irony generate is avoided in the citizens' and Rafe's refusal to allow any kind of gap to appear between themselves and their *attachments*. The contrasting position of the Blackfriars audience is that it is continually being displaced and detached from characters and ideals through the play's parodying of them. While the citizens try to make themselves comfortable in a theatre not theirs, the Blackfriars audience are offered the pleasure of being nowhere.

If the two audiences share anything in common then it is their unwillingness or inability to take risks. If Rafe embodies the citizens' desire *not* to have their illusions punctured, *not* to have their involvements put at risk, then the irony which locates the Blackfriars audience can be seen as a refusal of the risk of involvement. To allow oneself to get involved or be seduced attests to a certain openness towards experience. The risk of vicarious living presented by the theatre is resisted by the imagined Blackfriars audience in favour of a sustained irony. So. The citizens will not bring their illusionism into risky contact with its opposite and, likewise, the Blackfriars audience will not hazard their anti-illusionism to *its* opposite.

Something has happened to Marlowe's theatre of spectacle and judgement, a theatre which held illusionism and anti-illusionism, involvement and distance, identification and scepticism, seduction and judgement, charisma and critical debate in productive tension: illusionism cannot now brook any interference; the anti-illusionism which in *Tamburlaine* feeds ethical questions is siphoned off into sustained irony; illusionism and irony are completely polarised and there is consequently no traffic or dialogue between them.

To conclude this section, I want to reiterate the previously made point that it would be a mistake to characterise the private theatres solely in terms of their penchant for irony, satire, ventriloquism and metatheatrical discourse, and the post-Marlovian public theatres in terms of their naïve illusionism. Theatre styles and semiotics are more diversified than such simple schema will allow. As we have seen, even a single play may present contrasting notions of what it means to act and what it means to watch a play.

Such diversification is what we might expect from newly commercialised institutions partly released from their religious and
aristocratic heritage, and seeking new ways of attracting audiences and competing with each other for them. *The Knight of the
Burning Pestle* draws attention to an accelerated commercial
timescale whereby one theatre style may quickly be displaced
by another and made to look outmoded by a competitor. What I
want to suggest here is that irony and ventriloquism – two of
the features which characterise the *attempt* by *The Knight of the
Burning Pestle* to differentiate a sophisticated theatre public from
its popular counterpart – could be seen as being particularly
appropriate to this accelerated rate of turnover, for they suggest
an ongoing condition of disengagement from one or another style,
attitude, ideology, code and sign-system. Irony and ventriloquism
are, in other words, the marks of the versatile urban theatregoer
able to change and extend at will his/her repertoire of verbal/
theatrical resources without becoming committed to any one of
them. In this sense, then, irony is the mark of the sophisticated
urbanite which infiltrates private and public theatres alike. I am
not, of course, suggesting that this is the sole way to think about
irony and ventriloquism, only that this seems an appropriate way
of accounting for another influential inflection of the semiotics
of Renaissance theatre. We may call this theatre the theatre of
irony and ventriloquism, and its most eloquent and compelling
practitioner, Iago.

OTHELLO

Like the citizens of *The Knight of the Burning Pestle* who try to
make themselves comfortable in an alien environment, Othello
strives to make a home of his adopted culture.[28] That is to say,
Othello is to Venetian culture as the citizens are to the Blackfriars
theatre, as many Londoners may have been to London and/or
to each other: namely, strangers in a strange land.

Othello becomes central to a Venetian culture otherwise ready,
it all too often seems, to expunge him as the alien, through the
Tamburlaine-like impact of his rhetoric and theatrical presence.
In the scene (I.iii) where he is effectively put on public trial for
his supposed abduction of Desdemona, Othello charms his way
into the hearts and minds of an audience with a narrative which

not only overcomes *his* threatened exile, but also promises to heal the *Venetians'* own various experiences of alienation.[29] For Othello is far from being the only outsider in this play. Images and examples of displacement are rife: Iago complains about the way he has been displaced by Cassio as Othello's right hand man (I.i.8–33); he also suspects Othello of having cuckolded, or in other words, of having *sexually displaced* him (I.iii.384–6); Cassio is imagined as having cuckolded Othello; Roderigo throughout the play is alienated from his object of desire, Desdemona; Othello is, of course, ultimately separated from Desdemona, his 'other half' – the half which, in completing him, overcomes his sense of exile.[30] And in more general terms, Venice without the larger-than-Venetian-life Othello seems a divided and shoddily pragmatic city driven by greed and envy, and lacking in vision. It is upon the scene of this 'fallen', alienating city that Othello arrives as a kind of saviour who acts as a centring ideal. His epic, elevated narrative transcends the pragmatic and businesslike idiom of the Duke – 'Valiant Othello, we must straight employ you,/Against the general enemy Ottoman' (I.iii.48–9) – and begins to rewrite war as heroism, ambition as virtue. His speeches also reintroduce the pomp and ceremony of declamatory speech – 'Most potent, grave, and reverend signiors,/My very noble and approv'd good masters (I.iii.76–7) – where the head of state has discarded such language in favour of the harsher, brisker language of efficient statecraft.[31] In short, Othello's 'strange . . . passing strange' narrative reinvents Venice as charismatic public spectacle and promises to defeat his and their sense of exile. Theatre's power to transform and consecrate is once again in evidence.

Iago is the only Venetian who appears unperturbed by exile and utterly indifferent to the desire to overcome it. Where Othello, for example, does his utmost to become an accepted, card-carrying Venetian, Iago makes an art of the role of the outsider. *Potentially* the source of a Habermasian critical consciousness, Iago's detachment degenerates into cynicism. The way Iago describes his body – as a garden that can be replanted at will – exemplifies Iago's hard-headed rationality, for it demonstrates the extent of his scorn for the involuntary sensuality and intimacy into which the unschooled body may slip:

Virtue? a fig! 'tis in ourselves, that we are thus, or thus: our bodies are gardens, to the which our wills are gardeners, so that if we will plant nettles, or sow lettuce, set hyssop, and weed up thyme; supply it with one gender of herbs, or distract it with many; either to have it sterile with idleness, or manur'd with industry, why, the power, and corrigible authority of this, lies in our wills. If the balance of our lives had not one scale of reason, to poise another of sensuality, the blood and baseness of our natures would conduct us to most preposterous conclusions. But we have reason to cool our raging motions, our carnal stings, our unbitted lusts; whereof I take this, that you call love, to be a sect, or scion.

(I.iii.319–33)

The 'reason' invoked here is the instrumentalised, cynical counterpart to Habermas's critical reason. Critical reason is not opposed to emotion or desire, especially when it takes our emotional engagements with the world and with each other as its starting point. Psychoanalysis, as we shall see in Chapter 4, is one obvious example of a mode of critical enquiry which takes desire itself as one of its primary objects. Iago's reason instead takes flight from the emotions so that it may operate more efficiently as a machine for manipulating people. The body brought under the control of such a pitiless reason is an effective, sterile receptacle for the *mere accumulation* of attitudes, codes and linguistic resources. As linguistic entrepreneur, Iago is able to buy his way in and out of a variety of discursive and behavioural modes without fear of contamination by them.[32] Language does not detain Iago in the same way that it detains other characters in the play. Unlike Othello, for example, he does not try to overcome his sense of displacement by creating his *own* signifiers – one effect of which, in the case of Othello, is to make it difficult to think of Othello without thinking of the signifier honour. The signs and symbols appropriate to different status groups or to different cultural locations are instead appropriated by Iago without any psychic or emotional investment. He *ventriloquises* languages, for example, the language of the tavern (II.iii), of advice to rulers (III.iii), of masculine homosocial bonding (III.iii), of feudal service (II.iii), of friendship (II.iii), and so on, without these discourses leaving any permanent traces of inscriptions on a body and mind purged of passionate entanglements. When he announces in Act I that 'for necessity of present life,/I must show out a flag and sign of love' (I.i.155–7), he is in effect announcing the existence

of a self from whom signs have become totally alienated, disen-
gaged. It is for others to be moved, manipulated or seduced by
language. A nomadic traveller between tongues, Iago remains
an aloof observer of his own and others' verbal performances.
Signs thus become instruments for manipulation for Iago, by
virtue of being systematically drained of any emotional or psychic content. Where the citizens in *The Knight of the Burning Pestle*
over-invest in the language of chivalry to the extent that no alienating gap can possibly appear between self and sign, Iago evacuates
all such emotionally involving discourses the better to manipulate those who are 'caught' by them. And where the citizens treat
the theatre itself as a surrogate home in which characters become known quantities, Iago's meaningless 'flag[s]' of love and
friendship reconstruct the theatre as the scene of an empty ventriloquism and false intimacy. Iago is not only estranged from
others by virtue of his seeming friendship; he is also a stranger
to himself. Casual about his own motivation, to the point of re-
garding motivation itself as yet another conveniently manipulable
sign – 'I hate the Moor,/And it is thought abroad, that 'twixt
my sheets/He's done my office; I know not if't be true . . ./Yet
I, for mere suspicion in that kind,/Will do, as if for surety'
(I.iii.384–8) – Iago consigns one linguistic domain after another
to the market-place of disposable cultural capital liberated from
the angst of psychic investment.

The semiotics of theatre are thus hijacked by such compelling
performers as Iago to embody an empty form of role playing
which makes an art of the condition of exile. As this chapter has
shown, however, this is by no means the only meaning of theatre
present in Renaissance drama. Nor is protean role playing, as
Chapter 6 will show, always and everywhere the sign of a cynical
disengagement. Nevertheless, the domination of the meaning of
theatricality by the hollow player of multiple roles speaks to the
changeful nature of a theatre whose retrieval of a meaningful
metaphysics becomes increasingly difficult.

2

Structuralism
King Lear; The Duchess of Malfi; Hamlet; The Spanish Tragedy

'Her lips were as cherries.' Is it possible to understand individual acts of communication without simultaneously imagining the linguistic/poetic codes and conventions to which they belong? 'Her lips were as cherries' functions as a kind of cueing device which makes us think 'love poetry', or 'male love poetry', or perhaps 'outdated but still recognisable male love poetry'. 'Her lips were as cherries' belongs, that is, to a male poetic discourse in which it is conventional to compare one's mistress to one or another aspect of nature, using such standard metaphors as the following:

lips = cherries
neck = swanlike
eyes = sun
cheeks = roses
hair = gold

An example of the use of such conventional tropes for the female body is the following sixteenth-century poem by Thomas Watson:

Hark you that list to hear what saint I serve:
Her yellow locks exceed the beaten gold;
Her sparkling eyes in heaven a place deserve;
Her forehead high and fair of comely mould;
Her words are music all of silver sound;
Her wit so sharp as like can scarce be found:

42

Each eyebrow hangs like Iris in the skies;
Her Eagle's nose is straight of stately frame;
On either cheek a Rose and Lily lies;
Her breath is sweet perfume, or holy flame;
Her lips more red than any coral stone;
Her neck more white than aged swans that moan; . . .[1]

It is relatively easy to identify the dependence of Watson's poem upon a recognisable set of codes and conventions. For structuralists, however, *all* uses of language function in the way that 'Her lips were as cherries' does, for every speech act is always part of some larger network of meaning or symbolic code. Using the model of grammar, as structuralism often does, to describe the relationship between particular utterances and the larger language systems to which they belong, we could say that male love poetry constitutes the 'grammar' or syntax which makes possible and comprehensible the individual sentence 'Her lips were as cherries.' Without any familiarity whatsoever with the poetic and cultural convention which legitimises the idea that it is complimentary for a man to compare a woman's neck with a swan, the sentence 'Her neck was swanlike' might be thought rather odd or even insulting. Of course, it still can be thought odd or insulting, but that can only happen once the convention has been 'denaturalised' and exposed precisely as a convention. Denaturalising conventions by exposing their unwritten rules and artificiality is the province of structuralism, for, like semiotics, structuralism encourages us to become strangers to our own sign-systems.

THE SYSTEMIC AND THE INDIVIDUALISTIC

Although absolute distinctions between the concerns of semiotics and structuralism are thus difficult to draw, and indeed many critics treat them as one and the same thing, I have chosen to distinguish the two on the basis of structuralism's persistent emphasis on the priority of language *systems* over particular speech acts. It is not, in general, individual phenomena in all their apparent diversity and heterogeneity in which structuralism is interested, but the underlying rules or systems of meaning which constitute those phenomena in the first place. These rules or systems of meaning may be those of chess, or football, or fashion, or a literary text, or the genre to which a literary text belongs, or the discourse we call 'news' – any cultural practice, in fact, which may be seen to be constituted by an identifiable set of rules or structures. Jonathan Culler's claim, in *Structuralist Poetics*, that the 'cultural meaning of any particular act or object is determined by a whole system of constitutive rules' is characteristic of structuralism's gravitation away from the particular towards the typical, for it is the rules of a system which, according to structuralism, have to be consciously or unconsciously learned before any individual can function within that system.[2] If I were to go to an interview for the job of detective police superintendent wearing pyjamas, I would be showing my ignorance or deliberate transgression of the appropriate dress code. *All* acts and utterances are similarly rule-bound, or as Culler puts it, they are brought into existence in the first place by the rules pertaining to one or another symbolic system:

> The cultural meaning of any particular act or object is determined by a whole system of constitutive rules: rules which do not regulate behaviour so much as create the possibility of particular forms of behaviour. The rules of English enable sequences of sound to have meaning; they make it possible to utter grammatical or ungrammatical sentences. And analogously, various social rules make it possible to marry, to score a goal, to write a poem, to be impolite. It is in this sense that a culture is composed of a set of symbolic systems.[3]

For a structuralist, then, no individual thing exists entirely in and for itself, for individual things are always part of a larger structure or symbolic network.

The basis for structuralism's preoccupation with language systems is Saussure's distinction, in the *Course in General Linguistics*, between *langue*, translated below simply as language, and *parole*, translated as speech:

> By distinguishing between the language itself and speech, we distinguish at the same time: (1) what is social from what is individual, and (2) what is essential from what is ancillary and more or less accidental.
>
> The language itself is not a function of the speaker. It is a product passively registered by the individual....

Speech, on the contrary, is an individual act of the will and the intelligence, in which one must distinguish: (1) the combinations through which the speaker uses the code provided by the language to express his thought, and (2) the psycho-physical mechanism which enables him to externalise these combinations.[4]

Significantly – and *contra* some readings of him – Saussure grants more autonomy to the individual and individual speech acts than structuralism tends to, since Saussure takes for granted concepts of individual agency ('[s]peech' as 'an individual act of will') and self-expression ('code[s]' used to 'express . . . thought'). Saussure is not, in other words, as structuralist as some later structuralists take him to be, for the appeals to the individual and individualism qualify the tendency within structuralism to privilege the linguistic system *over* the individual who becomes a mere instrument or effect of that system. Structuralism is often much more unequivocally *anti*-individualist than Saussure. When Terence Hawkes in *Structuralism and Semiotics*, for example, invokes individualism, it is more often than not couched in negative terms: the 'illusions of individualism', according to Hawkes, are a regrettable, bourgeois phenomenon responsible for the reduction of the world to a '"single vision"'.[5]

Structuralism and individualism are both no doubt prone, as everything is, to excess, and in the early, heady days of literary theory, back in the 1970s and early 1980s, structuralism was given to making iconoclastic statements about the death of 'man', or in the phrase used for the title of an essay by Roland Barthes, 'the death of the author'. There Barthes writes:

We know now a text is not a line of words releasing a single 'theological' meaning (the 'message' of the Author-God) but a multi-dimensional space in which a variety of writings, none of them original, blend and clash. The text is a tissue of quotations drawn from the innumerable centres of culture.[6]

The extremism of Barthes's and other structuralist or poststructuralist manifestos was perhaps a necessary means of countering what he and others (such as Terence Hawkes) saw as the opposite extreme of an author-centred criticism tied to the notion that texts are simply the creative expressions of autonomous, language-independent individuals.

The usefulness of structuralism's assault upon such 'author-centric' criticism can be located by briefly glancing at a poem by Thomas Hardy and at the commentary which accompanies it in an edition of Hardy's poems published in 1975. The poem is 'In Time of "The Breaking of Nations"':

> Only a man harrowing clods
> In a slow silent walk
> With an old horse that stumbles and nods
> Half asleep as they stalk.
>
> Only thin smoke without flame
> From the heaps of couch-grass;
> Yet this will go onward the same
> Though Dynasties pass.
>
> Yonder a maid and her wight
> Come whispering by:
> War's annals will cloud into night
> Ere their story die.[7]

The short accompanying commentary by James Gibson takes it for granted that the origin and creator of the poem is Thomas Hardy:

> In this poem Hardy comments on the permanence of such simple things as work and love. Man must cultivate the earth so that he can eat, and he will continue to fall in love. Not even the madness of war can change these basic certainties. This has always been one of Hardy's most popular poems, probably because it states a great truth so simply and effectively.[8]

The supposed truths of the poem are presented as sacred, timeless truths, delivered from on high by an individual, Thomas Hardy, whose autonomous voice and vision are treated with reverential respect. The commentary is a perfect example of the kind of criticism that Barthes attacks in 'The Death of the Author', for it does indeed treat the text as a 'line of words releasing a single "theological" meaning (the "message" of the Author-God)'. An alternative, structuralist approach to this poem would begin by questioning the author as the origin of meaning and proceed to concentrate upon the 'rules' of the pastoral genre in which Hardy is writing and to which the poem belongs. 'Hardy', a structuralist might say, is not an autonomous 'speaker' but is instead 'spoken by' the literary tradition of pastoral. He is merely the 'effect' of a discourse which writes rural life in terms of its supposed simplicity, timelessness and spirituality.

The perspectives of author-centric criticism and structuralism can become unhelpfully polarised. On the basis of the account given so far, it would seem that analysis can begin *either* with the individual, *or* with the language system, and never the twain shall meet. However, although structuralism in some of its more belligerent moments may have pronounced the author and individual 'dead', its persistent use of the opposed but thereby interconnected terms, *langue* and *parole*, implies that a relationship of meaningful interaction *beyond simple opposition* may be seen to exist between them *depending on the nature of the language 'system' in question*. In other words, the kind of structuralism which privileges *langue* over *parole* may be entirely appropriate to certain very prescriptive and rule-bound symbolic systems (such as army uniform, for example), in which there is little or no room for the 'individual' to manoeuvre, but a different kind of structuralism would seem to be required by a *langue* with a high degree of variability. Literature, which post-Romantic criticism has often seen as the locus of individual creativity, would be an example of one such flexible and open-ended language system. It could be argued that within such a system the relationship between *langue* and *parole* is not one of simple, hierarchical opposition, but mutual and dynamic interaction. This is because generic rules are constantly being transgressed and/or rewritten by literary texts. As the structuralist critic Tzvetan Todorov puts it, 'The major work [of art] creates, in a sense, a new genre and at the same time transgresses the previously valid rules of the genre.'[9] The immense value of structuralism, from this perspective, is that it enables us to understand and appreciate the nature of those transgressions. For how can one break rules or know how they are being broken without a knowledge of what those rules are? One might intuitively sense that 'Her lips were as cherries' sounds 'right' whereas 'Her lips were like tomatoes' sounds 'wrong', but what structuralism can do is to disclose the nature of the rules which makes one sentence 'grammatical' and the other subversive of the grammar in question.

Structuralism's preoccupation with generic and other kinds of rules connects it not only to Saussurean semiotics (via the notion of *langue*), but also to older, pre-Romantic forms of genre criticism favoured by classical and neoclassical theorists. Where Romantic writers were themselves generally author-centric in their emphasis upon subjective imagination, creativity and radical innovation, pre-Romantic classical and neoclassical critics were more inclined to make the writer subservient to the rules of writing. Art, according to such a perspective, does not mysteriously originate from 'within' the individual psyche, but from 'without', through the explicit formulation of generic rules and conventions. These can be more or less prescriptive, depending on the kind of neoclassicism in question.

Structuralism can therefore be perceived as a kind of neoclassicism and, conversely, (neo)classicism as a kind of structuralism. Aristotle's *Poetics*, for example, a text which I will make use of later on in this chapter, can be thought of as a structuralist text by virtue of its concern with the *structure* and underlying 'grammar' of different forms of narrative. Likewise, Philip Sidney's late-sixteenth-century *A Defence of Poetry*, another text which I shall be discussing later, can be construed as structuralist in its preoccupation with the constitutive generic rules and conventions which make possible particular performances within one or another literary genre. Just as structuralism can be more or less amenable to the concept of the individual, likewise, the classical Aristotle's and neoclassical Sidney's rule-oriented conception of literary discourse can sometimes be more, and sometimes less, prohibitive of individual innovation.

THE SCOPE OF STRUCTURALISM

However, *un*like its classical and neoclassical predecessors, which focus mainly upon the conventional genres of literature (epic, tragedy, comedy, pastoral, lyric, and so on), modern structuralism's reach is much broader. Tzvetan Todorov and Franco Moretti, for example, have offered structuralist accounts of detective fiction; Vladimir Propp's *Morphology of the Folktale* focuses upon the narrative rules and conventions of the fairy story and folk tale; A. J. Greimas's *Structural Semantics* attempts to disclose the grammar not just of a single kind of narrative, but of all narratives, literary and non-literary, ranging from folklore to philosophy and Marxism.[10]

Applied to the study of the past, structuralism has also been used to excavate the 'deep' laws which underlie otherwise disconnected phenomena in a given historical period. An example of structuralist history – despite its author's denials of its structuralist provenance – is Michel Foucault's *The Order of Things*.[11] Foucault brilliantly discloses the underlying grammar or 'rules of formation' of the seemingly unrelated disciplines of economics, natural history and linguistics in three different periods of history (referred to by Foucault as the Renaissance period, the classical period and the modern period).[12] In each of these periods, what it means to study the natural world, money and language is governed by principles which change drastically from one discursive regime or *episteme* to another. Foucault calls his method 'archaeological'.[13] The use of this term connects Foucault (of *The Order of Things* at least) to the structuralist endeavour because structuralism likewise attempts to excavate beneath the surface layers of phenomena to discover their foundations, or, in Foucault's phrase, their 'rules of formation'.

One final example of structuralism's breadth of application is its impact on the analysis of contemporary popular culture. Roland Barthes's witty and sarcastic *Mythologies* is a series of reflections 'on some myths of French Daily life'.[14] In chapters dealing with such assorted topics as 'Steak and Chips', 'The Face of Garbo' and 'The New Citroën' Barthes uncovers the historically and culturally specific nature of sign-systems which would otherwise pass themselves off as timeless and natural. So wine, for example, is not just a drink which people naturally enjoy, it is a potent cultural myth suffused with symbolic meaning and an index of what it means to be French:

> Wine is part of society because it provides a basis not only for morality but also for environment; it is an ornament in the slightest ceremonials of French daily life, from the snack (plonk and camembert) to the feast, from the conversation at the local café to the speech at a formal dinner. It exalts all climates, of whatever kind: in cold weather, it is associated with all the myths of becoming warm, and at the height of summer, with all the images of shade, with all things cool and sparkling. There is no situation involving some physical constraint (temperature,

hunger, boredom, compulsion, disorientation) which does not give rise to dreams of wine.[15]

Barthes's task as structuralist *de*mythologist is thus to lay bare the hidden or partly hidden rules which govern the functioning of 'wine' as a signifier in French life.

BINARY OPPOSITIONS

There are numerous other examples, such as the structural anthropology of Claude Lévi-Strauss, of the scope of structuralism. What binds together these structuralisms is the search, amid the *apparent* randomness and heterogeneity of phenomena, for their hidden foundations in one or another *langue* or system of meaning. I drink a glass of wine because I feel like it. There appears to be no meaning to the event beyond that spontaneous personal impulse. But of course, says the structuralist, there is more – much more – to the meaning of the event than this spuriously personal one, for I am simultaneously participating in a symbolic code, the foundations of which can be discovered by methodical analysis. Structuralism thus retains a kind of foundationalism where other language-based theories – notably poststructuralism – eschew the notion that discourses can be referred back all the time to governing laws.

The foundational patterns of meaning which structuralism discovers beneath apparent diversity are often patterns of opposition. This again follows the insight of Saussure that words create meaning through their internal relationships (of opposition and similarity) with each other rather than to a reality which exists beyond them:

> what we find, instead of *ideas* given in advance, are *values* emanating from a linguistic system. If we say that these values correspond to certain concepts, it must be understood that the concepts in question are purely differential. That is to say they are concepts defined not positively, in terms of their content, but negatively by contrast with other items in the same system. What characterises each most exactly is being what the others are not.[16]

To briefly restate part of the argument of Chapter 1: concepts, according to Saussure, do not precede language. Prior to my learning of language, I do not have a concept of justice. Concepts are instead created through the system of differences and similarities which is language. We define words *relationally*, through their difference from, and similarity with, other words: 'yes' means 'not no'; loud is the opposite of soft; we can only define what is unconventional via reference to what is conventional, and so on. In their quest to discover underlying grammars of meaning, structuralists tend to pare down texts until they arrive at the binary oppositions or sets of oppositions which inform them. An example of structuralist criticism at work is the following account, by Jonathan Culler, of the binary oppositions which structure Balzac's *Sarrasine* (also discussed from a structuralist viewpoint in Roland Barthes' *S/Z*):

> The presentation of two heroines, one dark and the other fair, sets in motion an experiment in extrapolation in which the reader correlates this opposition with thematic oppositions that it might manifest: evil/good, forbidden/permitted, active/passive, Latin/Nordic, sexuality/purity. The reader can pass from one opposition to another, trying them out, even inverting them, and determining which are pertinent to larger thematic structures which encompass the other antitheses presented in the text. Thus, the first manifestation of the symbolic code in *Sarrasine* finds the narrator seated in a window with an elegant party on his one hand and a garden on the other. The opposition, as so often in Balzac, is explicitly developed in various ways, as the narrator traces possible symbolic readings: dance of death/dance of life, nature/man, cold/hot, silence/noise.[17]

STRUCTURALISM AS A SCIENCE

Structuralism – or at least some varieties of it – is also characterised by its quasi-scientific vocabulary. Eschewing the subjectivist impressionism and mystery of Romantic and post-Romantic criticism, structuralism often generates a plethora of technical terms to describe the various ways in which texts work. An additional quasi-scientific method used by structuralism is to make use of diagrammatic representations as a means of making visible a text's or discourse's underlying 'geometry'. What these characteristics make of structuralism is a cognitive, rationalist, 'objective' enterprise. The premise is that one can come to 'know' the grammar of a text objectively and communicate that knowledge to others.

STRUCTURALISM IN SUMMARY

- Structuralism has various classical and neoclassical precursors, but its direct antecedent is semiotics, and in particular Saussure's contrast between *parole* and *langue*, the latter becoming the special province of structuralism.
- Structuralism is preoccupied with the rules, structures, grammars, patterns of meaning, and so on, which underlie the apparent diversity and multiplicity of phenomena. A structuralist will try to pare down a text to its putatively essential components, and in doing so reveal its exemplary or typical generic characteristics.
- The underlying patterns of a text are often patterns of binary opposition. This follows Saussure's insistence upon the *relational* nature of language.
- The relationship between language *systems* and *individual* language users can be differently treated within structuralism. Although the relationship between *langue* and *parole* in structuralist manifestos has often been conceived in terms of hierarchical opposition (*langue* over *parole*, system over individual), there is scope within structuralism to re-conceive the relationship in terms of mutual and dynamic interaction. This latter conception is perhaps especially appropriate to literary discourse.
- Structuralism is a mainly *cognitive*, 'objective' enterprise, meaning that it assumes that its objects of enquiry are knowable, and that this knowledge can be communicated and generally recognised.

KING LEAR

This section will use Shakespeare's *King Lear* to attempt to identify the 'grammar' of tragedy. The account of *King Lear* will be, in structuralist fashion, fairly minimalist, for the focus will not be so much upon the complexities and specificity of the individual play (on what makes *King Lear* uniquely *King Lear*) but upon the underlying rules of the genre of 'tragedy' to which *King Lear* belongs. Having identified the syntax of tragedy (or at least one possible way of identifying tragedy's syntax), it will then be possible to think about the ways in which other Renaissance tragedies – and indeed *King Lear* itself – complicate or subvert this syntax. This will bear out the proposition made earlier that structuralism's emphasis upon the rules of formation of a given discourse is useful because knowing what the rules are enables us to make better sense of the ways in which rules are transgressed.

The grammar of tragedy might be defined as follows: *tragedy is the narrative of 'man', usually represented by an élite, male individual, pitting himself against forces which are beyond his control or comprehension.* This approximates the understanding of tragedy offered by the Renaissance poet, courtier and quasi-structuralist theorist of the genres of literature, Philip Sidney, in his *A Defence of Poetry*. There he writes of:

> high and excellent Tragedy that openeth the greatest wounds, and showeth forth the ulcers that are covered with tissue; that maketh kings fear to be tyrants, and tyrants manifest their tyrannical humours; that, with stirring the affects of admiration and commiseration, teacheth the uncertainty of this world, and upon how weak foundations gilden roofs are builded.[18]

My own structuralist definition of tragedy could be broken down into constituent parts and connected to Sidney's ideas as follows:

1. *In tragedy 'man' is usually represented by an élite individual.* Sidney's assumption, here and elsewhere in the *Defence*, that kings are the proper subjects of tragedy, is based upon tragedy's aspiration towards universality, the focus of tragedy being upon 'man' in general rather than upon particular men and women. This aspiration towards universality is met by the choice of kings (or other élite individuals) as tragic protagonists, for such is the power of the élite and therefore socially influential individual that he not only represents himself but the nation, and beyond this, 'mankind'. In tragedy, then, the fate of the (usually élite) individual is bound up with the fate of the nation and with the life of man.

2. *In tragedy man is usually represented by an élite, male individual.* Even though a queen (Elizabeth I) occupied the throne at the time of writing the *Defence*, Sidney makes kings, not queens, the subject of tragedy.
3. *In tragedy 'man' pits himself against forces* . . . Tragedy, according to Sidney, may make kings afraid of becoming tyrants, but the implication is that the line separating kingship from tyranny is often traversed. Such, in Sidney's terms, is the diseased, ulcerous nature of 'man' (as represented by élite individuals in tragedy) that he transgresses boundaries and opposes himself to forces which impose limitations on his sphere of influence, action and knowledge. The socially prestigious individual wants more prestige. Kings become tyrants.
4. *In tragedy 'man' pits himself against forces which are beyond his control or comprehension.* Despite 'man's' efforts to tame and/ or understand opposing 'forces', these forces remain impenetrable. In Sidney's phrase, tragedy 'teacheth the uncertainty of this world'.

If we take 'forces' to refer (as they do in *most* classical and *some* Renaissance tragedies) to God or the gods, then we might say that the central binary opposition of tragedy is between the androcentric (meaning human-centred) and the theocentric (meaning God-centred). A structuralist paring down of tragedy to its essentials might reveal this opposition to lie at the very heart of tragedy.

So to *King Lear*. The love test at the beginning of *King Lear* is one of many examples in Renaissance tragedy of a travestied ritual or ceremony – travestied, in the case of *King Lear*, because of Lear's androcentric assertion of his own supposed autonomy and will.[19] Rituals and ceremonies may be understood as attempts by a culture to connect its institutions and practices to some 'higher' truth or principle. The church wedding ceremony, for example, is an attempt to sanctify the otherwise 'merely' social institution of marriage. In Renaissance drama, there is a profusion of social ceremonies, in the form of banquets, entertainments, weddings, funeral rites, and so forth, designed to affirm a relationship between the secular and the sacred. Often such events have explicitly religious connotations. The wedding rites at the end of *As You Like It*, for example, are introduced by Hymen, the god of marriage, as follows:

Then is there mirth in heaven,
When earthly things made even
Atone together
Good Duke receive thy daughter,
Hymen from heaven brought her,
Yea brought her hither,
That thou mightst join her hand with his
Whose heart within his bosom is.[20]

Whereas harmony is affirmed, at the end of this and other comedies, between heaven and 'earthly things', the relationship between the human and the superhuman tends in tragedy to be much more antagonistic. This is because characters such as Lear, Faustus, Tamburlaine, Lady Macbeth and Macbeth usurp the divine in an attempt to achieve absolute sovereignty. Ceremonies are as a result emptied of their usual significance. Where the supposed meeting of personal desire and its public expression are celebrated and sanctified at the end of *As You Like It*, the love test in *King Lear* drives a wedge between the personal and the public. The effect is to make of public, ceremonial speech a mere sham – empty words cut off adrift from any meaningful emotional reality. If there is meaning to the love test, then it is Lear's and Lear's only: 'Mean time we shall express our darker Purpose.'[21] Ritual is thus appropriated to private purposes. It is designed to confirm Lear's subjectivity, to consolidate his ego. The disunity amongst 'earthly things' – the conflict, in this case, between the private and the public – forms part of a cycle of disconnection and binary opposition in *King Lear* between, words and things, the tongue and the heart, individual and community, secular and sacred, and androcentric and theocentric 'man' and God or the gods. Lear's use or misuse of ceremony contributes to the sense that, in tragedy, ritual and ceremony are somehow failing to express what they ought to express: namely a shared and sanctified sense of community, in which the personal is wedded to the public, and the public to the sacred.

Throughout Act I Lear systematically removes barriers which obstruct him. Those characters, such as the 'unmannerly Kent' (I.i 144), who appeal to 'higher' religious forces, such as good and evil, which they see Lear as transgressing, are chastised and then banished by Lear, so that no obstacle comes between him and his naming of the world according to his desire. Kent's plea

to Lear to 'Revoke thy gift; Or, whilst I can vent clamour from
my throat,/I'll tell thee thou dost evil' (I.i.162–4) meets with heavy
rebuke from Lear followed by a sentence of exile:

> Hear me, recreant!
> On thine allegiance, hear me!
> That thou hast sought to make us break our vow,
> Which we durst never yet, and with strain'd pride
> To come betwixt our sentence and our power,
> Which nor our nature nor our place can bear,
> Our potency made good, take thy reward.
> Five days we do allot thee for provision
> To shield thee from disasters of the world;
> And on the sixth to turn thy hated back
> Upon our kingdom: if on the tenth day following
> Thy banish'd trunk be found in our dominions,
> The moment is thy death. Away! By Jupiter,
> This shall not be revok'd.
>
> (I.i.165–78)

Like Tamburlaine, Lear's attitude towards language is talismanic:
once a reality has been named by the tyrant no one should attempt to un-name it. Lear's invocation of classical gods (here
Jupiter), further identifies him with tyranny and arbitrariness,
for the classical gods are notoriously capricious. Lear's invocation is from this perspective more like an identification: Lear is
becoming godlike, he is usurping the divine.

Such, however, is the play's retributive scheme that Lear is
punished for his presumption and relegated to the 'merely' human. In contrast with the aggrandised version of the human which
Lear represents early on in the play, exposure during the storm
scenes to the harsh reality of nature prompts Lear to construct
and universalise another version of the human, this time in terms
of the vulnerability of human beings: 'unaccommodated man is
no more but such a poor, bare, forked animal' (III.iv.104–5). Lear's
punishment for attempting to usurp the role of a god is thus to
be demoted to the status of a belittled human being, and for the
gods to resume an inscrutable, superhuman position. If Lear's
tyranny, early on in the play, is such that Lear's world and the
world beyond him totally *coincided*, then what Lear and other
characters subsequently experience are frighteningly 'other' realities

which resist the capacity of human beings to name or comprehend. Gloucester expresses the agony of an unintelligible universe thus: 'As flies to wanton boys, are we to th'Gods;/They kill us for their sport' (IV.i.36–7).

So *King Lear* corresponds, or can be made to correspond, to the structuralist definition of tragedy as: *the narrative of 'man', usually represented by an élite, male individual, pitting himself against forces which are beyond his control or comprehension.* I should reiterate that this is not the only way of thinking about tragedy, and not even the only *structuralist* way of thinking about it.[22] Neither does it exhaust what can be said of *King Lear*. Qualifications aside, the definition captures something of the nature of tragedy. Having identified a set of rules for the formation of the literary genre we know as 'tragedy', we can now move on to consider the way in which those rules are varied, complicated and/or subverted. We can consider, in other words, the *qualifications* I have just referred to.

THE DUCHESS OF MALFI

Structuralism, then, identifies the core elements of a discourse or genre. In the case of tragedy, the core is the opposition between 'man' and the 'forces' beyond his control or comprehension. Various permutations of this core are possible. Once the rules of a grammar have been learnt, an infinite number of sentences can be generated from that grammar. Thus each of the items in my structuralist definition of tragedy can be either replaced or supplemented by another item. For example, in John Webster's *The Duchess of Malfi* (to be discussed in greater depth and detail in Chapter 6), an élite, *female* individual replaces an élite, *male* individual. The kind of representativeness or universality towards which tragedy aspires correspondingly changes: the Duchess, that is, can be seen as representing herself, the plight of a woman in a male-dominated society and, beyond this, any individual oppressed by 'forces' seemingly beyond his or her control.

As this last set of points suggests, the 'forces' in question themselves change. In *King Lear*, I took 'forces' to mean superhuman or supernatural forces. In *The Duchess of Malfi*, these forces are secularised: it is society, and in particular male-dominated society, against which the Duchess struggles. In this tragedy, the

Duchess's freedom of movement and marriage partner are severely restricted by her brother Ferdinand, who hires the court lackey Bosola as a spy to observe the Duchess while Ferdinand is absent from court:

> Your inclination to shed blood rides post
> Before my occasion to use you. I give you that
> To live i'th'court, here: and observe the Duchess,
> To note all the particulars of her haviour:
> What suitors do solicit her for marriage
> And whom she best affects: she's a young widow,
> I would not have her marry again.[23]

The tyrannical Ferdinand is the secularised equivalent of the gods in *King Lear* and/or the equivalent of the godlike Lear who works at the beginning of Shakespeare's play in mysterious ways according to some unrevealed 'darker Purpose'. The greater concentration of focus, in *The Duchess of Malfi*, upon the secular, male-dominated environment of the court means that the central opposition in tragedy between 'man' and the forces beyond his/her control take on an altogether more worldly, gendered significance. For it is not so much the ways of God or the gods which are impenetrable to men and which men attempt to overcome, but the ways of men which are impenetrable to women and which women attempt to overcome. Moreover, rather than constituting a constraint or unfathomable mystery, God is frequently invoked by the Duchess as a source of authority, certainty and reassurance in a chaotic and brutal world in which religion has been manipulated by tyrants such as Ferdinand for their own ends. When Ferdinand infers that the Duchess's children are 'bastards' (IV.i.36), the Duchess, referring to her marriage, unequivocally responds:

> Do you visit me for this?
> You violate a sacrament o'th'Church
> Shall make you howl in hell for't
>
> (IV.i.38–9)

It is not God against whom the Duchess struggles, but men. Men and male-dominated society are the invisible forces which threaten to diminish her and which in other tragedies are represented by all-powerful and inscrutable gods.

The items within the grammar of tragedy have thus changed, such that for 'forces' we now read societal forces. So, too, has the meaning of the relationship between the grammatical items: if Lear's struggle against opposing forces constructs an image of the human as overreaching itself, then the Duchess's struggle is for a limited human agency and independence.

HAMLET

The grammar of tragedy which I have been exploring may also serve as a useful basis for discussing the nature of the complexities in one of the most intricate tragedies in the English language. *Hamlet* shares in common with other tragedies the same basic syntax of an élite, this time, male protagonist, who represents the life of 'man' as one of struggle against forces which he tries unsuccessfully to overcome or understand. The complexity of *Hamlet* is that the 'forces' are now multiple. For 'forces', we may now read any one, or any combination of, the following:

1. Supernatural forces (in the shape, primarily, of the ghost).
2. Societal forces (which are themselves multiple, because represented not only by the new court and new father figure, Claudius, but also by the old court and old father, Hamlet.
3. 'Internal', psychological forces, mysteriously at work within Hamlet himself.

Adding still further to the complexity of *Hamlet* as a tragedy is the fact that each of these forces can be read as metaphors for each other. Thus the ghost can be understood as an 'external' physical phenomenon but also as a signifier of Hamlet's state of mind. Precisely what 'state of mind' the ghost may be said to represent is the site of yet further questions and complexity. Does the ghost represent Hamlet's desire for the return of the 'real', biological father and the 'seemingly' less complicated world which old Hamlet 'seems' to represent? Or is the ghost of old Hamlet part of the problem rather than the solution, in that it only contributes to the world of shadowy illusions and 'seeming' realities which Hamlet inhabits? Or, to glance fleetingly at Freud's interpretation of *Hamlet*, is the ghost a signifier of Hamlet's secret guilt? On this reading, Hamlet is haunted by guilt in the form of the ghost because Claudius has done what Hamlet himself subconsciously wished to do, namely murder his father in order to be with his mother. In *The Interpretation of Dreams*, Freud writes:

> Hamlet is able to do anything – except take vengeance on the man who did away with his father and took that father's place with his mother, the man who shows him the repressed wishes of his own childhood realized. Thus the loathing which should drive him on to revenge is replaced in him by self-reproaches, by scruples of conscience, which remind him that he himself is literally no better than the sinner whom he wishes to punish.[24]

The Oedipal scenarios invoked by psychoanalysis will be fully explored in Chapter 4. Suffice it to say here that the psychoanalytic supposition of a Hamlet driven by a subconscious desire to be the sole object of his mother's affection infinitely complicates any understanding of the nature of the 'forces' at work in *Hamlet*. Are the impenetrable and invisible 'gods' to be understood as supernatural, social or psychological? Or are they an unholy alliance of all three?

Confronted with a play such as *Hamlet*, structuralism teeters on the brink of collapse. The grammar of tragedy is still just about legible, but such is the complexity of the play that a structuralist reduction of *Hamlet* to its essential components is highly problematic. The play, from this perspective, is precisely about the breakdown of stable meaning and structures.

Hamlet is nevertheless persistent in his struggle to reveal the hidden core of the tragic experience and to restore 'truth' to a fallen world of 'seeming truths'. In this he resembles numerous other tragic protagonists who likewise work towards clarification and redemption of meaning. 'Something', it seems, has been lost: some ideal order, some overarching, shared meaning, some ideal balance between humanity and humanity's 'others' (the 'gods', society, the subconscious). Tragedy's compulsion towards the restoration of shared meaning defines one further element of its grammar. Tragedy, that is, seeks to replace the antagonistic relationships which exist between competing 'truths' and realities – 'man's' truth *versus* God's truth, the world according to Lear *versus* the world according to Kent or Cordelia, reality as defined by men *versus* reality as redefined by women, 'private' *versus* public realities – with a more singular and universally recognisable conception of truth. This drive towards the recovery of authentic foundations and 'true' as opposed to sabotaged universals is especially felt during moments of finality when characters utter their dying or near-to-last words. The sense of an impending end, emphasising 'lastness' and last chances, puts pressure upon characters to achieve some momentous recognition of the truth about the meaning of life. Othello, for example, asks the future to speak of 'one that lov'd not wisely, but too well' (V.ii.345–6). Flamineo, in Webster's *The White Devil*, confesses that he has 'liv'd/Riotously ill, like some that live in the court/And sometimes, when my face was full of smiles/Have felt the maze of conscience in my breast'.[25] Lear, some time before his end, appears to recognise the error of his ways: 'Pray you now, forget and forgive: I am old and foolish' (IV.vii.84). Tragedy generally works up to these and other such climactic moments of clarification when values such as compassion, in the case of *King Lear*, or 'conscience', in the case of *The White Devil*, are recognised and/or re-established as timeless, universal verities. Where tragic protagonists live and often die, as Bosola in *The Duchess of Malfi* puts it, 'in a mist' (V.v.93), tragedy's epiphanies recover or attempt to recover authentic values and authentic knowledge. Insight into the true nature of things – including the true nature of the causes of tragedy – enables transcendence of the world of 'false' appearances and access to a metaphysical realm of 'pure' essences.

If tragedy, however, is an essentialist discourse, which works towards the recovery of essential truths, then its essentialism is severely and persistently threatened. So we can add one final item or binary opposition to the grammar of tragedy, namely the opposition between essentialism and anti-essentialism, or, in the Aristotelian terms elaborated in the following section, between recognition and ignorance/astonishment.

ARISTOTLE AND TRAGEDY

No account of tragedy would be complete without some reference to the influential ideas of the first theorist of Western tragedy, Aristotle, and so I want to turn briefly to Aristotle in order to complete this structuralist account of tragedy. Like Sidney's *A Defence of Poetry*, which is itself influenced by Aristotelian ideas,

Aristotle's *Poetics* can be seen as a precursory form of structuralism. When Aristotle describes tragedy as 'a representation of an action which is serious, complete, and of a certain magnitude ... and through the arousal of pity and fear effecting the *katharsis* of such emotions', he is in effect attempting to identify the narrative structure and generic characteristics of tragedy.[26] The identification of Sidney and Aristotle as quasi-structuralists bears out the point made earlier that pre-Romantic critics tend to be more interested in genre and generic conventions than in the expressive author. However, if the *Poetics* is structuralist, then it merely *gestures* at a structuralist account of the grammar of tragedy. The *Poetics* is a short and sparse text, and the terms Aristotle uses to describe tragedy in particular are not fully developed. They are suggestive, inspirational and open to a variety of interpretations. If the *Poetics* thus offers an explanation of tragedy, then it is an extremely foreshortened explanation. The point I want to make about the sparseness of Aristotle's account of tragedy is that it seems *appropriate* to the genre to want to try to explain it, but not be able fully to do so. The simultaneous desire for, and threat to, knowledge, are especially present in one of the terms Aristotle uses to define tragedy: recognition.

Of all the terms that Aristotle uses to characterise tragedy, it seems to me that *anagnôrisis*, or 'recognition', is the key term, because of its central relevance to all of the others. Recognition is defined, in a beguilingly straightforward way, as a 'change from ignorance to knowledge'.[27] Although knowledge is then qualified as the disclosure of 'either a close bond, or enmity' between characters, knowledge is not substantially or momentously predicated by Aristotle.[28] It may be that historical distance prevents us from 'recognising' the full implications, to a Greek audience, of the discovery of a close relationship or enmity. Nevertheless, Aristotle's writing, here and elsewhere in the *Poetics*, is cursory and technical, rather than explanatory and climactically expansive. Recognition is one of tragedy's techniques, one of its formal devices, but its effects, in terms of significance and meaning, are not densely elaborated. Thus the question of knowledge, the question of what we are to recognise through the unfolding of the tragic narrative, *remains* a question, which then unsettles the other terms used by Aristotle. For example, what is the nature of the *hamartia*, often translated as tragic flaw, which tragedy encourages us to recognise? Is error the result of *individual* or *collective* hubris? By collective do we mean a particular society or humanity in general? Aristotle does not answer these or any other questions which later critics have sought to answer. As Timothy Reiss puts it, 'what we have [in the *Poetics*] is simply the expression of some *fact* about how to construct a tragedy. To translate the word as "tragic flaw" is to make of a later particular reading of some tragedies a Principle of Tragedy.'[29] Reiss subsequently makes the point that 'Tragedy *performs* . . . equilibrium in its own action, it resolves the ignorance of a protagonist, the insolubility of a conflict between mutually exclusive ethical or social imperatives, or the more general absence of meaningfulness *by the order of its own performance.*'[30] Relating this insight specifically to the question of recognition, we could say that the answer to the problem of what we are to recognise is not given in advance of the particular tragedy in which it is worked out. Truth and knowledge are, in other words, conditional upon individual performances – and individual interpretations – of tragedy.

To conclude this brief account of Aristotle's structuralism: the fact that the *Poetics* does not provide an exhaustive and complete explanation of the grammar of the genre corresponds to the threat to explanation, cognition and foundations which takes place within tragedy itself. This brings me to one further Aristotelian category, namely wonder, or *to thaumaston*, to which I have already briefly referred. Of wonder, Aristotle writes:

> Since tragic mimesis portrays not just a whole action, but events which are fearful and pitiful, this can best be achieved when things occur contrary to expectation yet still on account of one another. A sense of wonder will be more likely to be aroused in this way than as a result of the arbitrary or fortuitous, since even chance events make the greatest impact of wonder when they *appear* to have a purpose (as in the case where Mitys's statue at Argos fell on Mitys's murderer and killed him, while he was looking at it: such things do not *seem* to happen without reason). So then, plot-structures which embody this principle must be superior.[31]

Tragedy may reveal a pattern – a kind of 'poetic justice' – but the recognition that there *is* a just pattern to life will be astonishing and unexpected, the implication being that lack of pattern is more the tragic norm.

RECOGNITION, ESSENTIALISM AND ANTI-ESSENTIALISM IN *KING LEAR* AND *HAMLET*

Briefly revisiting two of the three plays already discussed in the light of the account given of Aristotle, we might usefully ask: what are the essential truths which tragedy encourages us to recognise in its attempt to overcome oppositions between competing realities and kinds of truth?

In the case of *King Lear*, is the folly of human presumption the lesson that tragedy teaches? Does the nothing that Lear becomes speak to the reality of the human condition and the absolute 'something' to which he aspired, the unreality? Does *King Lear* show us our humble place in the universe? Or does the play, in showing us the tyranny of the forces that control us, only encourage us to defeat them? A third option might be to suggest that the balance that *King Lear* seeks lies somewhere between these extreme androcentric and theocentric, or humanist and antihumanist, perspectives.

The first words in *Hamlet* – 'Who's there?' (I.i.1) – are an early signal of the difficulties of *recognition* which characters will experience in this play. The beginning of the play also presents the first of several of the play's travestied rituals, for Barnardo, the guard who is about to relieve Francisco, is the one who asks 'Who's there?' when we might reasonably have expected the guard already on duty to have been given this line. Where the 'correct' form of the military ritual would have allowed Francisco and Barnardo to recognise themselves and each other (as guard on duty and relief guard), recognition through communication is straightaway threatened. Little and large errors of recognition continue to be made throughout the play.

Recognition, to recall Aristotle, is a 'change from ignorance to knowledge', but in *Hamlet* this change never appears to take place. Instead, ignorance of any 'true' state of affairs prevails. *Mis*-recognition is, in other words, a permanent condition. The catalogue of questions asked by Marcellus, another of the King's guards, is typical of the murkiness which surrounds virtually everything and everyone in this play:

> Good now, sit down, and tell me, he that knows,
> Why this same strict and most observant watch
> So nightly toils the subject of the land,

And why such daily cast of brazen cannon
And foreign mart for implements of war,
Why such impress of shipwrights, whose sore task
Does not divide the Sunday from the week.
What might be toward that this sweaty haste
Doth make the night joint-labourer with the day,
Who is't that can inform me?

(I.i.73–82)

The state of Elsinore, presided over by Claudius, is evidently a secretive state, which keeps its subjects uninformed. Put more theoretically, Elsinore is a world in which the relationship between signifiers and signifieds, appearances and realities, surfaces and depths, causes and effects has been disrupted. Guards are on round-the-clock duty without knowing why. The state makes preparation for war but its subjects are ignorant of the reasons. It therefore seems entirely appropriate to the state of Elsinore that a ghost should appear and that its appearance is so ambiguous that it generates further crises of recognition: 'What art thou', asks Horatio, echoing the opening question of the play 'that usurp'st this time of night,/Together with that fair and warlike form/In which the majesty of buried Denmark/Did sometime march?' (I.i.49–52). The ghost is an unknown quantity, an *unrecognisable* other, generating one after another question as to its identity and provenance. It epitomises the 'mystery' (III.ii.357) which virtually every figure in the play at one time or another, or indeed at all times, embodies.

Of course the guilty secret upon which the Claudian state is built – namely Claudius's murder of old King Hamlet – is eventually exposed, and the tragedy consequently becomes legible within an Aristotelian grammar as the story of a change from ignorance to knowledge. The identification of Claudius as the villain of the piece might be seen as signalling the tragedy's restoration of moral foundations. It replaces appearances – of truth, virtue and villainy – with their essences. It provides the tragedy with a definite cause and catalyst – Claudius being the origin of Elsinore's dis-ease. And it puts a stop to the seemingly interminable problem of recognising who is who and what is what.

However, matters are always more complicated in this most complicated and inexhaustible of plays. For example, the Freudian reading, referred to earlier, obliges us to reconsider the assumption that Claudius is the sole villain and catalyst of the tragedy, for Hamlet is also guilty. Now the cause of tragedy is Oedipal, with tragedy originating in unresolved childhood traumas, and what we are encouraged to recognise are not so much *moral* as *psychological* truths.

Thus I recognise, as Hamlet does, what seems to be *the* truth only to find that there are other truths and other stories to tell around its central tragic 'core': *Hamlet* as a story of Oedipal rivalry; *Hamlet* as a story about indecision, indecision being the cause of the tragedy; *Hamlet* as a story about the shift from one kind of world (old Hamlet's) to another (Claudius's), the shift being the cause of the exile's feeling that he belongs to neither. Recognition does not work in the explicit and obvious way that it does in the early Renaissance English tragedy *Gorboduc*. *Gorboduc*'s use of allegorical dumbshows at the beginning and choric commentaries at the end of each act clarifies the design and truth of the play for an audience who are thereby not called upon to exercise their judgement to any great extent.[32] By contrast, *Hamlet* participates in what I referred to in Chapter 1 as the theatre of human judgement. This is a theatre which *does* create active participants of an audience estranged, like Hamlet himself, from metaphysical and moral certainties and thereby placed in the position of having to think and judge for themselves.

THE SPANISH TRAGEDY

There are many ways of applying structuralist ideas and mobilising the concepts of *langue* and *parole*. Thus far, I have been thinking about the genre tragedy as an example of a *langue* and individual tragedies as *paroles*. Whilst continuing some of the themes of the previous analyses, this section will offer a different application of the concepts of *langue* and *parole*, by using them to explore problems of language and communication within a single play, *The Spanish Tragedy*. In what follows, *langue* will generally refer to the possibility of shared language and shared socio-linguistic codes, while *parole* will refer to the privatisation of meaning which can be seen as occurring in the play. In *The Spanish Tragedy*, *parole* takes precedence over a destroyed *langue*, or else, socio-linguistic structures are so alienating that individuals retreat into their own private *paroles*.

The story of Hieronimo in *The Spanish Tragedy* is the story of a man vainly attempting to overcome his enforced exile into a world of his own. As a result of the murder of his son Horatio, who is stabbed to death and left hanging in the arbour where he and Bel-Imperia were making love, Hieronimo is shocked into contemplation of an act whose special enormity defeats comparison. It is an 'incomparable murder', a murder which maroons Hieronimo:[33]

Where shall I run to breathe abroad my woes,
My woes whose weight hath wearied the earth?
Or mine exclaims, that have surcharged the air
With ceaseless plaints for my deceased son?
The blustering winds, conspiring with my words,
At my lament have moved the leafless trees,
Disrobed the meadows of their flowered green,
Made mountains marsh with spring-tides of my tears,
And broken through the brazen gates of hell.
Yet still tormented is my tortured soul
With broken sighs and restless passions,
That winged mount, and hovering in the air,
Beat at the windows of the brightest heavens,
Soliciting for justice and revenge;
But they are placed in those empyreal heights,
Where, counter-mured with walls of diamond,
I find the place impregnable; and they
Resist my woes, and give my words no way.

(III.vii.1–18)

The second half of this speech effectively cancels the first. Against the image of an animate universe premised upon the existence of sympathies and continuities between microcosm ('my woe', 'my lament') and macrocosm (the lament of Nature), there is the opposing image of an indifferent universe composed of discontinuous, incomparable realms. Hieronimo's 'still tormented' soul is not relieved of its particular sorrow by his conceit of a sympathetic nature. Instead of emptying itself out through the perception of correspondences, Hieronimo's grief remains persistently his to endure. The reality of widening gaps between the personal and the general, *parole* and *langue*, is explicitly attested to in the second half of a speech which concludes by turning in upon itself.

Hieronimo's woeful 'words' seek company, but they find none. They are outward-reaching in their aspired-to embrace of a timeless and universal order of justice, but the path from the particular to the universal is decisively blocked. The heavens are 'impregnable'. Despite the withdrawal of God or the gods from human affairs, Hieronimo continues to 'breathe abroad [his] woes' in his ever more desperate pursuit of justice. As long as Hieronimo's desire for revenge/justice manifests itself in pleas and entreaties, as long as it assumes, that is, a public character, then the extreme personal passion for revenge may be assimilated with a commonly recognised system of justice. However, the king, ideally the secular representative of divine justice, is, like the heavens, deaf to the call for 'Justice, O, justice to Hieronimo' (III.xii.27). The reason for the king's impregnability is 'business': 'Who is he that interrupts our business?' (III.xii.30). Sealed off from Hieronimo because of his own abiding preoccupation with cementing an alliance with Portugal, the king epitomises the self-absorption and immersion in immediate affairs which pervade the world of the play.

The play is full of examples of characters immersed in their own private worlds. The ghost of Andrea, for example, who forms an on-stage audience with the figure of Revenge, periodically complains to Revenge that the play he is watching seems to have little to do with *him* and *his* desire for revenge: 'Come we for this from depth of underground,/To see him feast that gave me my death's wound?' (I.v.1–2). Likewise, the secret Machiavellian plotter Lorenzo systematically disconnects his public from his solitary, private self – 'I'll trust myself, myself shall be my friend' (III.ii.118) – to become absorbed in his own self-made world. And Hieronimo, whose access to the king is blocked by both Lorenzo and by the king's own self-absorption, himself becomes ever more introverted and secretive. The possibility of revenge finding legitimate expression through an official and universally recognised exercise of justice becomes increasingly remote. Like virtually everything else in the play, things, people and concepts fall apart from one another. 'Justice', says Hieronimo, 'is exiled from the earth' (III.xiii.140), and thus revenge and justice, private and public, become utterly distinct.

The dubiously compensatory 'pleasure' left to Hieronimo is his elaborate, idiosyncratic and undiscriminating performance of revenge. In the sudden and spectacular transformation of courtly entertainment into a scene of vengeful bloodletting, Hieronimo, like the revengers who succeed him in subsequent plays, becomes a connoisseur of violence. He puts on, as he promised he would, 'a strange and wondrous show' (IV.i.185). Revenge, within this entertainment designed to amaze, has little or nothing to do with justice, and everything to do with the satisfying imposition of a highly personalised scheme of values which surpasses the ingenuity and introvertedness of all the preceding secret plots. The question, of Hieronimo's show, which we are encouraged to ask (and which the on-stage witnesses themselves repeatedly ask) is not 'is the action just', but 'why does Hieronimo do it?' It is not justice but again *psychology* which is now the centre of interest. And I would argue, further, that such is the privatised nature of this psychology that it cannot be fully comprehended by a mode of analysis devoted as much to principles of relationship and connection as to the concrete particulars of individual characters. We can, of course, say that Hieronimo's course of action is purely reactive, and that he is driven to extremes by the situation in which he finds himself. But what this neat wedding of individual psychology to social situation fails to take account of, is the total collapse of communication between people, concepts and levels of explanation and analysis dramatised by Hieronimo's show and the ensuing reactions to it. Hieronimo becomes an unknowable *other* in a world of unknowable others. 'Each one of us', announces Hieronimo in the planning stages of the performance, 'must act his part/In unknown languages,/That it may breed the more variety' (IV.i.172–4). The unintelligibility of the play within mirrors the actual or potential unintelligibility of the play without. Stranded in linguistic worlds of their own, the actors in Hieronimo's play will only be acting out their own alienation and isolation.

The proof, if proof were needed, that communication has become seriously threatened is the on-stage audience's response to Hieronimo's explanation, which proves to be no explanation, of the reasons for his actions. The King, Viceroy and Duke of Castile hear but evidently do not understand Hieronimo's long speech of justification (IV.iv.73–152), for they begin to ask questions which Hieronimo has only just answered. Speech has lost its communicative function along with its basis in any transcendent or universal principles. Having delivered yet another speech which fails to infiltrate the impregnable fortresses of others' hearts and minds, Hieronimo signals his total disaffection and withdrawal from the possibility of shared speech and principles by biting out his tongue. *The Spanish Tragedy* accumulates further negative examples of separating plots and insular consciousnesses through its bifurcating topographies. Andrea's framing narrative of his journey through the underworld sets the tone, here, for Hell is rigidly, claustrophobically parochial. Lovers are sent to the '"fields of love"' (I.i.42), martialists to the '"martial fields"' (I.i.47), and 'either sort [is] contained within his bounds' (I.i.62). Likewise, usurers are appropriately punished by being 'choked with melting gold' (I.i.67); 'wantons' are 'embraced with ugly snakes' (I.i.68); and 'murderers groan with never-killing wounds' (I.i.69). Myopia is punished with myopia. The inhabitants of the underworld can never escape the places to which they have been everlastingly consigned. Andrea himself meets his destiny and obsession in the figure of Revenge, who leads him out of the underworld to witness several further examples of monadic enclosure.

There is, however, a glimmer of hope in this play which pessimistically testifies to the destruction of all shared grammars of meaning. Up until the moment of his total withdrawal from communication, Hieronimo is virtually the only character in the play who attempts, though not always successfully, to maintain a balance between the individual and the typical, the particular and the general, *parole* and *langue*. The balance is expressed in his desire to publicly stage, exemplify and make a didactic point about the world's disintegration into 'sundry languages' (IV.iv.74). To publicise the evacuation, by individuals, of meaningful forms of public life is to reanimate that threatened public realm by revealing the otherwise unrevealed fact that there is, after all, a pattern to be grasped, a general trend to be located in the movement *from* justice *to* revenge, *from* relationship and shared meaning *to* disconnection, *from* universals *to* particulars. It would be a mistake, therefore, to see Hieronimo's play as a *purely* personal statement, for its larger aim is arguably to encourage its audiences, both on stage and off, to recognise those general patterns which exist beyond individualised perception.

In this respect, Hieronimo could be seen as the play's beleaguered spokesperson for further Aristotelian ideas about tragedy, ideas which are again revisited in Philip Sidney's *A Defence of Poetry* (written at approximately the same time as Kyd's *The Spanish Tragedy*). I am not arguing, here, for the direct influence of either Aristotle or Sidney upon Kyd, but for a conception of tragedy at least partly shared by classical and Renaissance theorists and practitioners of the genre in the face of the *specific* fragmentation of theatre styles and genres discussed in Chapter 1 and the *general* phenomenon of fragmentation thematised in *The Spanish Tragedy*. In the *Poetics* Aristotle argues as follows for the relationship between philosophy, history and poetry/tragedy (tragedy being a subdivision of poetry):

> poetry is both more philosophical and more serious than history, since poetry speaks more of universals, history of particulars. A 'universal' comprises the *kind* of speech or action which belongs by probability or necessity to a certain *kind* of character – something which poetry aims at *despite* its addition of particular names. A 'particular', by contrast, is (for example) what Alcibiades did or experienced.[34]

Sidney takes up these differences and wittily elaborates them thus:

> The philosopher, therefore, and the historian are they which would win the goal, the one by precept, the other by example. But both, not having both, do both halt. For the philosopher, setting down with thorny arguments the bare rule, is so hard of utterance and so misty to be conceived, that one that hath no other guide but him shall wade in him till he be old before he shall find sufficient cause to be honest. For his knowledge standeth upon the abstract and general, that happy is that man who may understand him, and more happy that can apply what he doth understand. On the other side, the historian, wanting the precept, is so tied, not to what should be but to what is, to the particular truth of things and not to the general reason of things, that his example draweth no necessary consequence, and therefore a less fruitful doctrine.[35]

Mediating between the abstract universals of philosophy and the concrete particulars of history, poetry offers the best of both worlds. Himself a writer of 'fruitless poetry' (IV.i.72) and the author of the tragedy which he presents to the court, Hieronimo could be seen as a metaphor for the playwright, Thomas Kyd himself, and the tragedy which he has performed by his players in 'sundry languages' as the condensed, and more 'philosophical' (as in abstract) version of Kyd's play. Hieronimo's tragedy is, in other words, Kyd's tragedy in miniature. It is a gathering place for otherwise scattered meanings, a final 'speaking abroad' by Hieronimo of the ills and fragmentation of society. It is as though Kyd, via Hieronimo, is encapsulating and reiterating the moral or 'precept', as Sidney calls it, of the play, for fear that that moral might have been obscured by the play's own pull towards the particular.

The play thus has an identifiable structuralist *grammar* even if that grammar is to point to the increasingly *un*grammatical nature of society. At the same time, the abstract design of the play is given, in Aristotle's phrase, the 'addition of particular names'. Abstract issues, that is, receive concrete embodiment. *The Spanish Tragedy* is thus not philosophical according to Sidney's or Aristotle's definition of that term. It does not present the issues with which it is concerned in the dryly abstract way that, again, *Gorboduc* does. Characters in Kyd's play are not simply conduits for ideas and arguments.

Thus even as public and private, *langue* and *parole* threaten to part company, the play just about makes it possible to reconnect them. The play's underlying structures of opposition between speech and speechlessness, private and public *are* clarified by, and condensed in, Hieronimo's play-within-the-play. This is the abstract version of the play itself. It is the play in shorthand. It is the play pared down, in the manner of a structuralist analysis, to its essentials. In Aristotelian terms, it is the moment of *recognition*, the change from 'ignorance to knowledge' which allows us to see the big picture, and understand what is at risk. By contrast, the play as a whole is more 'historical', meaning, in Aristotle's and Sidney's use of the term, that its design is concretely embodied in the lives of particular individuals.

Structuralism itself tends towards the abstract and the 'philosophical'. It tends, that is, to understand language in terms of impersonal structures and systems rather than direct, 'face-to-face' communication. Such understanding is often shorn of any reference to psychology. Meanwhile, 'psychology' is frequently thought about in wholly individualistic terms, and shorn, in turn, of any reference to society. Structuralism thus inherits oppositions between private/public, personal/impersonal, psychology/society which could be said to have originated, or at least intensified, in the sixteenth and seventeenth centuries and which are so strikingly dramatised in *The Spanish Tragedy*.

3

Poststructuralism
A Midsummer Night's Dream; Hamlet; The Alchemist

'Let us wage a war on totality; let us be witnesses to the unpresentable.'[1] Thus speaks the influential rabbi of postmodern/poststructuralist thought, Jean-François Lyotard. The introductory section of this chapter will explain how hostility to totality and sympathy for the unpresentable or unseen constitute two key features of poststructuralist thinking which differentiate it from such totalising and cognitively inclined theories as structuralism. Put summarily, where structuralism looks for systems of meaning, poststructuralism questions systematic thought. Where structuralism seeks to lay bare a text's or language's workings, poststructuralism advances a sense of the text's mystery.

This introductory section will also situate poststructuralism within a broader historical framework by glancing at its affinities with Romanticism.[2] This is not, of course, the *only* way to situate poststructuralism, but it will help to make clear the contrasting intellectual and cultural traditions to which structuralism and poststructuralism may be seen as belonging. The contrast I have in mind here is roughly that between science and art, or the knowable and the mystical. What poststructuralism brings to a scientifically minded structuralism eager to map the text through diagrams and technical vocabulary is a Romantic sense of the sublime. In this respect poststructuralism is the most recent variation on a tradition which starts at least as far back as the Romantics and continues through modernism and the New Criticism of the 1940s and 1950s. This tradition insists upon the ineffability of the literary text, upon the resistance of the literary text to translation into utilitarian facts. As the New Critic Cleanth

Brooks once said of the effect of the use of paradox in John Donne's poetry: 'Deprived of the character of paradox with its twin concomitants of irony and wonder, the matter of Donne's poems unravels into "facts", biological, sociological, and economic.'[3] Though less admiring of literary artefacts than New Criticism, poststructuralism similarly resents the scientistic reduction of writing to facts or structuralist grammars.

Poststructuralism also challenges structuralism's scientistic tendency to 'de-psychologise' and dehumanise language. If language, within structuralism, tends to be regarded as an impersonal system, then language, for many poststructuralists, is the very site of human subjectivity. Language, after all, makes it possible to say 'I', it allows us to locate ourselves as subjects. However, if language enables or promises subjectivity, then it also postpones it, for we are constantly being dislocated and unsettled by language due to its inherent instability. To insist upon the way language puts us into process is, of course, to pose questions about who we are. How can the 'I' be ever fully knowable to itself or to others when that signifier 'I' can be used in any number of different sentences and contexts? Poststructuralism thus *questions* subjectivity as much as it *confirms* it, but this questioning itself identifies the difference of structuralist and poststructuralist attitudes to language, for in structuralism, or at least some versions of it, the question of the subject simply does not arise. It is the impersonal sign, not the subject, which is the primary object of analysis, whereas, in poststructuralist writing, sign and subject are brought into much closer relationship.[4] Reading a text is not a distanced, objective, quasi-scientific enterprise, for when we read a text, we are in effect reading ourselves, and experiencing in a particularly acute and intense way the effects that signs have upon subjects.

I do not want to imply that the concerns of structuralism and poststructuralism are utterly distinct, for both take the linguistic turn that much of modern literary theory in general takes, and both could be described as having decentred the subject. Neither do I wish to imply that structuralism and poststructuralism fall into neatly divided schools, for structuralist writing often contains within it the seeds of poststructuralist ideas, and, conversely, poststructuralism often retains structuralist concepts. An example of such interpenetration is Barthes's essay, 'The Death of the Author', to which we have already referred. It is often not clear, for instance, whether Barthes's decentring of the subject is done in the name of a structuralist science of the text, or a poststructuralist conception of the subject as process. Witness, as an example, the following passage:

> In his story *Sarrasine* Balzac, describing a castrato disguised a woman, writes the following sentence: *'This was woman herself, with her sudden fears, her irrational whims, her instinctive worries, her impetuous boldness, her fussings, and her delicious sensibility'.* Who is speaking thus? Is it the hero of the story bent on remaining ignorant of the castrato hidden beneath the woman? Is it Balzac the individual, furnished by his personal experience with a philosophy of Woman? Is it Balzac the author professing 'literary' ideas on femininity? Is it universal wisdom? Romantic psychology? We shall never know, for the good reason that writing is the destruction of every voice, of every point of origin. Writing is that neutral, composite, oblique space where our subject slips away, the negative where all identity is lost, starting with the very identity of the body writing.[5]

Does the subject – as *fixed entity* and origin of meaning – 'slip away', as Barthes puts it, only to return – as *process*? Or does it vanish to make way for the 'objective' concepts and categories of structuralism?

Given these complicating questions, it would be simplistic to divide theorists and the ideas associated with one or another theory into completely separate 'schools'. On the other hand, it would equally be a nonsense to eliminate both the marked and the more subtle differences between theories. While structuralism and poststructuralism both decentre the subject, privilege language, subvert essentialist thinking, and so forth, they do so to different ends. The differences outlined above, between the scientism of structuralism and poststructuralism's neo-Romantic emphases upon the question of the subject and upon the 'unpresentable', constitute *some* of the points of tension between the two styles of theorising.

Because of poststructuralism's partial rehabilitation of the subject, the first application of poststructuralist criticism which follows later will explore a topic – namely, love – conventionally associated with the affective life of the subject. Love seems an appropriate topic for poststructuralism because it solicits the subject through its promise of fulfilment and subjectivity ('I love, therefore I am!'), at the same time as it puts the subject into process, and makes of subjectivity a question ('what does being in love mean?'). Love thus mirrors some of poststructuralism's own concerns in that it simultaneously *subjectivises* language: meaning that it invites us to think that language is not just an impersonal medium but has to do with 'us'; and it also makes of the subject a linguistic process.

The second application of poststructuralist criticism directly confronts the question of what we mean by the subject, and explores the different ways in which the 'self' can be signified in language. I am not suggesting that subjectivity is the only concern of poststructuralism. My point is rather that, unlike structuralism, poststructuralism overcomes the signifier/subject divide by treating language as something that matters intimately to us. In the discussion of poststructuralist ideas which follows, the notion that language and subjectivity are coterminous will hopefully emerge.

LANGUAGE IN POSTSTRUCTURALISM

Let me now begin to explore the above ideas in greater depth and detail by focusing on some of the work of probably the most influential of poststructuralist thinkers, Jacques Derrida.

For Derrida, language, or 'writing' as he prefers to call it, is an adventure into the unknown. How will the plot unravel? How will the next sentence terminate? Where will you have been taken by the end of this chapter? These questions are not so much the concern of structuralism. Structuralism tends to emphasise the *predictability* of language and narrative, by revealing their conformity to underlying rules and structures. Contrastingly, poststructuralism places greater emphasis upon the *unpredictability* and creativity of language.

However, Derrida's writing itself does not simply explain the proposition that writing is an adventure. It *enacts* that proposition. Thus the Derridean equivalent to my humble and reasonably intelligible 'writing is an adventure into the unknown' is the following conclusion to his essay on the shortcomings of structuralism:

Writing is the outlet as the descent of meaning outside itself within itself: metaphor-for-others-aimed-at-others-here-and-now, metaphor as the possibility of others here-and-now, metaphor as metaphysics in which Being must hide itself in order to appear. Excavation within the other toward the other in which the same seeks its vein and the true gold of its phenomenon. Submission in which the same can always lose (itself). *Niedergang* [descent], *Untergang* [down-going]. But the same is nothing, is not (it)self before taking the risk of losing (itself). For the fraternal other is not first in the peace of what is called intersubjectivity, but in the work and the peril of inter-rogation; the other is not certain within the peace of the *response* in which two affirmations *espouse each other*, but is called up in the night by the excavating work of interrogation. Writing is the moment of this original Valley of the other within Being.[6]

This passage is not entirely characteristic of Derrida's style and the hope of making sense of it is not helped by quoting it out of context of the rest of the essay. Nevertheless, the passage is still to some extent typical of a writer who sees writing in terms of risk, unpredictability and danger, and practices what he preaches by putting meaning and intelligibility at risk. What do we gain from thinking about writing in this way?

Feeling 'at a loss' or 'at sea' is probably how quite a few readers initially respond to Derrida and other poststructuralist writing. Moments when we lose our way in an argument or dense section of prose threaten our capacity to make sense. We may reasonably think of such moments as moments which we will need to overcome if we are to come to 'know' the text, master its arguments, communicate those arguments to others, and so on. Often, however, the difficulty is itself part of the argument. The medium *is* the message. This is particularly so of poststructuralist writing. Thus it is worth considering further the experience of being 'at a loss'. For doesn't this phrase indicate that we are being removed from our normal places, divided from what we already know? I know how the word 'other' can ordinarily be used. Likewise the words 'writing', 'being' and 'valley'. But the combination of these words within the enigmatic Derridean sentence 'Writing is the moment of this original Valley of the other within Being' obliges me to suspend and/or extend previous knowledge. What I claimed about tragedy in the last chapter, that tragedy involves a crisis of knowledge or *anagnôrisis* (recognition) applies here, but now more positively, because for Derrida the loss or temporary suspension of the already known is exhilarating. Like the experience of vertigo, writing's (metaphorical) removal of the ground from beneath our feet mobilises us. Roland Barthes refers to this experience of dislocation as *jouissance* or bliss: 'Text of bliss: the text that imposes a state of loss, the text that discomforts (perhaps to the point of a certain boredom), unsettles the reader's historical, cultural, psychological assumptions, the consistency of his tastes, values, memories, brings to a crisis his relation with language.'[7]

Poststructuralism could thus be said to advocate the ecstasy of unknowing. Or, more precisely, it values unknowing as an indispensable condition of the possibility of knowing. This is what I take Derrida as meaning when he writes that the 'moment of decadence . . . is the period proper to all movement of consciousness'.[8] Only through the decadence or *'destructuring'* of what is already conceived can consciousness become active, and knowledge become dynamic and non-finite, rather than static and finite.[9] Only by opening oneself to 'the Valley of the other' – to what is beyond present knowledge, and therefore beyond the present self – can the self think, feel, know, see differently. The subject is thus put into process. Against those forms of knowledge, such as structuralism, which aspire to know their objects of knowledge in some ideally complete and exhaustive way, poststructuralism emphasises the hidden and the occulted. It values that which resists being brought to consciousness, because what we do not or cannot fully know entices curiosity, entices the desire to know otherwise.

Language, within poststructuralist thought, itself becomes mysterious. A medium of *communication* within structuralism, language within poststructuralism is an opaque medium which is forever subverting the communicability of concepts. There are two key Derridean tropes upon which I want to focus in order to specify further poststructuralism's view of knowledge and language as arcane. One is the notion of the supplement; the other, closely related notion is that of absent presence. There are various other related terms, such as *trace, dissémination, écriture, différance* and *pharmakon*, which Derrida uses to 'describe' – though describe is too static a word – the workings of language, but these two will serve to indicate the poststructuralist Derridean ethos.

For Derrida, language operates according to a principle of supplementarity. There are two meanings of supplement which Derrida suggests cannot be firmly distinguished. Supplement is first defined by Derrida as an addition to something which is already complete. According to this definition, the supplement 'adds itself, it is a surplus, a plenitude enriching another plenitude'.[10] But the supplement, says Derrida, does more than simply add, for 'the supplement supplements. It adds only to replace. It intervenes or insinuates itself *in-the-place-of*; if it fills, it is as if one fills a void.'[11] The example Derrida uses is the failed attempt in the writings of Jean-Jacques Rousseau to inscribe Nature as a 'self-sufficient' notion.[12] The example I want to briefly make use of is the reflection on human need in *King Lear*. In response to Goneril's question about her father's need to retain his own followers – 'What need you five-and-twenty, ten, or five/To follow in a house where twice so many/Have a command to tend you?' (II.iv.259–61) – Lear answers:

What need one?
O! reason not the need; our basest beggars
Are in the poorest thing superfluous:
Allow not nature more than nature needs,
Man's life is cheap as beast's. Thou art a lady;
If only to go warm were gorgeous,
Why, nature needs not what thou gorgeous wear'st,
Which scarcely keeps thee warm. But, for true need . . .
(II.iv.262–8)

What human beings need is not so obvious as to preclude the possibility that they might 'need' the presumed opposite of need; namely, superfluity, luxury, excess. Superfluity is the supplement that 'adds to' the notion of need, making it an equivocal rather than self-sufficient and self-evident concept. However, I am not sure that I would want to take the further Derridean step and suggest that superfluity 'supplements' in the secondary sense of *replacing* the previously existing concept of need. To do so would be to imply that concepts are *so* much in lack of their own identity that they may be arbitrarily exchanged for any number of other identity-less notions. Lear may equivocate the word 'need', but he has enough of the universalising soothsayer in him to want to recover a sense of the true identity of concepts: 'But, for true need . . .'. And although he may begin to build his definition of true need on the back of a misogynist satire on the inauthentic needs of fashionable women, that 'wrong' move is for us to recognise precisely as an error which keeps alive the possibility of discovering what the truth about human needs might ultimately look like.

Derrida's notion that the supplement, in its secondary sense, totally voids the concept which it is supplementing may thus require some qualification. Derrida himself fluctuates between the extreme view that the 'substitute does not substitute itself for anything which has somehow existed before it' and the more temperate notion that 'Nothing . . . is anywhere ever simply present or absent.'[13] This, for me, is a vitally important distinction. It is the difference between saying, on the one hand, that all concepts are equally absent, anonymous and therefore substitutable, and, on the other, that *some* concepts may be more substitutable than others, and that all concepts in any case achieve some level of 'presence' which makes them recognisable as that concept and no other. Steering a line somewhere between these two positions, we might conclude that concepts do have recognisable identities, but that these identities are never so static or Platonic as to be completely immovable. Thus it could be suggested, for example, that most of the time Hamlet has a reasonable grasp of the concepts of, and therefore difference between, justice and injustice, but that does not stop him wondering about the justice or injustice of revenge. Hamlet's idea of justice is, in other words, complicated and compromised by revenge, but it is not so compromised as to become a totally meaningless or 'absent' category which may be simply supplemented/supplanted by revenge.

I have dealt in some detail with Derrida's notions of supplementarity and absence/presence because much hinges upon them. Infinite play of meaning and deferral of presence constitute what Derrida refers to as the fall or loss of the '"transcendental signified"'.[14] Because meanings or signifieds can never be definitively located, we are forever separated from the certainties associated with one or another transcendent principle. Rather than stabilising signification, such putatively transcendent signifieds as God, Science, and 'Man' are as prone as any other signifier to the vagrancy of language. Poststructuralism's view of language is worth contrasting once again with that of structuralism. In structuralism, words are weighed down with meanings as a result of the albeit shifting sets of oppositions and differences which exist between them and hold them in place ('man' *versus* the gods, private *versus* public, appearance *versus* reality, and so forth). Contrastingly, in poststructuralism, words are much 'lighter'. Concepts are not so anchored as to form the basis of expansive, large-scale narratives about the warring principles at work in the world or society. Words float free of the oppositional structures which burden them with meaning.

POSTSTRUCTURALISM AND THE SUBLIME

As I have already indicated, I would not want to go all the way down the poststructuralist road and see all concepts as equally absent. Nevertheless, a little absence may be a good thing, especially when it comes to freeing up some of the more stultifying tendencies of an excessively cognitive approach to literature. For where does an account which reduces the text to a totally known quantity leave notions of creativity, surprise and astonishment? Tragedy, for example, may make us hungry for knowledge and explanation, but that is only because it has succeeded in disturbing our cognitive maps, our assumptions, our usual ways of making sense. Surely all great literature should in some way 'astonish', which is the Aristotelian way of putting it, or induce a state of *jouissance*, which is Roland Barthes's equivalent term for describing the thrill of being transported. The Romantic term is 'sublime'. Emmanuel Kant, key nineteenth-century theorist of the sublime, argued that the contemplation of such awesome natural phenomena as 'shapeless mountain masses towering one above the other in wild disorder' is an example of a sublime moment when our capacity to reason is disturbed but thereby called upon to rise to the challenge of the extraordinary and 'employ itself upon ideas involving higher finality'.[15] Derrida's notion of writing as 'the moment of [the] original Valley of the other within Being' is not so very far removed from Kant's embrace of the indispensability of mystery to reason. Closer still, perhaps, to Derrida's sense of the ineffable are the following lines from Wordworth's *The Prelude*:

Visionary power
Attends upon the motions of the winds
Embodied in the mystery of words;
There darkness makes abode, and all the host
Of shadowy things do work their changes there
As in a mansion like their proper home.
Even forms and substances are circumfused
By that transparent veil with light divine,
And through the turnings intricate of verse
Present themselves as objects recognised,
In flashes, and with a glory scarce their own.[16]

Poststructuralism, it could be argued, builds a sense of Romantic mystery into its theory of language by virtue of the way it treats concepts as 'shadowy things', haunted by the alien presence of other concepts.

Thus conceived – and there are, of course, numerous other ways of conceiving of it – poststructuralism can be used either to question the identity of literature (the concept of literature itself being an absent presence) or to give an account of its identity precisely as mysteriously elusive to conceptualisation. For poststructuralism, from this latter perspective, brings into focus an important, but often overlooked, aspect of our experience of literature: no matter how exhaustive our understanding of a literary text may become through the worthwhile attention we devote to its formal properties, its literary, intellectual and socio-historical contexts, and so on, one of the reasons for valuing literature may be the residue that escapes or continues to challenge conceptualisation.[17] As with jokes, or erotic experience, so also with aesthetic experience: explanation of 'how it works' can seem inappropriate and clumsy. The antidote to structuralist or formalist accounts of the rules and conventions governing literary production is thus the poststructuralist insistence upon the play, creativity and ineffability of writing. Such an insistence naturally makes of subjectivity a process.

Looking further afield, beyond literature – as poststructuralism with its emphasis upon the ambiguity of *all* writing itself does – the uses and/or implications of poststructuralism are many and varied. To insist that no concept is ever fully present or fixed may offer the personally and politically liberating message that concepts are always and everywhere open-ended and contestable.

Or it may lead to a debilitating kind of obscurantism. The sections to follow will consider these several sides of the poststructuralist story. The politics of poststructuralism will also be discussed in Chapter 6, on feminism.

POSTSTRUCTURALISM IN SUMMARY

- Poststructuralism questions the binary oppositional thinking of structuralism, its desire to pare down texts to their essentials, its emphasis upon the already given rules which individual texts exemplify, and its excessively cognitive approach whereby the literary text is rendered fully visible and known.
- Poststructuralism offers an alternative, more dynamic as well as arcane view of language based upon the notion that concepts are never fully present, are never completely 'themselves'.
- The notion that meaning is to a greater or lesser extent occulted connects poststructuralism to the Romantic notion of the sublime. Poststructuralism therefore lends itself to a view of literature which takes account of the ineffability of aesthetic experience.
- Poststructuralism's Romantic inheritance also contests structuralism's tendency to view language as an impersonal system which carries on regardless of the subject.
- The wider political and social implications/uses of poststucturalism's aesthetics of the sublime are varied: insistence upon the metaphysical absence and instability of concepts may be either liberating (because concepts become contestable) or debilitatingly obscurantist (because nobody can finally know anything).

A MIDSUMMER NIGHT'S DREAM

A Midsummer Night's Dream brilliantly plays the poststructuralist game of 'now you see it, now you don't', for love, the central theme of the play, simultaneously proffers and withdraws its meaning. Love, that is, is an elusive signifier, an absent presence, promising a sense of fulfilment as far as the subject is concerned but defying his/her desire to name and know the nature of desire. Let me begin with the play's bizarre erotic comedy. . . .

Is it possible to fall in love with a wall? Can walls come? In the entertainment put on by Bottom and company to celebrate the wedding of Theseus and Hippolyta, such strange happenings can apparently occur. Here is Thisbe speaking first to the Wall which separates her from the ostensible object of her desire, Pyramus:

> *Thisbe.* O wall, full often hast thou heard my moans,
>   For parting my fair Pyramus and me!
>   My cherry lips have often kiss'd thy stones,
>   Thy stones with lime and hair knit up in thee.
> *Pyramus.* I see a voice; now will I to the chink,
>   To spy and I can hear my Thisbe's face.
>   Thisbe?
> *Thisbe.* My love thou art, my love I think!
> *Pyramus.* Think what thou wilt, I am thy lover's grace;
>   And like Limander am I trust still.
> *Thisbe.* And I like Helen, till the Fates me kill.
> *Pyramus.* Not Shafalus to Procrus was so true.
> *Thisbe.* As Shafalus to Procrus, I to you.
> *Pyramus.* O kiss me through the hole of this vile wall.
> *Thisbe.* I kiss the wall's hole, not your lips at all.
> *Pyramus.* Wilt thou at Ninny's tomb meet me straightaway?
> *Thisbe.* 'Tide life, 'tide death, I come without delay.
>   *Exeunt Pyramus and Thisbe [, severally].*
> Wall. Thus have I, Wall, my part discharged so;
>   And, being done, thus Wall away doth go.
>
> (V.i.186–203)

There are several kinds of comic confusion here: of the senses ('I see a voice'); of the inanimate and animate (for Wall is a walking, talking wall, played by Snout); and of names ('Helen' and 'Limander' instead of the Hero and Leander, who are the central protagonists in Christopher Marlowe's adaptation of the classical myth). The inspiration for all these comically incongruous misplacements, and the biggest confusion of all, is the confusion as to who is really in love with whom – or what. Thisbe's unsure 'My love thou art, my love I think!' and Pyramus's equally equivocating 'Think what thou wilt' are the tell-tale signs of the radical ambiguity at the heart of this particular discourse of love.[18] *Is* Thisbe in love with Pyramus? Or is she really enamoured of the Wall: 'My cherry lips have often kiss'd thy stones'; 'I kiss the wall's hole, not your lips at all'? And is it any surprise, given the unexpected attention lavished upon Wall, that Wall then refers, punningly, to sexual orgasm: 'Thus have I, Wall, my part discharged so'. Situations *almost* as strange as walls getting excited as a result of the novel experience of becoming objects of desire have arisen in the play 'proper'. Witness Titania's crush on Bottom, semi-transformed as an ass. So what is the point of all this strange sexual comedy? What does it mean to fall in love with a wall? Is there a 'deeper' meaning to the fun of seeing Snout stalwartly attempting to maintain the pretence of being stonily inanimate in the face of Thisbe's desire for him?

A cliché about love – that love thrives on obstacles – is being literalised in this scene, such that the wall separating Pyramus and Thisbe becomes the object of the two lovers' desire. How can 'love', then, ever be itself when it is subject to such comical category mistakes? How can lovers ever know the nature of their desire when desire shows them that it is not the other that they desire, but the boundary separating them from their ostensible love object? Another way of saying this – and the play, as we shall see, takes so much delight in other ways of saying things that 'things' increasingly lose their substance and solidity – is to suggest that lovers love their projections of each other more than they do the actual flesh and blood 'reality' of the other. Physically present, the 'solid object' Pyramus may exert some influence over the way he is imagined by Thisbe. Physically absent, he is as she likes him, as she wants him to be. The physical absence of Pyramus is the key to the creation of another Pyramus, a Pyramus who is 'present' to Thisbe's erotic contemplation of him. This narcissistic, auto-erotic aspect of love surfaces in another of the scene's sexual innuendoes when Thisbe says to Pyramus that she has kissed 'the wall's hole, not your lips at all'. The kissing of holes which are associated with female sexuality suggests masturbation, and implies that Thisbe is content, at least for the time being, with the fantasies of Pyramus which she projects in his (physical) absence. Thisbe does not necessarily want the real, live Pyramus. She wants – as well as hates – the wall which separates her from Pyramus, because this allows her to imagine 'her' Pyramus.

Pyramus is partly complicit with his own 'disappearance', for he gives permission to Thisbe to 'think what thou wilt'. This line is edged, however, with the suggestion that Thisbe will not be able to enclose him totally within her narcissistic projections, for think what she will, he will always be to some extent other to her perceptions of him. Bottom as Pyramus is as eager to be different people as Bottom as Bottom is: 'like Limander am I trusty'; 'Not Shafalus to Procrus was so true'; 'let me play Thisbe too' (I.ii.46); 'Let me play the lion too' (I.ii.66). Thus if narcissism promises to make present to consciousness that which is physically absent, the actual presence of Bottom as Pyramus as 'Limander' and then 'Shafalus' disturbs the narcissistic fantasy and generates more absence (and so more desire). Wall, as the signifier of absence, thus fuels compensatory narcissistic projections which are in turn undermined by the realisation that the loved one is still desirably missing.

Like Thisbe, Pyramus has a similar love/hate relationship with Wall because of its creation of an ever fluctuating relationship between presence and absence. For Pyramus, as for Thisbe, the wall is 'sweet' and 'lovely' for promising to reveal through its 'chink' (V.i.174–5) a tantalising glimpse of his beloved. Because it will only reveal some and not all of Thisbe, love will maintain its alluring mystery, its otherness. Partial visibility is more erotic than total exposure. 'Is not the most erotic portion of a body *where the garment gapes?*', asks Roland Barthes. 'It is intermittence', he continues, 'which is erotic: the intermittence of skin flashing between two articles of clothing (trousers and sweater), between two edges (the open-necked shirt, the glove and the sleeve); it is this flash itself which seduces, or rather: the staging of an appearance-as-disappearance.'[19] Wall, or more precisely, the hole in the wall becomes desirable in its own right because it prevents the object of perception from becoming fully transparent to the perceiver. Wall stages, in Barthes's terms, an 'appearance-as-disappearance'.

The same is true of the actors playing the parts of Pyramus, Thisbe, Wall, Moonshine and so on, for they are never so fully absorbed in their roles as to be unable to step outside them to speak to the on-stage audience about the play in which they are acting. Throughout the artisans' performance, Bottom, for example, slips easily in and out of his role as Pyramus, speaking sometimes as Pyramus, at other times as Bottom, about the scene he has just been performing. In other words, neither Bottom nor Pyramus is fully absent or fully present, because the one is always visible in or through the other. Bottom is visible as Bottom even as he plays the part of another; and his 'own' personality is never suppressed for long by the part he plays. But if we were then to reach the conclusion that Bottom can never create the illusion of being something other than himself, this would also be problematic because so much of Bottom's personality is based upon his zest for experimentation, his desire to be other. The ass's head that he is transformed into by Puck speaks to the paradox of Bottom, for Bottom is at once the most and the least transformed of all the characters.

The duality of Bottom – his all too palpable presence combined with his embrace of the idea of being other – is perfectly mirrored in his ambivalent attitude towards theatrical illusion. On the one hand, he is keen to remind the audience that the artisans' play *is* a play and that illusion should not be mistaken for reality. Thus in one of the rehearsals, he recommends that the prologue to their play should 'tell [the audience] that I, Pyramus, am not Pyramus, but Bottom the weaver' (III.i.19–20). Likewise, the illusion of the lion, which seems to kill Thisbe, must not be so potent as to frighten the 'ladies' (III.i.29) in the audience:

> *Snout.* Therefore another prologue must tell he is not a lion.
> *Bottom.* Nay, you must name his name, and half his face must be seen through the lion's neck; and he himself must speak through, saying thus, or to the same defect: 'Ladies,' or 'Fair ladies, I would wish you,' or 'I would request you,' or 'I would entreat you, not to fear, not to tremble: my life for yours! If you think I come hither as a lion, it were pity of my life. No, I am no such thing; I am a man, as other men are': and there, indeed, let him name his name, and tell them plainly he is Snug the joiner.
>
> (III.i.35–44)

On the other hand, this anti-illusionist desire to remind the audience that the actors are not really the characters they are impersonating rests upon a belief in the power of the role to transform the actor so utterly that no trace whatsoever is left of the actor's identity. Bottom is thus an example of that mixture of illusionism and anti-illusionism explored in Chapter 1. He is suspicious of illusion and the imagination, yet enthusiastically embraces them. He is always but never quite 'himself' because an aspect of his self is his desire to be other. As Pyramus is simultaneously visible and invisible to Thisbe through the chink in the wall, so Bottom is likewise present and absent, solid and unsolid. It is no surprise, given this duality, that the play's most seemingly grounded character should be one of its most compelling spokespeople for its philosophy of the inexpressible. Here is Bottom's response to the 'dream', as he refers to it, of being half-transformed into an ass and then doted on by the queen of the fairies:

> I have had a most rare vision. I have had a dream, past the wit of man to say what dream it was. Man is but an ass if he go about to expound this dream. Methought I was – there is no man can tell what. Methought I was – and methought I had – but man is but a patched fool if he will offer to say what methought I had. The eye of man hath not heard, the ear of man hath not seen, man's hand is not able to taste, his tongue to conceive, nor his heart to report, what my dream was. I will get Peter Quince to write a ballad of this dream: it shall be called 'Bottom's Dream', because it hath no bottom.
>
> (IV.i.203–15)

Bottom truly realises his desire to be other here, for if he is almost always, despite this desire, visible as down-to-earth, anchored Bottom, keen to reassure the 'ladies' of the true identity of things and people, then this faltering, astonished description of his indescribable dream shows him taking leave of his habitual foundationalism. This is a moment of decadence, menace and exhilaration, a moment when 'meaning' is tantalisingly beyond the reach of the knower. Like Wall, who places a bar between subject and object, perceiver and perceived, the dream, with its suggestion of momentous, but undisclosed knowledge, lies on the outer rim of consciousness. At once pressingly concrete and disturbingly vacant, the dream insists on being told at the very same moment as it scuppers interpretation.

Bottom's evocative account needs to be set alongside other accounts of awakenings from or into the odd, dreamlike experiences induced by Puck's love drug. This is Lysander, for example, on waking to discover that he is fallen out of love with Hermia and in love with Helena:

Content with Hermia? No. I do repent
The tedious minutes I with her have spent.
Not Hermia, but Helena I love:
Who will not change a raven for a dove?
The will of man is by his reason sway'd,
And reason says you are the worthier maid.
Things growing are not ripe until their season:
So I, being young, till now ripe not to reason;
And touching now the point of human skill,
Reason becomes the marshal to my will,
And leads me to your eyes, where I o'erlook
Love's stories, written in love's richest book.

(II.ii.110–21)

There is nothing of Bottom's hesitation in Lysander's *immediate* rationalisation of his new object of desire. The sudden change of heart does not pose a challenge to conceptualisation; it does not suggest to Lysander that love might be that absent presence, that very 'real' yet unreal, tangible yet intangible experience which the play elsewhere shows or describes it as being. The unpredictability of love is tamed by Lysander, and the regulated language is a sign of the domestication of what appears, in Bottom's speech, as wild.

As Lysander's references to 'love's stories' and to 'love's richest book' imply, the well-read courtier has a number of amorous scripts to hand which enable him to deal eloquently with the equally numerous scenes of love. Lysander does not mangle *his* literary references, for he, as an educated courtier, has a greater familiarity with, and command of, literary culture. The reason that love does not discomfort Lysander to the same extent that it discomforts Bottom has partly to do with the more excessive nature of Bottom's transformation, but also with the always and already *scripted* nature of Lysander's responses. From this perspective, characters get or 'deserve' the transformation which is appropriate to their character. Bottom is miraculously transformed because he believes in miracles. Lysander is only slightly transformed because he has mastered the unpredictable, and is never flummoxed. In the courtier's A–Z of amorous topoi, a swift change of partner can be dealt with as a narrative of sudden enlightenment. Thus it dawns on Lysander that, 'of course', Helena is the real thing, and Hermia the inauthentic simulacrum. We've heard this one before, and before the play is through, we'll hear it again, from Demetrius.

In Derridean terms, Lysander's pat response constitutes a refusal to acknowledge the hiddenness to consciousness of being in love. Rather than acknowledging love to be an absent presence, Lysander thinks that the meaning of love is present in the words that he uses, and the 'texts' of love that he quotes. The courtiers' reliance upon ready-made scripts which seem to encapsulate love is everywhere apparent. In the very first of the play's numerous lovers' dialogues, Lysander and Hermia exchange their knowledge of texts thus:

> *Lysander.* How now, my love? Why is your cheek so pale?
> How chance the roses there do fade so fast?
> *Hermia.* Belike for want of rain, which I could well
> Beteem them from the tempest of my eyes.
> *Lysander.* Ay me! For aught that I could ever read,
> Could ever hear by tale or history,
> The course of true love never did run smooth;
> But either it was different in blood –
> *Hermia.* O cross! too high to be enthrall'd to low.
> *Lysander.* Or else misgraffed in respect of years –
> *Hermia.* O spite! too old to be engag'd to young.
> *Lysander.* Or else it stood upon the choice of friends –
> *Hermia.* O hell! To choose love by another's eyes.
> *Lysander.* Or, if there were a sympathy in choice,
> (I.i.128–41)

Lysander begins here with the standard male poetic device, discussed at the beginning of Chapter 2, of comparing his mistress with nature. The ossified procedure of comparing cheeks with roses, necks with swans, eyes with sun, and so on – is parodied in Shakespeare's Sonnet 130 ('My mistress' eyes are nothing like the sun') and made a mockery of in *A Midsummer Night's Dream* itself in the artisans' play. Thisbe's catalogue of comparisons between Pyramus and nature ends with the line: 'His eyes were green as leeks' (V.i.322). Likening eyes to leeks lays bare the convention – the structuralist grammar – of amorous poetic comparison, which has become routinised to the point of burying love and the love object under the weight of ready-made formulae.

What is, then, interesting about the above dialogue is the way Hermia introduces an element of excitement and unpredictability by *speeding up* Lysander. Interrupting his sluggish and again text-based exposition of the trope that true love never runs smoothly, Hermia engages him in a quick-fire and more frenzied exchange of motifs about star-crossed, tragic love. Amenable, to begin with, to Lysander's discourse of love, in responding appropriately to his standard poetic 'cue' – 'How now, my love? Why is your cheek so pale?/How chance the roses there do fade so fast?' – Hermia then takes the lead in what becomes a quickstep rather than slow waltz. There is now more of an erotic charge to the dialogue, as courtly eloquence and wit are put on trial and the lovers compete to outdo each other's or their own previous hyperbolic extravagance. This saying 'more than' (in the case of Hermia's climactic series of exclamations) or saying differently (in the case of Lysander's 'Or . . . Or . . . Or . . .') temporarily turn Lysander and Hermia into excessive figures whose *last* word is never their *final* word. As the self-perpetuation and alternation of stichomythia imply, there will always be something more or something different to say. There will always be a motif to add to or to supplant another motif, for the permutations of amorous discourse and experience are many and varied. The boys from court might want to contain love through their eloquent mastery of love's varied repertoire, but something nearly always escapes, for love is a signifier, so the play's romantic embrace of the ineffable insists, which is always in excess of signifiers.

The exchange between Lysander and Hermia poses the further question of whether love belongs to the realm of 'existential' truth or of seductive fiction, for the possible existence of parody in the hyperbolic language which is used by the lovers to express the hyperbolic emotional reality of love, would undercut the pretensions of romantic discourse to the status of a kind of secular religion. Parody would make us wonder whether love is a heightened reality or a massive illusion, an authentic truth or a compelling lie.[20] Performed or read 'seriously', love becomes the site of hushed reverence. Performed or read parodically, love equates to folly. We do not and perhaps should not choose between these readings or imagined performances, for the writing, in line with the play overall, suggests a double perspective which treats love with both reverence and irreverence. In poststructuralist terms, we could say that love is haunted by the presence of contradictory signifiers. It is a sign that seems to lack for nothing, but which simultaneously signifies lack.

In the forest scenes, the fast dance of love which is begun in the first act by Hermia and Lysander gathers further momentum as lovers move to a rhythm which they neither control nor understand. Attempts to explain changes of affection are stillborn as love constitutes an ever more acute problem of knowledge. Who is *really* in love with whom? Can one ever be certain of the desire of the other? Does 'I love you' always mean what it says, or is the meaning of being in love always hiding itself so that, as Derrida puts it, 'the Valley of the other within Being' can appear? Does the phrase 'I love you' not encompass such a cornucopia of possibilities that its meaning is always menaced? Within the context of *A Midsummer Night's Dream*, 'I love you' can variously mean:

1. I love me, I love my conception, my poetic conceit of you.
2. I love the boundary separating us. I love what I cannot see of you, I love your otherness, that which lies tantalisingly beyond my knowledge and experience.
3. I am incomplete, at a loss, in exile without you as a foundation.

Only in the last instance does love offer itself as a position of knowledge, but even this foundationalist conception is rocked in the play. Thus the 'ancient love' which has made of Hermia and Helena 'a double cherry, seeming parted,/But yet an union in partition' (III.ii.215, 209–10) is threatened by what Helena sees as Hermia's malicious baiting of her. Not even this love, grounded as it is in lifelong friendship, escapes the unruly influence of that other kind of love we call romantic passion.

The variability of love in *A Midsummer Night's Dream* does not mean that it is an utterly empty, absent concept which can be simply supplemented/supplanted by any number of other concepts. As I suggested earlier, a concept can have many facets yet still remain recognisable as that concept and no other. Or perhaps it is truer to say that the play *experiments* with different principles of supplementarity, some of which leave no trace whatsoever of the supplemented object, while others add to the object without entirely effacing it. Lysander's substitution of one love object for another is an example of the first principle, for it leaves no trace of his former identity as Hermia's lover, while

Bottom's visibility as Bottom while playing the part of Pyramus is an example of the second. It is the kind of double vision generated by this second principle which the play seems to me to embrace, for therein lies both the strange sensation of something being near and far, present and absent, itself and not itself, as well as the possibility for multiple interactions between illusion and reality. 'This green plot shall be our stage' (III.i.3) announces Bottom as the artisans begin their rehearsal in the wood *which the play has already transformed from a stage*. The stage can thus be many things – a wood, a wood which is then imagined as a stage – but amid these various transformations the play is keen to remind us, through such references to its own processes, of the original thing which is paradoxically so capable of being imagined in many other ways. Love can be seen as occupying the same relationship of the stage itself to the idea of an original meaning veiled by the layer upon layer of illusion superimposed upon it. The play periodically reminds us that the stage is a stage, because we are all too liable to suspend our disbelief and parenthesise (rather than *totally* forget) that primary reality. Likewise, we may know or we may think that we know what the true meaning of love is, but that primary meaning may be concealed by the play's multiple variations upon its central theme. The meaning of love is absent, but not *so* absent as to preclude a sense that it has an authentic essence – if only we could speak it or see it. To quote out of context a phrase from another play preoccupied by the relationship of appearances to invisible or non-existent realities, love is 'an essence that's not seen' (*Othello*, IV.i.16).

The same could be said of the experience of the aesthetic. For how can one put into words and thus make visible the essence of the aesthetic experience which the play affords? What diverse kinds of paraphrasing can adequately 'translate' the sublime – for me – line, 'I know a bank where the wild thyme blows' (II.i.249). An evocative line, but evocative of what? Longing? Nostalgia? Escape? Some part of ourselves from which we have been divided? Probably all these things and more besides, always more, because if the phrase does communicate escape, then it enacts it by suggesting as well as escaping definite meaning. Such language creates of the play a dream, like Bottom's, which speaks powerfully of we know not quite what. As 'imagination', says Theseus, 'bodies forth/The forms of things unknown, the poet's

pen/Turns them to shapes, and gives to airy nothin
habitation and a name' (V.i.14–18). If the poet makes ab:
present, then those located, named things may still bea ... _
of their former invisibility. There may still be a wall separating
us from complete understanding. And there is little reason, from
the poststructuralist perspective which I have been pursuing in
this chapter, why we should ever want the wall to be destroyed,
for as long as the person, concept or feeling is *partially* and therefore mysteriously visible through the wall's chink, then therein
lies the erotically tantalising *possibility* of knowledge, certainty
and fulfilment.

HAMLET

As the above account implies, the insistence of poststructuralism
on the inherent instability of language can have the effect of
deinstitutionalising concepts. Wherever the meaning of a concept
seems to have become cosily settled and agreed upon, poststructuralism can open up the term to a variety of alternative
possibilities. In 1980s Britain, for example, the term 'individualism' was institutionalised through its appropriation by the specific
class and political ideology that became known as Thatcherism.
The outcome of this appropriation was that 'being individual' in
the 1980s came to be associated with entrepreneurialism, enterprise culture and weaning oneself off of a welfare state which
was thought to have turned us into unhealthily needy depend-
ants who expected everything to be done for us. So close was
the association of the term 'Thatcherism' with 'individualism'
that the latter virtually came to mean one Thatcherite thing and
one thing only. In short, individualism became institutionalised.

Although there is a particular paradox about the fact that *individualism* should have become institutionalised, there is in general
nothing unusual about any of this. Words are constantly being
placed in the service of one or another socio-political agenda.
What poststructuralism makes visible is the way that any attempt to monopolise the meaning of a word always takes place
within a context of *struggle*. Words, that is, are sites of contestation, whose 'natural' open-endedness must be overcome if they
are to become available as ideological monosyllables.

Hamlet has often been assigned a central role in the history of individualism, sited as a key moment in the formation of the modern subject. For Catherine Belsey, in *The Subject of Tragedy*, for example, *Hamlet* 'has begun to define an interiority as the origin of meaning and action, a human subject as agent'. Yet the play, she continues, 'cannot produce closure in terms of an analysis which in 1601 does not yet fully exist'.[21] Belsey means by this that the ideology of individualism is emergent in *Hamlet* rather than fully developed. Although she does not pursue the notion that individualism, in this emergent state, may be open to very different interpretations, her insight lends itself to such a post-structuralist perspective. *Hamlet*, one might say, is 'about' the very problem of being an individual, it is 'about' the different, contradictory ways there are of signing the self.

Hamlet presents a world in which traditional hierarchies are collapsing, a world in which attempts to ascribe and determine identity from on high repeatedly fail. In his opening speech, Claudius projects himself as the unifying representative of the new court and nation, in an attempt to effect a smooth transfer of allegiance from the old to the new regime. The situation of a new monarch attempting to establish himself as the embodiment of a new social and political unity is familiar from several other of Shakespeare's plays. The focus upon this key moment of *formation* of a new regime signals an instability, a need for continual construction and reconstruction of social order. Order, it seems, is never something which can be relied upon, or which can be established once and for all. As Machiavelli's *The Prince* advises, the successful leader must employ a variety of strategies to gain and maintain a fragile stability.

Central to this legitimisation crisis is the problem of the individual. As a new king, Claudius cannot afford to be complacent about his subjects. Given the prospect of individuals aligning themselves differently (with the old regime, for example), the loyalty of subjects and their place within the scheme of things have themselves to be continually reconstructed.[22] This problem is compounded by the fact that the meaning of individualism, as already suggested, is very differently inflected in the play, for what it means to be an individual has not yet been contracted to any particular class ideology. Individualism is in the process of formation, and so is an open-ended rather than closed signifier.

In playing several variations upon the theme of taking the law into one's own hands, the revenge narrative in *Hamlet* itself suggests the open-endedness of individualism. From one perspective, the individualism of revenge can be seen as the expression of a macho aristocratic code of personal honour. As Robert Watson suggests, this form of self-assertion was coming under increasing threat in the late sixteenth and early seventeenth centuries from a centralising state bureaucracy:

> Duels of honour would become a serious problem among the Jacobean aristocracy, but they are probably a secondary manifestation of a more basic shift that was already troubling the Elizabethan populace. Local justice, based in the competing interests of families, was rapidly giving way to a centralized legal bureaucracy in which personal passions and honour counted for little and patronage and rhetorical skill became all-important. Little wonder that the revenger is usually a powerless outsider avenging an inflammatory offence to a lover or close kin.[23]

Watson's view offers a useful corrective to the notion (supplied by Catherine Belsey, for example) that individualism appeared for the first time as a mainly bourgeois phenomenon in the sixteenth and seventeenth centuries, for individualism, or at least a certain version of it, is instead associated by Watson with an aristocratic code of personal honour. This suggests that individualism has not one but several histories, and that the meaning(s) of individualism secreted in each of these histories may either combine or enter into conflict with other, emergent meanings. This is arguably the case in *Hamlet*, where revenge as an aristocratic code of personal honour conflicts with other inscriptions, within the discourse of revenge, of subjectivity. Thus if revenge, for Hamlet, signifies an aristocratic form of self-assertion of which he finds himself, for most of the play, incapable, then revenge simultaneously expresses several other kinds of individualism or, indeed, *anti*-individualism. Revenge variously signifies filial duty prescribed from on high by the ghost of Hamlet's father; a populist, independent form of justice made necessary by the corruption which exists at the top of society; the devolution of moral agency, as well as moral *questions*, on to the individual; wanted autonomy; unwanted autonomy; and so on. The 'meaning' of revenge (like the meaning of love in *A Midsummer Night's Dream*) is constantly deferred, and the individualism which revenge embodies – or negates – is likewise the site of competing inflections.

Beyond revenge, the self signifies in several further ways. Subjectivity equates at times, for example, with a narrow-minded subjectivism which blocks access to universal truths and thereby generates an atmosphere of parochialism and claustrophobia. To Hamlet, for example, Denmark is a 'prison' (II.ii.243) whose inmates are *too* located, too anchored within their own little worlds of ambition or power politics. Images of frames, prisons and confinement pervade the play. The ghost speaks of the 'prison-house' (I.v.14) of his current existence and of being 'confin'd' by day 'to fast in fires'. (I.v.11). Guildenstern advises Hamlet to 'put your discourse into some *frame* [my emphasis]' (III.ii.300). Claudius, in sacrificing friendship to expediency, *confines* contact with others to manipulation. The welcome he gives to Rosencrantz and Guildenstern is therefore no authentic welcome: 'Moreover that we much did long to see you,/The need we have to use you did provoke/Our hasty sending' (II.ii.2–3). Only in soliloquy, or in feigned madness, can Hamlet temporarily escape the confinements of Denmark, speak in a more expansive, metaphysical register, and fleetingly entertain the possibility of releasing his soul from the confines of its worldly prison: 'O that this too too sullied flesh would melt,/Thaw and resolve itself into a dew' (I.ii.129–30). And in his mocking reminders to Claudius of the ultimate fate of all human flesh – 'we fat ourselves for maggots' (IV.iii.22–3) – Hamlet attempts to make the king see the broader picture, the bigger realities from which he has divided himself in making of himself a world unto himself.

Perspective, then, in Elsinore is limited by the confinement of self within narrow boundaries. Even Hamlet's generalisation that 'Denmark's a prison' (II.ii.243) is almost immediately qualified, and made relative to a particular, limited point of view: 'To me it is a prison' (II.ii.250–1). Statements with aspirations to generality cannot, it seems, escape the limitations of their particular conditions of utterance. Denmark is a prison, but only because the melancholic Hamlet thinks it so. It may be any number of other things, for *thinking* that something is so is no guarantee that it *is* so. Such is the nature of the subjectivisation of knowledge in the play that thinking can make revenge good, bad, indifferent, necessary, heroic, just or unjust. Thinking can turn a cloud into a camel, a weasel or a whale:

Hamlet. Do you see yonder cloud that's almost in shape of a camel?
Polonius. By th' mass and 'tis like a camel indeed.
Hamlet. Methinks it is like a weasel.
Polonius. It is backed like a weasel.
Hamlet. Or like a whale.
Polonius. Very like a whale.
Hamlet. Then I will come to my mother by and by.

(III.ii.366–74)

To pass a subjective interpretation off as the truth Hamlet fulfils the criterion for truth which is dominant in Denmark. Polonius says yes to every new interpretation because he is a sycophant who defers to the truth as those in authority choose to define and redefine it. Hamlet, on the other hand, does not want the truth conveniently reshaped according to one or another subjective impression. He wants to discover *the* truth – the truth about Claudius, the truth about revenge, the truth about himself – beyond all partial and limited mediations of it.

Claustrophobia; parochialism; partiality. These negatives identify one way of conceiving of subjectivity in the play. There are, as we have seen in the case of revenge, other ways of thinking the subject. Hamlet works through these, sometimes defining self as limitation and partiality; sometimes as unfathomable interiority: 'I have that within which passes show' (I.ii.85); sometimes as the place where beliefs and identities given from elsewhere are tested, and the place, simultaneously, where 'internal' dispositions are themselves questioned. Hamlet's calling into question of the knowledge and identity (as revenger) prescribed by the ghost makes reference to his own 'weakness' and 'melancholy' at the same time as it maintains a degree of confidence in the ability of individuals to try out and test truths for themselves:

The spirit that I have seen
May be a devil, and the devil hath power
T'assume a pleasing shape, yea, and perhaps,
Out of my weakness and my melancholy,
As he is very potent with such spirits,
Abuses me to damn me. I'll have grounds
More relative than this. The play's the thing
Wherein I'll catch the conscience of the King.

(II.ii.594–601)

In the context of *Hamlet*, then, being an individual can variously mean ambition (and killing your brother to achieve your ambition), violent usurpation, myopia, fragmentation, taking the law into your own hands through murder and/or revenge, refusal to conform, exile, madness, exercising your own judgement and being healthily suspicious of what ghosts and other aspiring voices of authority tell you to think and do, and exercising your own judgement as an independent member of an audience. Subjectivity is an elusive signifier, which is never fully present to itself. The multiple inscriptions of self in *Hamlet* anticipates poststructuralism and poststucturalism's own conception of the subject as process.

THE ALCHEMIST

The politics of poststructuralism can cut in more than one direction. The notion that concepts are never fully present because never identical with themselves may be a useful antidote to attempts to institutionalise concepts, but poststructuralism's anticonceptualist aesthetics of the sublime or of the 'unpresentable' have various other implications. In a society, for example, which is becoming ever more complex, opaque and 'sublime', it may be that Lyotard's appeal to the unpresentable is less the radical statement of a progressive, avant-garde thinker than a mere sign of the times, a symptom of the increasingly mysterious workings of a culture nobody really understands. Do economists really understand the economy? Can the vast and dispersed system of capitalism ever be fully 'present' to consciousness?

We should perhaps be wary, then, of universalising poststructuralism's neo-Romantic aesthetics of the sublime, for the fate of those with an attachment to the inexplicable may be that of the duped victims presented in Ben Jonson's *The Alchemist*.

Jonson's play satirises both the agents and the victims of the obscurantist language of alchemy. Alchemy in the play is at once science, pseudo-science, cosmology, religion and philosophy. Underlying its various mutations, however, is the assumption that the professors of alchemy, Subtle and Face, do not have fully to explain themselves to the aspiring beneficiaries of the transformation of base metals into gold. In response to the unbelieving Surly's accusation that alchemy's multiplicity of strange

ingredients and cryptic terms would 'burst a man to name', Subtle
and Mammon defend the obscurity of the art thus:[24]

> *Subtle.*   And all these, named,
> Intending but one thing: which art our writers
> Used to obscure their art.
> *Mammon.*   Sir, so I told him,
> Because the simple idiot should not learn it,
> And make it vulgar.
> *Subtle.*   Was not all the knowledge
> Of the Egyptians writ in mystic symbols?
> Speak not the Scriptures oft in parables?
> Are not the choicest fables of the poets,
> That were the fountains and first springs of wisdom,
> Wrapped in perplexed allegories?
> *Mammon.*   I urged that,
> And cleared to him that Sisyphus was damned
> To roll the ceaseless stone only because
> He would have made ours common.

> (II.iii.199–209)

This is close to the view of the poet put forward by Theseus in *A
Midsummer Night's Dream*, only here the alchemist's knowledge of
things not 'commonly' seen is associated with a quasi-aristocratic
attitude towards knowledge based upon the arrogance of exclusivity
and possession. Whereas the special ability of the poet to see differently takes the form of a proposition (the poet *might* be able to
see things not normally seen), the alchemist, combining pseudo-
scientific, religious and aristocratic discourse, claims absolute
possession of secret and remarkable knowledge. The actually sound
or otherwise foundations of this knowledge are not available for
inspection. They are to be taken on trust, as a matter of faith.

Faith in mysterious knowledge requires the suppression of all
other kinds of knowledge. On the eventual return of Lovewit,
the master of the house, several of his neighbours tell of the
strange comings and goings which have taken place during his
absence. As the lies of Doll, Face and Subtle look as though they
are about to be exposed, Face – reverting to his normal identity
as the trustworthy servant, Jeremy – persuades Lovewit and the
neighbours that the neighbours must have been hallucinating and/
or drunk: 'I should believe my neighbours had seen double/

Through the black-pot [beer-mug], and made these apparitions'
(V.ii.31–2). Face's version of events is believed (initially at least)
and the neighbours begin to doubt the evidence of their own senses
(V.ii.36–46). Characters in *The Alchemist* are routinely taught *not*
to trust to what can be seen, heard and empirically tested, but
to believe in the invisible shadow world to which only the initiated few have access. Dapper, one of the benighted visitors to
the tricksters' house, spends almost half of the play blindfold in
the privy. Such is his willingness to block out the evidence – in
this case, the smell – of his immediate surroundings that he thinks
he is in 'Fortune's privy lodgings' (III.v.78) awaiting the arrival
of the Queen of Fairies. This, at any rate, is the illusion he has
been sold by those who make of the invisible a profitable business. The visitors' fantasies may be tangible, and the motivations
of the tricksters' conspicuously materialistic, but this does not
prevent the duped visitors from wilfully ignoring any 'facts' which
might get in the way of their fantasies. The actual condition of
the house which Doll, Face and Subtle have managed to subdue
is described by Lovewit towards the end of the play:

> Here I find
> The empty walls worse than I left 'em, smoked;
> A few cracked pots and glasses, and a furnace;
> The ceiling filled with poesies of the candle,
> And madam with a dildo writ o' the walls.
>
> (V.v.38–42)

In terms of the varieties of theatre semiotics discussed in Chapter 1, it is the illusionist theatre of spectacle which Subtle and
company can be seen as having successfully sold – with no come-
back and no questions asked – to their clients. Customers' absolute
suspension of their disbelief ensures that the actual nature of
their surroundings goes unnoticed.

Faith in the unseen, rather than that which can be validated
by 'vulgar' sensory experience, is additionally generated by the
alchemists' use of specialised language and by the invisibility of
the production process. Jargon referring to complex technical
processes consolidates Subtle's special status as a master of an
arcane art whose mysterious workings are never seen, the elaborate
alchemical apparatus being always off stage – elsewhere – referred
to but never actually witnessed:

Subtle.   Look well to the register,
  And let your heat still lessen by degrees,
  To the aludels.
Face.   Yes, sir,
Subtle.   Did you look
  O' the bolt's head yet?
Face.   Which? On D, sir?
Subtle.   Ay.
  What's the complexion?
Face.   Whitish.
Subtle.   Infuse vinegar
  To draw his volatile substance and his tincture,
  And let the water in glass E be filtered,
  And put into the gripe's egg. Lute him well,
  And leave him closed in *balneo.*
Face.   I will, sir. [*Exit*]
Surly. What a brave language here is, next to canting!
                                            (II.iii.33–43)

In the burgeoning capitalist world which Jonson's play depicts, production is alienated from consumption, which is to say that the consumers of the benefits of the creation of gold know nothing about the (imagined) processes of its production. Ignorance of technical as well as social conditions of production is intrinsic to capitalism, as commodities appear as if by magic. However, it would be a mistake to identify alchemy exclusively as a metaphor for capitalist production, because of the various other forms of occultation with which it is associated. The alchemist's knowledge is not just a matter of the technical *expertise* required for one or another form of specialised capitalist production. It is not just a set of technical procedures which can be learnt by virtually anyone. Subtle's knowledge is imagined as more recherché, more exclusive, more *subtle* than this, the implication being that the alchemist is tuned to mysterious, invisible forces not penetrable by ordinary mortals. Associated by Subtle with poetry, alchemy is aestheticised knowledge, knowledge which cannot be acquired solely through explicitly formulated rules.

To reiterate some previous points and to bring this chapter to a close: poststructuralism's emphasis upon the unpresentable may usefully liberate meaning from the 'tyranny' of the concept, but this anti-conceptualism is not without its problems. Poststructuralist writing, like alchemy, is itself often arcane, impenetrable, and resistant to conceptualisation. As Brian Vickers, one of Derrida's critics, writes, to 'discuss [Derrida's] theories you are virtually compelled to use his terminology, and once you are inside his system you have no external purchase on it, no means of judging it in independent terms'.[25] That the same could be said of the language of alchemy in *The Alchemist* is worrying enough not to want to fall totally prey to poststructuralism's aesthetics of the sublime.

4

Psychoanalysis
Bartholmew Fair; 'Tis Pity She's a Whore

Once 'inside' a developed theory with its own particular house
style it may be difficult to see it, let alone criticise it, from the
outside. On the other hand, to remain on the outside looking in
may fail to do justice to a theory's internal dynamics. So is it
better to be an insider or outsider – or both? This question has
already cropped up in different guises and different contexts in
previous chapters: Othello as outsider wanting to be insider; the
citizens in *The Knight of the Burning Pestle* wanting to feel at home
in a theatre not theirs; reading understood in terms of identification, on the one hand, and critical distance, on the other. The
question of insides and outsides, intimacy and estrangement,
identification and alienation, will appear again, in this and subsequent chapters, in still further different guises.

For a while I want to remain an *outsider* to psychoanalysis in
order to consider its relationship to the other theories so far discussed.[1] Like structuralism and poststructuralism, the form of
psychoanalysis which has mainly influenced modern literary theory
is language-based. However, there are some striking differences
in the way structuralism, poststructuralism and psychoanalysis
understand language. Where structuralism, as we have seen, tends
to regard language as an impersonal system, psychoanalysis shares
in common with poststructuralism a conception of language as
the very site of subjectivity. Psychoanalysis, that is, never for-
gets that if subjectivity is a *linguistic* affair, then language is at
the same time a *subjective* affair.

Psychoanalysis, however, also looks beyond language and the
linguistically constructed subject to the pre-linguistic, pre-social
world which we leave behind us but which according to psychoanalysis we never entirely abandon. To be more precise, then,

105

psychoanalysis is interested in the place of intersection between 'history' and 'pre-history', in the moment of transition from the pre-linguistic to the linguistic. It is preoccupied with the individual's traumatic entry into history, culture and language: traumatic because the arrival on to the scene of culture involves the jettisoning of childish things and childish ways. Not the least of the infantile ways which have to be cast aside is the experience of continuity between self and world, subject and object, self and (m)other. The account of childhood which psychoanalysis has offered us is that infant and mother or mother figure exist in a state of dyadic union and that, modelled upon this bond, the world is experienced as continuous with the infant as plaything rather than 'external' reality. The infant, then, has no concept of an 'outside' world. For there to be an outside there would have to be an 'inside', an integrated and differentiated sense of self. But again, what sense of differentiated integration can the corporeally uncoordinated infant possibly experience? Jacques Lacan, the French psychoanalyst who has had a considerable influence on literary studies in recent years, punningly describes the pre-social infant as an 'hommelette',[2] a term which, as Mary Eagleton suggests, simultaneously invokes 'little man, a manlet or homunculus; an omelette, or an eggy mess of possibilities; and finally a Hamlet, or a scrambled Oedipus'.[3] What the 'hommelette' in Hamlet is subconsciously keen to eradicate, what the pre-social infant is at first oblivious to, and what psychoanalysis sees as characterising socialisation, is *difference* and *division*.

There is thus a price to be paid for individualisation and that price is separation: separation from the maternal body; separation from the experience of the continuum of self and world; separation from the pulsations and excitations of an unschooled body, careless of the self's later concern with body image and integration. Thus if, by subjectivity, we mean an awareness of our difference and separateness from others, then psychoanalysis remembers a 'time' or 'no-time' before difference and before separation.

However, even as psychoanalysis looks beyond the subject, it does not abandon categories associated with interiority and the affective life of the human subject. The narrative which psychoanalysis tells is nearly always about 'us' and our fears, desires, anxieties, attachments, compromises, and so on. The separated subject may disappear at times from the narrative but a human drama remains.

But I shall now stop being an outsider and get on more intimate terms with the details of the narrative which psychoanalysis tells of our loves and losses. Amid the intricate twists and turns of this narrative, it will be important not to lose sight of the main plot or, in structuralist terms, of the underlying grammar of psychoanalysis: which is the continual tension between the principles of differentiation and non-differentiation.

DIFFERENTIATION AND NON-DIFFERENTIATION

There are various ways in which the amorphous infant, blissfully unaware of difference and otherness, gets its act together and becomes integrated and separate: through the formation of *erotogenous zones*, which begin to mark off distinct areas of the body from each other; through *cathexis*, that is, the attachment of otherwise chaotically undirected drives to particular objects; through the *Oedipal stage*, at which point a third party, in the shape of the father or father figure, intrudes upon the intimate scene of infant/mother bonding and obliges the child to become aware of an outside world with its laws, conventions and taboos; and through *language*, which, to recall Saussure, is a system of differences, a system which, in other words, encourages us to think discontinuously in terms of distinctions and separations. At the same time as these forces for differentiation and organisation impinge upon the infant's world, there is a countervailing desire to overcome or compensate for separation and loss. Many of the scenarios described by Freud and later psychoanalytic theorists involve a continual toing and froing between the principles of differentiation and non-differentiation, discontinuity and continuity, organisation/integration and disorganisation/non-integration. One or two examples will help to show how this oscillation specifically works.

In his *Three Essays on the Theory of Sexuality*, Freud suggests that children have an innate aptitude for being 'polymorphously perverse'.[4] The 'sexual instinct', writes Freud, 'is *not unified*' and 'any sense-organ – probably, indeed, *any* organ – can function as an erotogenic zone'.[5] Sensual pleasure can be variously experienced through the stimulation of, for example, the oral (breast-feeding), the anal (holding on and letting go), the autoerotic (thumb-sucking) and the voyeuristic (I'll show you mine if you show me yours). While these and other forms of sensuality speak to the variousness of childish excitability, they are nonetheless erotogenous *zones*. That is, they begin to mark out a topography of the body whereby the extreme disorganisation of the new-born child gets to be partly, but only partly, contained and channelled. *Contra* Freud, or at least certain emphases in the *Three Essays* upon the objectless and therefore undirected nature of early infantile experience, it may also be the case that at an early stage a cathexis takes place whereby the child learns to recognise a particular source/object of gratification in the shape of the mother or mother figure. Freud himself seems to acknowledge this in the following passage:

> At a time at which the first beginnings of sexual satisfaction are still linked with the taking of nourishment, the sexual instinct has a sexual object outside the infant's body in the shape of his mother's breast. It is only later that the instinct loses that object, just at the time, perhaps, when the child is able to form a total idea of the person to whom the organ that is giving him satisfaction belongs. As a rule the sexual drive then becomes auto-erotic.[6]

The infant who knows no difference, who thinks that the breast appears as though it were as extension of itself, who does not sharply distinguish the breast from any other of its own or others' erotogenous zones, may nevertheless begin from an early age to recognise a special other – the mother – which is different from itself.

However, there is at the same time a swerve away from this early realisation of difference and division, for, according to Freud, the glimpsing of a world of distinct entities is accompanied by a turn towards autoeroticism ('As a rule the sexual instinct then becomes auto-erotic'), which keeps the infant's world intact and seamless. It is at this point that I want to look towards the work of some of the structuralist and poststructuralist revisionings of Freud's ideas which bring language explicitly into the frame of psychoanalysis. For what some of these later theories suggest is that the mother becomes a 'metaphorical' mother – a fantasy mother of the mind – as a way of compensating for those early stirrings of doubt about the indivisibility of the infant's world. So, for Jean Laplanche, for example, the autoerotic has everything to do with fantasy and nothing or little to do with 'actual' breasts and bodies. The 'object linked to the autoerotic turn' writes Laplanche 'is a 'fantasmatic breast'.[7] It is a breast which exists as much in the mind as it does in reality, and therefore a breast which *as* an internalised fantasy overcomes the sense of the separateness of the real thing. Thus begins the infant's initiation into the art of substitution, whereby the separateness of objects can be compensated for by replacing them either with other objects (dummies, bits of cloth, teddy bears) *metonymically* associated with the maternal body, or else with symbols and *metaphors*. Metaphor is from this perspective more displacing than metonymy, since metonymy (usually understood as a part of something substituting for the whole of that something), maintains more intimate, contiguous contact with the substituted object or concept than does metaphor. This is so even though we may dispute what constitutes a metaphor or metonym: to compare a small child to an omelette may seem a ridiculous metaphor until the comparison is explained – at which point it may seem more metonymically 'in touch with' its primary object of attention (childhood) rather than metaphorically out of touch. For Laplanche, however, sexuality becomes an increasingly and undisputedly metaphorical affair: anchored at first to biological need by virtue of the way the breast gratifies hunger as well as the senses, sexuality takes its leave of the realm of necessity to enter the decorporealised domain of subjective, autoerotic fantasy where anything may become anything through the operation of metaphor.[8]

LANGUAGE AS EXILE

The invocation of metonymy and metaphor means that we have now reached the point where classic Freudian psychoanalysis meets the structuralist/poststrucuralist emphasis upon language to form a revised psychoanalytic theory which insists that language is through and through a psychically charged activity intimately bound up with the experiences of plenitude and lack, non-differentiation and division. Witness, for example, Julia Kristeva's evocative encapsulation of the illusion or fantasy that the lost plenitude of the maternal body might be adequately recovered in word and symbol:

Signs are arbitrary because language starts with a *negation* *(Verneinung)* of loss, along with the depression occasioned by mourning. 'I have lost an essential object that happens to be, in the final analysis, my mother,' is what the speaking subject seems to be saying. 'But no, I have found her again in signs, or rather since I consent to lose her I have not lost her (that is the negation), I can recover her in language.'[9]

Once again, however, we see that with every attempt to restore presence, plenitude, oneness, continuity, there is an accompanying sense of exile and division. The infant can 'make do' with surrogate, symbolic versions of the maternal body but loss of the real thing is nevertheless apparent, for, as Kristeva implies, to *consent* to lose something is to acknowledge the loss involved in the act of a metonymic or metaphoric substitution of it. If that were not the case then we would become fetishists attached to objects or security props in the belief that they lacked and substituted for nothing whatsoever. Which, as it happens, will form part of my later discussion of Ben Jonson's *Bartholmew Fair*.

Like Kristeva's speaking subject, Laplanche's sexual self also experiences loss. As already suggested, this is because sexuality, which was originally in continuity or at least (metonymic) contiguity with the maternal body, becomes increasingly detached from its origin and 'metaphoric':

The sexual *aim* is . . . in a quite special position in relation to the aim of the feeding function; it is simultaneously the same and different. The aim of feeding was ingestion; in psychoanalysis, however, the term used is 'incorporation'. The terms may seem virtually identical, and yet there is a slight divergence between the two. With incorporation, the aim has become the scenario of a fantasy, a scenario borrowing from the function [of feeding] its register and its language, but adding to ingestion the various implications grouped under the term 'cannibalism,' with such meanings as: preserving within oneself, destroying, assimilating. . . . Thus from the aim of the function to the sexual aim, a transition exists which may still be defined in terms of a certain kind of displacement: one which, this time, follows an analogical or metaphorical line, and no longer an associative chain through contiguity.[10]

Instead of feeding and through feeding *actually* being part of the maternal body the child may *fantasise* about eating his/her mother. Sexuality in this way loses its material/maternal base even as it tries to recover it. The endless displacements and substitutions which poststructuralists see as taking place through the operation of metaphor and metonymy provoke Jacques Lacan into thinking of language itself as the unconscious. 'Since Freud,' writes Lacan, 'the unconscious has been a chain of signifiers.'[11] For Lacan, to 'be' in language is to be in a state of unspecifiable – and therefore unconscious – lack. To paraphrase the above quotation of Kristeva's into more Lacanian terms: 'it seems that I have lost something vital, necessary and essential but because language has transformed need into the more elusive, metaphorical phenomenon of desire, I cannot return to that prior state where need and desire were happily wedded and both were simultaneously satisfied'. Language cannot replace what came before it, it cannot compensate for that original state of oneness, not least because it cannot definitively name what preceded naming.

Having delved into *some* of the details and intricacies of Freudian and post-Freudian theory, I want to make two final points, of a more general kind, before concluding this section. First, the imagined pre-historical and pre-linguistic being that psychoanalysis describes is not a chronological 'stage' which we simply pass through and outgrow. The past or pre-past may return to haunt us and indeed, in the modern psychoanalytic conception of 'adult' language as psychically charged, the early experiences of loss and its negation are continually being re-experienced in displaced form. Even intellectual attachments or 'passions' may be thought of as replaying some old childish traumas and settlements. Which brings me to my second general point. Psychoanalytic accounts of both early childhood experiences and their survival as haunting memory into adulthood, will not strike everybody as self-evidently true. If *something* rings true, then so be it. An avid psychoanalytic theorist might say that scepticism is a symptom of denial/repression. But a different perspective, one which allows for a degree of scepticism, and one which also allows us to use psychoanalytic insights *against* psychoanalysis itself, would start by suggesting that psychoanalysis, despite some implicit or explicit claims to the contrary, is neither a faith nor a positivist science, and that to treat it as though it were either of these things would be to believe in it and identify with it so totally that it would become a fetish: some 'thing' that becomes everything and will not admit to any kind of insufficiency. Total identification with, and absorption into, psychoanalytic (or any other kind of) discourse would be to deny the sense of loss and separateness which Lacanian and other forms of psychoanalysis suggest it is our fate as divided social beings to experience. What I am suggesting, then, is that a form of scepticism which holds back from identification (of any kind) can be thought about from a psychoanalytic viewpoint as an acknowledgement of our state of exile from each other, from things, from beliefs and systems of knowledge which might otherwise seek to recruit us. This does not mean that we have to become total loners or isolates, distrustful, to the point of Iago-like cynicism or the extreme irony of *The Knight of the Burning Pestle*, of all intellectual and other attachments, for this would be to create yet another fetish: namely, a fetish of the self and *its* supposed separateness and self-sufficiency. Somewhere between these positions there is a mean. That mean goes by the name of *Bartholmew Fair*.

PSYCHOANALYSIS IN SUMMARY

- Like other theories which have influenced modern literary studies, psychoanalysis has taken a linguistic turn. Unlike structuralism, however, psychoanalytic understanding of language acknowledges the psychically charged dimension of language, meaning that it treats language as the locus of experiences and emotions conventionally associated with the interior lives of individuals.

- Because it concerns itself with the fluid and amorphous human 'stuff' that history, language and culture subsequently set to work upon, the object of enquiry of psychoanalysis can be located as the very *intersection* of 'pre-history' (understood, in so far as it can be understood, as a state of oneness, plenitude, indivisibility and non-integration) and history (understood in terms of difference, separation and integrated – to various degrees – subjectivity).

- Oscillation between the principles of differentiation and non-differentiation, loss and negation of loss, coordination or cathexis and disorganisation/uncathected 'energy' can be seen as characterising the various stages of infant development described by psychoanalytic theory.

- The difference modern psychoanalytic theory makes to classic Freudian psychoanalysis is to bring language into focus as the site of a continuing psychic drama in which plenitude is rediscovered only to be lost once again because language is itself based upon difference, lack and displacement/substitution. Metonymy and metaphor are seen as especially significant here, as both displace (though in different ways and to differing degrees) and so fail to offer a means of recovering the imagined lost plenitude of childhood.
- Childhood does not suddenly stop. Even though we are required to put our childhood traumas and attachments behind us, the dramas of childhood are replayed in displaced form in adulthood. Our pre-historical being continues to influence and disturb our historical being. For example, 'absolute' intellectual as well as other attachments (including an attachment to psychoanalysis) may be seen from a psychoanalytic perspective as a denial of the reality of loss and insufficiency.

BARTHOLMEW FAIR

Bartholmew Fair opens with a comic preamble to the play proper in which a contract or mock contract is drawn up by the character of the scrivener between 'the spectators or hearers at the Hope on the Bankside, in the County of Surrey, on the one party, and the author of *Bartholmew Fair*, in the said place and county, on the other party'.[12] One of the agreements to which the audience is obliged to subscribe is 'that every man here exercise his own judgement, and not censure by contagion, or upon trust, from another's voice or face that sits by him ... as also that he be fixed and settled in his censure' (ll. 94–8).

The play begins, then, with an authorial injunction enjoining upon the audience the need for law, order, constancy and segregation. For the purposes of this psychoanalytic interpretation of *Bartholmew Fair*, 'author' will be read as Oedipal father/father-figure; audience as the father's wayward children conscripted by the father at the beginning of the play to the principle of solitary, independent spectatorship – 'It is ... agreed that every man here exercise his own judgement'; and the play, representing a fair, as the occasion for sensual release, enjoyment and libidinous attachments forbidden by the father. Members of the audience are obliged to keep their distance from the play/fair, play as fair, and likewise to remain distant from each other. Only by doing so will they be prevented from lapsing into the pre-Oedipal world which the fair re-presents. Justification for reading the play in this psychoanalytic way is Jonson's own use of the vocabulary of fathers and children, in relation to fairs and fairings, in his prose work *Timber: or Discoveries*:

> What petty things they are, we wonder at! Like children, that esteem every trifle; and prefer a fairing before their fathers: what a difference is between us and them, but that we are dearer fools, coxcombs, at a higher rate? They are pleased with cockleshells, whistles, hobby-horses, and such like: we with statues, marble pillars, pictures, gilded roofs, where underneath is lath, and lime; perhaps loam. Yet, we take pleasure in the lie, and are glad we can cozen ourselves. Nor is it only in our walls and ceilings; but all that we call happiness is mere painting, and gilt: and all for money: what a membrane of honour that is! And how hath all true reputation fallen, since money began to have any![13]

As the contract set out at the beginning of *Bartholmew Fair* implies, respect for the Law of the Father, and the values which that Law promotes of integrated selfhood and independent judgement, are endangered by the prolongation into adulthood of a capricious and volatile infantilism.

We need to remember, though, that the contract in *Bartholmew Fair* is a mock contract, or at least not a totally serious one, and that consequently the endorsement of complete, Oedipal independence, together with the attendant prohibition of promiscuous intermingling, are being wholly or partly ridiculed. However much the ideals of independence and constancy *look* as though they may be seriously intended, the manner of representing them does not itself remain constant. Witness the following deterioration of the ideal of constancy into ignorance and stagnancy:

> It is also agreed that every man ... be fixed and settled in his censure, that what he approves or not approves today, he will do the same tomorrow, and if tomorrow, the next day, and so the next week, if need be; and not to be brought about by any that sits on the bench with him, though they indict and arraign plays daily. He that will swear *Jeronimo* [refers to the

Hieronimo of Kyd's *The Spanish Tragedy*] or *Andronicus* [refers to Shakespeare's *Titus Andronicus*] are the best plays yet, shall pass unexcepted at here as a man whose judgement shews it is constant, and hath stood still these five and twenty or thirty years. Though it be an ignorance, it is a virtuous and staid ignorance; and next to truth, a confirmed error does well.

('Induction', ll. 94–109)

A man impervious to changing fashions and tastes may become almost as ridiculous as the social butterfly – but only 'almost', because in the end the man who makes of himself and his self-sufficiency an absolute virtue is probably more worthy of Jonsonian admiration than the capricious man – or 'hommelette' – who is childishly delighted by the newfangled. Neither of these types, however, is able to acknowledge loss, for if one makes a fetish of the self, then the other, as we shall see, makes a fetish of the object.

The fair itself is an example of those forms of folk humour and carnival explored by Mikhail Bakhtin in his influential book, *Rabelais and His World*. I have already briefly invoked carnival (in Chapter 1). Here I want to set out one or two further ideas which closely link carnival to psychoanalytic themes.[14] According to Bakhtin, the carnival festivities which took place on high days and holy days during the medieval and Renaissance periods constituted a release from the constraints of official reality. '[C]arnival', writes Bakhtin, 'celebrated temporary liberation from the prevailing truth and from the official order; it marked the suspension of all hierarchical rank, privileges, norms, and prohibitions.'[15] Carnival is marked, continues Bakhtin, 'by the peculiar logic of the "inside out" (*à l'envers*), of the "turnabout", of a continual shifting from top to bottom, from front to rear, of numerous parodies and travesties, humiliations, profanations, comic crownings and uncrownings'.[16] Carnival's mockery of hierarchical and other distinctions, many of which are based upon the supposed superiority of mind to body, spirit to flesh, is fuelled by what Bakhtin refers to as 'the material bodily principle' or 'the material bodily lower stratum'.[17] The 'leading themes' of the bodily principle are 'fertility, growth, and a brimming-over abundance'.[18] Carnival is, in short, the pre-modern equivalent of Freud's polymorphously perverse pre-Oedipal child whose bodily drives have not yet been regulated.

Bartholmew Fair manifests several of the carnivalesque motifs described by Bakhtin.[19] The fate of Zeal-of the-Land Busy (stage Puritan) and Adam Overdo (Justice of the Peace), which is to be put in the stocks, is an instance of the comic uncrowning and humiliation of actual or aspirant figures of authority. The pervasiveness of a 'low', body-based language of abuse speaks to the prioritisation of a volatile and unrestrained 'material bodily principle' over polite and reasonable discourse. Likewise, the bizarre game, played by several of the characters, of 'vapours', which involves contradicting one another for the sake of contradiction, suggests, amongst other things, the discharge of undirected and nameless bodily energies. Finally, the abundant figure of the 'pig-woman' Ursula, who is variously invoked as 'Body o' the Fair' (II.v.67), 'mother o' the pigs' (II.v.68) and 'fatness of the Fair' (II.ii.112), and whose sharp business practices are described by Adam Overdo as 'the very womb and bed of enormity gross as herself' (II.ii.102–3), evokes both Bakhtin's ideas about carnival fertility and psychoanalytically oriented perspectives on the infantile desire for absorption by the maternal body. Quarlous, one of the more aloof and circumspect visitors to the fair, likens Ursula to a 'quagmire' and 'bog' into which a person 'might sink . . . and be drowned a week ere any friend he had could find where he were' (II.v.82; 85–7). From the Oedipalised Quarlous's perspective, Ursula is that enveloping and gargantuan womblike space which would draw him back into a state of non-differentiation.

As the reaction of the quarrelsome Quarlous makes clear, not all of the characters are prepared to 'let go' and give themselves over to the sensual delights of the fair. Attitudes to the fair vary considerably: from Zeal-of-the-Land Busy's hypocritical condemnation to the utterly unequivocal and rapt enthusiasm of *Bartholmew* Cokes, whose name indicates his complete identification with *Bartholmew* fair. This range of reactions suggests a more equivocal attitude to carnival than Bakhtin's mainly positive celebration of carnival as an expression of popular resistance to official culture. And there is good reason for the play's more ambivalent attitude. That reason is money. The aim of Ursula and company is to make money out of the fair's visitors by fair means or foul. In other words, this is a commercialised version of the carnivalesque, or, to revert to the psychoanalytic idiom, it is *a capitalist simulation of the blissful state of pre-Oedipal indivisibility not to be confused with the 'real' thing.* The real thing – if it ever existed even in more 'authentic' versions of carnival – is past. All we can do is acknowledge its loss.

Which, of course, several of the visitors, notably Cokes, conspicuously fail to do. Cokes is the epitome of Freud's child, a polymorphous, unregulated infant who infuriates his guardian Wasp because his attention is captivated by each and every capital object on sale at the fair:

> *Cokes.* Those six horses, friend, I'll have –
> *Wasp.* How!
> *Cokes.* And the three Jew's trumps; and half a dozen o' birds, and that drum – I have one drum already – and your smiths – I like that device o' your smiths very pretty well – and four halberts – and, le'me see, that fine painted great lady, and her three women for state, I'll have.
> *Wasp.* No, the shop; buy the whole shop, it will be best; the shop, the shop!
>
> (III.iv.67–75)

'What do you lack? What is't you buy? What do you lack?' (II.ii.28–30). Such is the repeated refrain of the market, in the shape of Leatherhead, whose shop it is to which Cokes is drawn. As the ideal consumer, Cokes takes to heart the sales pitch of the trader which promises that lack may be filled by material objects. Even though the goods on offer at the fair are shoddy goods – 'Froth your cans well i' the filling' (II.ii.92–3) is Ursula's instruction to her tapster, Mooncalf – such is the extent of Cokes's desire to overcome desire that he cannot acknowledge the insufficiency of the fair. Its illusory plenitude, passed off as real, is treated totally at face value by a Cokes anxious to overcome the gap separating him from the objects which he thinks will fulfil him.

Thus if the spectator contracted by the author at the beginning of the play is all distance, independence and containment, then Cokes is all volatile empathy and identification with the sights and sounds of the fair. His appetite for forms of identification which are absolute and complete is at its most pronounced – and ridiculous – in the conversations he has with the puppets during the puppet show put on by Leatherhead and Littlewit. 'I am in love with the actors already, and I'll be allied to them presently' (V.iii.116–7), he tells Littlewit on hearing from Littlewit of the delights which the play will offer. Mindless of the differences between theatre and world, illusion and reality, inanimate and animate, Cokes, like the citizens in *The Knight of the Burning Pestle*, gets thoroughly caught up in the fiction of the puppet show. The world according to Cokes has no seams or divisions. There is nothing from which he is separate. This is true of the fair which bears his name; the objects in it to which he becomes childishly attached; the puppet show in which he becomes immersed; and the puppets with whom he converses as though they are real. For Cokes there is no 'inside' or 'outside'. There is no reality outside the way he imagines it to be. If, as Jean Laplanche suggests, the mother becomes for the infant a metaphorical, fantasmatic mother whose metaphoricity simultaneously compensates for and accentuates the loss of the real thing, then Cokes's imaginary world knows no insufficiency. Even when disillusionment with the fair (as a result of being cheated and robbed) threatens to puncture Cokes's idyll and separate him from what he perceives to be the source of all sensual pleasure and satisfaction – 'Methinks the Fair should not have used me thus, an 'twere but for my name's sake' (IV.ii.7102) – his 'faith' is only temporarily shaken. Moreover, the personification of the fair as ideally protective of its *own* kin or kind constitutes a refusal to see the fair as an impersonally separate commercial phenomenon. The fair has let him down, but like a friend or parent, it will have opportunities to shelter Cokes once more.

The complete inability of the pre-Oedipal Cokes to tolerate any kind of absence or loss is wonderfully illustrated in the following exchange between himself, Wasp (nicknamed 'Numps') and Leatherhead:

> *Cokes*. Come, Mistress Grace, come sister, here's more fine sights yet, i'faith. God's lid, where's Numps?
> *Leatherhead*. What do you lack, gentleman? What is't you buy? Fine rattles? Drums? Babies? Little dogs? And birds for ladies? What do you lack?
> *Cokes*. Good honest Numps, keep afore, I am so afraid thou'lt lose somewhat. My heart was at my mouth when I missed thee.
> *Wasp*. You were best buy a whip i' your hand to drive me.
> *Cokes*. Nay, do not mistake, Numps, thou art so apt to mistake; I would but watch the goods. Look you now, the treble

fiddle was e'en almost like to be lost.

Wasp. Pray you take heed you lose not yourself.

(III.iv.1–12)

The play's repeated insinuation, through Leatherhead, of a condition of lack, combined with Cokes's determination to lack for nothing, makes the play almost irresistible to psychoanalytic interpretation.

But what of us? What of the spectator or, now, the reader of this play whose psychoanalytic motifs, once noticed, proliferate? What of *our* loss/desire for completion? Is it not possible to psychoanalyse our/my relationship to the play, an analysis which might have something to say about the desire to arrive at a satisfyingly complete psychoanalytic or otherwise interpretation? These questions seem especially pertinent given the play's own drawing of attention in its Induction to the role of the spectator.

If the childlike Cokes gets too immersed in the fair and subsequently in the puppet play, and if the idea of absolute Oedipal self-sufficiency and detachment is also mocked, then how are we to position ourselves in relation to the play or to plays in general – or, more generally still, to works of art? I spoke earlier of the way intellectual attachments may be so absolute as not to admit of any insufficiency. The same could be said of works of art, for which many people still declare a love and a passion (see the Introduction). Is it possible that the utopian dimension of works of art, which is a transgression/transcendence of ordinary time, puts us in touch with something more primordial and essential than our 'merely' historical selves? When we enter the imaginative world of a play, that world might seem less brutally 'external' than the real one which exists outside the play. The imaginative play world is, in other words, one which *we* are enabled to control, manipulate and interpret. It therefore approximates the subjective playground that characterises the infantile fantasy world where lost objects can be found. As such, the theatre becomes the site of considerable emotional investment. This is how Cokes treats the fair and, later, the puppet play.

Contrastingly, the Induction mockingly or half-mockingly advises against infatuation, for the Oedipal father, in the shape of Jonson the Author, forbids us the pleasure of involvement. We must not forget ourselves in the way that Cokes gives himself over to pre-Oedipal narcissistic fantasy – which is, of course, a kind of subjectivity, but one that consumes the other as part of the self and so eradicates difference. There is a further problem here, however. For would we not also be losing ourselves if we were to submit unquestioningly to the 'external' authority of Ben Jonson? Automatic compliance with the master's *instruction* to be independent would make passively dependent subjects of us. We are asked to become separated subjects not through 'personal' choice but by 'impersonal' legalistic contract. If subjectivity is to be any kind of attractive proposition – and prevent us from reeling away back to the pre-Oedipal realm – it will have to be less prescriptive, less 'external' than this.

So. On the one hand, we have a father-figure – an 'external' authority – impersonally contracting us to division and independence, and, on the other, a refusal (by characters within the play) of separation and externality. And there is also, as part of this equation, the play/work of art which potentially acts as a surrogate 'object' of emotional investment amenable to pre-Oedipal 'subjective' fantasy – amenable, in other words, to the dissolution of a strict subject/object polarity. The question once again arises: where are we in relation to these various Oedipal and pre-Oedipal dramas of differentiation and indivisibility?

The play can be seen as imagining not one but two Oedipal scenarios, one rigid, impersonal and contractual; the other, more flexible. In *Bartholmew Fair* an overly strict and authoritative Oedipal scenario whereby differentiation entails subjection to *prescribed* laws of difference is displaced through mockery so that another, more flexible form of Oedipalisation may emerge. This less legislative form of Oedipus complex may also be seen as taking a more 'relaxed' attitude towards the pre-Oedipal. Given that no figure of authority inside or outside the play escapes ridicule, we are encouraged to become, as it were, our own masters or mistresses, and 'test' ideas (such as the desirability of constancy, for example) for ourselves. However, this does not mean that we should be so certain of or pleased with our empowered selves as to preclude uncertainty or displeasure. A certain openness – which includes, in the context of *Bartholmew Fair*, an openness to the other as a hidden or buried part of the self, an openness to Cokes, for example, as an aspect of the child in us – prevents the stasis, closure and absolute autonomy/authority of the self.

Thus, in conclusion, we can say that the delicately poised mean of *Bartholmew Fair* involves: a questioning of external authority and *its* preconceived, externally imposed 'laws' of difference; an endorsement, instead, of subjective testing as part of a less strict Oedipal process; and an embrace, which falls some way short of being total, of fantasies of pre-Oedipal oneness. Central to the Jonsonian 'vision', seen from the perspective of psychoanalysis, is the importance of recognising loss. It is only with such recognition that an obsessive fetishism of subject or object may be avoided.

'TIS PITY SHE'S A WHORE

'Tis Pity She's a Whore knows no such Jonsonian means or neo-classical balance. If Jonson requires us to examine as well as to vicariously participate in pre-Oedipal, carnivalesque excess (or at least in post-Oedipal, capitalist simulations of it), then John Ford's play encourages us to identify with its central character's complete identification with the pre-Oedipal, only for that sympathy to turn belatedly to repugnance. The 'orgy' and extremity of illicit identifications and couplings that is *'Tis Pity She's a Whore* reaches out to the audience to make conspirators rather than observers of its members.

Giovanni, the play's central protagonist, is, as it turns out, a monster of pre-Oedipal narcissism. If, in most modern psychoanalytic accounts, fully differentiated subjectivity is the effect of language's organisation of the world into systems of difference, then Giovanni returns subjectivity to a pre-Oedipal state which literally consumes the other as part of a self and so makes of two potentially separate things one self-same entity. Giovanni's consumptive self is in many ways the culmination of that high-profile Renaissance egomania, one long-term effect of which has been to limit the ways we may think about subjectivity. Faced with such narcissistic appropriations of subjectivity by the likes of Tamburlaine, Faustus, Vindice, Giovanni and others, it is difficult to conceive of subjectivity as being anything less than the sovereign thing that these characters imagine it to be.

The play dramatises an incestuous relationship between brother and sister. Incest belongs to the realm of the pre-Oedipal. It transgresses the laws of post-Oedipal sexual and linguistic difference, by in this case confusing the names of brother and sister with the name of lover. The beginning of the play sees Giovanni attempting to unwrite the given laws of difference and insisting upon his own version of right and wrong based upon a pre-Oedipal 'morality' of oneness. The opening scene takes the form of an exchange between the Friar, addressed by Giovanni as 'father' and Giovanni, referred to by the Friar as 'son'.[20] The exchange resembles a Catholic confession, with the father/priest attempting to relocate his wayward son within the hierarchically differentiated structure of a permanent, metaphysically underpinned family:

> Dispute no more in this, for know, young man,
> These are not school points; nice philosophy
> May tolerate unlikely arguments,
> But Heaven admits no jest: wits that presumed
> On wit too much, by striving how to prove
> There was no God, with foolish grounds of art,
> Discovered first the nearest way to hell,
> And filled the world with devilish atheism.
> Such questions, youth, are fond; for better 'tis
> To bless the sun than reason why it shines;
> Yet He thou talk'st of is above the sun.
> No more; I may not hear it.
>
> (I.i.1–12)

The Friar is the representative of law. This law is God-given. The Friar asserts that the world and its rules and regulations have been created 'elsewhere', by God. The world is God's text, not man's. God is the ultimate father-figure, who allocates roles and identities from on high. As a psychoanalytic trinity, God is at once Oedipal father, breaking his children's contact with the fleshly things of this world, including the maternal body; 'son', that is to say (according to Christian exegesis of the Bible), God's Word, as law, corporealised and made *present* both in the shape of Christ and also in the shape of his representatives on earth, like the Friar; and, finally, he is holy-ghostly/spectral immateriality, producing desire by virtue of his simultaneous *absence*. God thus conforms perfectly to the modern psychoanalytic understanding of language as a system of difference based upon lack and desire!

The family invoked by the Friar may be said to be *over*-Oedipalised. It brooks no questioning. The rules of difference are a matter of external imposition, like Jonson's legalistic contract at the beginning of *Bartholmew Fair*. As representative of God's law, the Friar speaks a curt, authoritative language of differences, differences which are intended to systematise and regulate forever the speaking subject's moral and social position in the world: Heaven versus Hell; right versus wrong; God versus 'man'; the divine versus the human. Ours is not to reason why, or to question this system of differences. To question it would be to submit God to 'mere' human reasoning or 'wit'. The Friar's God is the equivalent of the external authority of Jonson's author figure, in that he imposes identities and names upon us, and inscribes us within a predetermined system of differences. In his difference from the human, he is also elusive – 'above the sun' – an absent object pointing to the inadequacy and emptiness of any sign which might attempt to stand in for him. This extends to the Friar himself, who purports to speak for a God whom he suggests cannot be spoken for. The Friar's words are empty as a result of his virtual admission of the way human signs are always in (hopeless) pursuit of the things they purport to make present. Although God promises reconciliation between the human and the divine in a final achievement of pre-Oedipal oneness, humanity's 'fall' into difference, division and exile means that continuity with an undifferentiated being (God the mother as well as father) is not ours to experience in this world. Veiled, God cannot be revealed within human language and human understanding.

The Friar's assumption of a God-given universe, based upon regulatory differences and an alienating sense of absence or lack, comes under severe pressure from Giovanni. Rebelling against his externally fashioned subjectivity, refusing the law and language of the Father, Giovanni proceeds to dismantle and render arbitrary the conventions which alienate men and women from what he sees as their 'natural' inclinations:

> Shall a peevish sound,
> A customary form, from man to man,
> Of brother and of sister, be a bar
> 'Twixt my perpetual happiness and me?
> Say that we had one father, say one womb
> (Curse to my joys) gave both us life and birth;
> Are we not therefore each to other bound

So much the more by nature? by the links
Of blood, of reason? nay, if you will have't,
Even of religion, to be ever one,
One soul, one flesh, one love, one heart, one all?

(I.i.24–34)

In employing a form of human 'wit', prohibited by the Friar, to construct an argument in defence of incestuous love, Giovanni displaces God as divine author of the world and asserts the right to fashion himself and a moral 'order' responsive to his pre-Oedipal desire. In place of the language of differences which create seemingly unbridgeable gaps between people (brother/sister), between moral categories (right/wrong) and between objects of desire/devotion (God himself) and their attainability or knowability, Giovanni reiterates the notion of oneness ('one womb . . . One soul, one flesh, one love, one heart, one all'). Where the Friar speaks of separations and exclusions, Giovanni speaks of coupling and conjoining, and of removing the 'bar[s]' that prohibit the amorous merging of subject and object, self and other. For Giovanni, the flesh-and-blood, here-and-now Annabella is an attainable object of love/devotion, an attainable, full source of meaning which promises to obliterate the sense of division and lack which lie at the heart of the linguistic subject. She is, as Giovanni himself suggests in his reference to the 'one womb' shared by brother and sister, the closest Giovanni can come to recovering the primordial love object of the maternal body.

Love symbolically castrates Giovanni. He speaks of love wounding him, of his 'incurable and restless wounds' (I.ii.143). The loss of the phallus (marker of difference) exiles him from a clearly demarcated public identity and masculine self, and moves him to a state approximating that of pre-genital, pre-linguistic non-differentiation. The oceanic imagery he uses – 'It were more ease to stop the ocean/From floats and ebbs than to dissuade my vows' (I.i.64–5) – indicates, through its evocation of a condition of flux, an absence of boundaries and separations. And with the onset of passionate love between Giovanni and Annabella, brother and sister begin to mirror one another in both their words and deeds. In Act I Annabella gazes upon Giovanni from 'above' (I.ii.28), and in Act III this act of voyeurism is repeated by a Giovanni similarly transfixed by, and transfixing of, Annabella. Theatrical space is utilised in such scenes to signal Giovanni's

and Annabella's break with 'ordinary' reality – the realm of socially permitted identities played out 'below' on the main part
of the stage – and their gradual immersion into a world of their
own. As this world materialises and is granted mimetic presence, so Annabella and Giovanni begin to usurp the main stage
and enact upon it their own reality. Appropriating religious discourse, their feelings are solemnised in incantatory language and
ritualistic actions which defy separateness and celebrate the union
of kindred spirits. The heaven of a self completed by its other
half can, it seems, be rediscovered on earth:

> *Annabella.*   On my knees,   *She kneels*
>   Brother, even by our mother's dust, I charge you,
>   Do not betray me to your mirth or hate,
>   Love me, or kill me, brother.
> *Giovanni.*   On my knees,   *He kneels*
>   Sister, even by my mother's dust, I charge you,
>   Do not betray me to your mirth or hate,
>   Love me, or kill me, sister.
>
>   (I.ii.249–55)

Significantly, the mother is invoked to consecrate a love which
now clearly announces its repudiation of the Law of the Father
and reactivates the continuity and unity of pre-Oedipal relationships. Incorporating the image of the other into the self – 'Go
where thou wilt, in mind I'll keep thee here,/And where thou
art, I know I shall be there' (II.i.35–8) – Giovanni and Annabella
establish an emotional and physical interdependency associated
with the lost bond of mother and child.

Giovanni also seeks unity of another kind: unity between sign
and referent, language and reality. Unlike the Friar, whose attitude towards the flawed and fallen nature of human understanding
and language drives a wedge between (human) words and the
(divine) realities which they unsuccessfully attempt to capture,
Giovanni affirms that his words are in direct contact with (emotional) realities. The sense of language as a form of estrangement,
of it being given from elsewhere and being forever in pursuit of
a referential 'base', is counteracted by Giovanni's insistence upon
the inseparability of tongue and heart, language and emotional
truth:

Giovanni.   . . . The poets feign, I read,
That Juno for her forehead did exceed
All other goddesses: but I durst swear
Your forehead exceeds hers, as hers did theirs.
Annabella.   Troth, this is pretty.
Giovanni.   Such a pair of stars
As are thine eyes would, like Promethean fire,
If gently glanced, give life to senseless stones.
Annabella.   Fie upon 'ee.
Giovanni.   The lily and the rose, most sweetly strange,
Upon your dimpled cheeks do strive for change.
Such lips would tempt a saint; such hands as those
Would make an anchorite lascivious.
Annabella.   D'ee mock me, or flatter me?
Giovanni.   If you would see a beauty more exact
Than art can counterfeit or nature frame,
Look in your glass and there behold your own.
Annabella.   O you are a trim youth.
Giovanni.   Here.   *Offers his dagger to her*
Annabella.   What to do?
Giovanni.   And here's my breast, strike home.
Rip up my bosom, there thou shalt behold
A heart in which is writ the truth I speak.

                                            (I.ii.186–207)

The appearance (and Annabella's implications) that Giovanni is
merely imitating the voices of other poetic lovers is belied by
the reality to which Giovanni says his words refer. Poets may
feign, lovers may use words to flatter and seduce, but Giovanni
means and owns what he says. Where the 'customary form[s]'
of conventional morality and conventional love alienate the self
from its natural inclinations and expression, true love creates an
authentic self and a correspondingly authentic language, produced from the heart and soul of that self. Language is no mere
external phenomenon, but written on/in the body's seat of emotion. The self-fashioning practised by Giovanni constitutes a
rejection of all 'external' influences and cultural constructs and
an attempt to rediscover an authentic pre-historical self within
the intimate and incestuous space where all outsides, externali-
ties and differences are abolished.

However, language continues to separate Giovanni from the

object of this love. It continues to distance and alienate him from his sister even as it attempts to overcome this distance. For Annabella suspects, as the audience/reader also suspect, that Giovanni (like Lysander and Demetrius in *A Midsummer Night's Dream*) only succeeds in writing his beloved as a conventional poetic text. Giovanni's language creates a 'bar' (the bar of poetic conventions) between himself and his sister, even as it speaks, idealistically, of the removal of all bars and barriers. The above dialogue, for example, takes the form of a disrupted sonnet. Giovanni's fourteen lines of adulation in which he attempts to 'make a sonnet' of his sister are interrupted by Annabella's gently mocking interruptions. These interruptions indicate Annabella's partial or total refusal to see herself in Giovanni's inscriptions of her. They signal her difference from Giovanni's conceit of her – a conceit imagined by him to be continuous with her.

Giovanni's frustration at his inability to secure in language utter unity between self and other erupts eventually into violence. The series of references in the play to the violent excavation of interiorities – 'Rip up my bosom . . .' (I.ii.206), 'I'll rip up thy heart . . .' (IV.iii.53), 'You have unripped a soul . . .' (III.vi.2) – culminate in Giovanni's violent response to the demise of his relationship with his sister. Unable to cope with the loss of the now penitent Annabella to Soranzo, and refusing any kind of return to social reality, Giovanni excavates the heart of Annabella (by this time pregnant by him), and enters the final 'banquet' scene with her heart 'upon his dagger' (V.vi.7). In one of his disclosures to the on-stage audience, he refers to the nine-month period he enjoyed in the secrecy of Annabella's bed:

> For nine months' space in secret I enjoyed
> Sweet Annabella's sheets; in nine months I lived
> A happy monarch of her heart and her.
> Soranzo, thou know'st this; thy paler cheek
> Bears the confounding print of thy disgrace,
> For her too fruitful womb too soon bewrayed
> The happy passage of her stol'n delights,
> And made her mother to a child unborn.
>
> (V.vi.44–51)

The exact equivalence between the term of Annabella's pregnancy and the term of their relationship suggests that what Giovanni has himself been experiencing is the enclosure of a womblike existence, a return to the maternal body. As he enters the final scene, 'trimmed in reeking blood' (V.vi.9), after having terminated Annabella's life and pregnancy, it is as if he has perversely taken the place of the child, as if he is the product of the nine month-long pregnancy. Determined to be sole 'monarch' of Annabella's heart and womb, Giovanni will brook no rival, neither Soranzo nor even his own child. Replacing the 'official' feast with his own grotesque, privately carnivalesque version: 'You came to feast, my lords, with dainty fare;/I come to feast too, but I digged for food/In a much richer mine . . . 'tis a heart,/A heart, my lords, in which is mine entombed' (V.vi.24–8), Giovanni compensates for being separated from Annabella by impaling the heart which feeds the womb upon his dagger and continuing to feast upon them.

Giovanni's violent response to the trauma of exile (exile from Annabella's life, heart, womb and sheets) is thus to destroy in order to retain for himself everything which threatens to become, or which has already become, separate. This denial of difference extends to the interpretative monopoly which Giovanni seeks to impose upon the final act. The visual spectacle of heart upon dagger is accompanied by a series of verbal commentaries by Giovanni. This suggests an attempt to create an interpretative continuity between the visual and the verbal, to possess the meaning of his action and subdue the difference of other voices, other interpretations:

> Here, here, Soranzo; trimmed in reeking blood,
> That triumphs over death; proud in the spoil
> Of love and vengeance! Fate or all the powers
> That guide the motions of immortal souls
> Could not prevent me
>
> (V.vi.9–13)

> Be not amazed; if your misgiving hearts
> Shrink at an idle sight, what bloodless fear
> Of coward passion would have seized your senses,
> Had you beheld the rape of life and beauty
> Which I have acted?
>
> (V.vi.16–21)

The glory of my deed
Darkened the midday sun, made noon as night.
You came to feast, my lords, with dainty fare;
I came to feast too, but I digged for food
In a much richer mine than gold or stone
Of any value balanced; 'tis a heart,
A heart, my lords, in which is mine entombed

(V.vi.23–8)

'Tis Annabella's heart, 'tis; why d'ee startle
I vow 'tis hers: this dagger's point ploughed up
Her fruitful womb, and left to me the fame
Of a most glorious executioner

(V.vi.31–4)

Giovanni shocks his on-stage audience, if not into silence, then into a series of virtually monosyllabic responses: 'What means this?' 'Son Giovanni!', 'What strange riddle's this?' (V.vi.14, 15, 30). The dramatic coup staged by Giovanni ensures that his words dominate, so that while others are lost for words, Giovanni assumes linguistic mastery. The (temporary) dependency of other characters upon Giovanni undermines any autonomy they may themselves lay claim to and eliminates the threat posed by the difference of other plans, realities, subjectivities. To acknowledge difference is not only to acknowledge the social and linguistic laws of difference; it is also to recognise the actual or potential difference of other people from their socially constructed subjectivities. Giovanni neither recognises the subjectivities endorsed by society nor any other form of separateness different from his own. His pre-Oedipal narcissistic fantasy is based upon the utter eradication or absorption of others. In making a spectacle, an icon of himself in the final scene, Giovanni is reaffirming the world according to Giovanni and obliterating all competing realities. The show-stopping spectacle constitutes, for him at least, a heroic act of conquest and (re)possession.

Giovanni's desire for possession, in the face of dispossession, thus takes various forms: possession of meaning; possession of Annabella's and his own 'true' primordial, pre-historical being; possession of his own narrative; possession of theatrical space; and possession of words as physical objects. The threat of a return to the world of socially regulated differences and positions

(positions which are ostensibly being reconsolidated by a banquet scene in which characters are invited, by the stage direction at the beginning of the scene, to 'take their places'), generates a mania for repossession of what Giovanni sees as being inalienably 'his'. A penitent Annabella may have agreed with the Friar to conform once again to the normal rules and roles of society and marry Soranzo, but Giovanni forcibly returns her to his reality. This return is total. While Annabella existed, there was always the possibility of her refusing Giovanni's inscriptions of her and asserting her autonomy. But a dead Annabella is now Giovanni's Annabella. And the amorous language which created a bar between self and other because of its substitution of poetic signs and symbols for the 'real' Annabella is now violently literalised. Carrying out his promise to tie signs to sensuous physical reality, metaphors of true union are now made bloodily concrete.

Yet for all of Giovanni's attempts, as an 'oracle of truth' (V.vi.52) to possess the meaning of his action, that meaning eludes him. As Michael Neill has suggested, the emblem of heart upon dagger is open to a variety of different meanings:

> It may be either a conventional Petrarchan emblem of his own passion, or a 'glorious executioner's' bitter quotation from the spectacular imagery of public justice – though in the light of Giovanni's vindictive rage against his rival, the audience may be more inclined to recognise in it the often-used emblem of Envy devouring a heart.[21]

Rather than conclusively owning the meaning of the image of heart upon dagger, Giovanni is caught in a web of conflicting signifiers. His language in the last scene is riotously metaphorical, as he restlessly substitutes one image of the murder of the love object for another. He is, in other words, prey to the differentiating and substitutive effects of language even as he is once again attempting to eliminate difference and metaphoricity. Instead of uniting signifier with referent, metaphor with physical organ, the superfluity of metaphorical associations has the effect, as Neill suggests, of 'driving a wedge between sign and signification, word and thing'. Annabella's heart, despite being impaled upon Giovanni's weapon, remains 'other', signifying nothing but itself and its 'atrocious physicality'.[22]

Giovanni is not alone in his pre-Oedipal narcissistic fantasies. *'Tis Pity She's a Whore* is littered, as are many other Italianate plays of the period, with revenge narratives. Most of these narratives focus upon the trauma of loss/separation and the attempt to compensate for loss by murdering and/or victimising the lost object. For example: Hippolita, Soranzo's erstwhile mistress, seeks vengeance upon Soranzo for abandoning her; Richardetto, Hippolita's husband, seeks vengeance on Hippolita for her abandonment of him; Giovanni, as we have seen, takes vengeance upon Annabella for her perceived betrayal of their relationship; when Soranzo finds out that Annabella is pregnant by another man, he rants at her and threatens to 'rip up [her] heart' (IV.iii.53) in order to discover the name of her previous lover. We can add to these examples those from other plays already discussed: Othello's revenge upon Desdemona for her supposed abandonment of him; Hamlet's upon Claudius for separating him from his mother, and so forth. What we find in all of these examples is an *insurgence against externality*, a refusal to recognise the other *as* other, a pre-Oedipal denial of loss and expulsion.

Psychoanalysis seems to me to function in a *somewhat* similar fashion to Giovanni and Batholmew Cokes, for if on the one hand it suggests the inevitability – because of the nature of language – of difference and separation, then on the other it counteracts the total alienation of subject from object, private from public, self from other. I suggested earlier that psychoanalysis builds a human story – around language – about our loves and losses. Does this human story not counteract the tendency, within some modern theories, like structuralism, to treat language as an impersonal, trans-subjective medium? As Giovanni tries unsuccessfully to overcome the externality of language by thinking of language as produced from within the heart and soul of the feeling subject, so psychoanalysis likewise attempts to bring language within the orbit of the feeling, desiring 'I'.

5

Historicism
The White Devil; As You Like It; Henry V

To do literary criticism nowadays almost always involves doing history. No longer seen as the locus of transcendent human values, the literary text is understood to be the product, as well as sometimes the producer, of history. But what does it mean to 'do history'?[1] History can be done and/or mediated in diverse ways, through archival research, professional textbooks, statistics, graphs, economics, oral testimony, history plays, historical novels, biography, autobiography, theme parks, re-enactments, and so forth. And history can be told from different class, gender and ethnic points of view. Are some of these ways of doing history 'better' or 'truer' than others? For example, is autobiography, which is often thought to offer its readers an insight into what it *felt* like to live at a certain time and place, 'truer' to historical experience than, say, the putatively more 'objective' yet impersonal statistic? Is history to be understood, on the model of art, as an imaginative re-creation of the past which plays out a drama, similar to the drama of psychoanalysis, of identification and estrangement, estrangement being the means of *dis*-identifying with the present in order to experience other selves from other times and places? Or is history to be understood, on the model of science, as an 'objective', *disinterested* discipline which should ideally edit out that problematic entity/process called the 'subject' in order to study the past 'as it was' rather than 'how it appears' to a subject simultaneously alienated from, yet drawn towards, his/her historical others?

If, as I shall go on to argue, the common denominator between these concepts of history is the notion that historical consciousness is consciousness of the *difference* of one time and place from other times and places, then the variety of approaches

132

to the study of the past might be said to constitute *different ways of thinking about historical difference.* These different discourses of difference – these different ways of thinking about historical difference – will be explored in detail later on. First let me consolidate the *general* claim that modern historical consciousness involves consciousness of difference.

HISTORY AS DIFFERENCE

An obvious but nevertheless useful point of entry here is simply to bring to attention the concept of periodisation: the way we mark off periods thought to be distinct from one another: Medieval, Renaissance (more recently referred to as Early Modern), Modern, Postmodern, and so on. These, of course, are very basic markers of difference which may seem cumbersome and overly homogenising. So we can add more differences: Romantic, Enlightenment, Victorian, and so forth. And we can also understand a given period as *internally* differentiated. The effect of this is to question further the homogenisation implicit in the appeal to historical blocks and to initiate exploration of the diverse levels of culture within a given so-called period. Did the meaning of the Renaissance change from one social group to another? Was the Renaissance class-specific? Did people in the provinces experience the Renaissance in the same way that European city-dwellers did? Was the Renaissance an urban phenomenon? Did everyone in the Renaissance know that they were living through a period called the Renaissance? Were there several different renaissances? Did one version of the Renaissance come to dominate by disseminating itself through the medium of print? Is the homogenised concept of 'the Renaissance' the effect of a print culture able for the first time to disseminate a standardised period-concept? . . .

I think I see a phenomenon – called the Renaissance – only for that phenomenon to fracture. I think I see a time and a place different from my own time and place only for that different culture to become so *internally* differentiated as to be even more lost, even further removed. Consider the additional example, explored in Chapter 1, of the Renaissance theatre. There I argued that the theatre, no longer under the *direct* auspices of the Church or aristocracy, created its own complex and internally differentiated space and semiotics. The increasingly complex internal history of the theatre means that it is not possible to treat the drama as though it were simply expressive of something else: such as religion.

However tempting and viable it is to unify 'the Renaissance' under one or another umbrella concept, the insistence upon history as difference means that the signifier 'Renaissance' will always be in excess of any one single, definitive signified to which it is attached. Let us briefly imagine that religion *does* present itself as one such definitive signified to which all things Renaissance can be attached. Religion can quite validly be seen as the mastercode of the Renaissance: the code that makes sense of all other codes. It is, as Debora Shuger suggests, the 'cultural matrix for explorations of virtually every topic: kingship, selfhood, rationality, language, marriage, ethics, and so forth'.[2] But if this is true, then so is the opposite. For example, in Machiavelli's *The Prince* – a text often held to be a seminal 'Renaissance' text – religion seems to be parting company with the new autonomous practice of politics.[3] In the theatre the Machiavellian separation of ethics from politics, sacred from secular, is one of the drama's most persistent preoccupations. Individual plays may refute such a separation but, as I have already suggested, the secular commercial theatre is itself complicit with the process of separating spheres. Religion may still heavily influence the drama, but the drama is relocating religion on its own terms. The theatre of human judgement, as I referred to it in Chapter 1, can be seen as rewriting religious discourse in such as way as to *disempower* God as omniscient spectator and judge and *empower* the theatre audience as moral agents. Theatre thus disconnects itself from one kind of orthodox religious belief (that God is supreme agent and judge) in order to resituate religion in its own distinctive way.

Examples of separating cultures and separating practices *within* cultures could be endlessly cited. All such examples suggest that historical consciousness might best be understood, as indicated earlier, as the consciousness of difference. For many contemporary theorists and practitioners of history, consciousness of history and consciousness of difference are indeed one and the same thing. If it was once possible to write the history of Western civilisation as the history of Progress and Enlightenment; or to speak of 'our country's history' as though that history formed a continuous and unified narrative;[4] or, less ambitiously, to appeal confidently to such umbrella period-concepts as the Renaissance, then these grand or semi-grand narratives have in recent times given way to history as a discourse of difference.

VERSIONS OF HISTORY AS DIFFERENCE

But what of the different ways, referred to earlier, of understanding difference? Do all discourses of difference equally repudiate the concept of a continuous human being? Is it possible to think in terms of continuity and discontinuity at the same time? Is the insistence upon historical difference *expressive* of human possibility or does it negate any connection whatsoever between the human and the historical? Does difference *communicate* something about what it means to be human or does difference instead tell us that there is no such thing as the human? As approaches to history differ, so, too, will the answers to these questions. For the purposes of this chapter, three contrasting 'discourses of difference' may be identified, as follows:

1. *The objective view.* This view assumes that the present, consciously or unconsciously held beliefs, values and attitudes of the historian are different from those held by people in the past, and that these present beliefs can and should be overcome so as not to obstruct a clear, impartial, objective description of the past.
2. *The anti-humanist constructionist view.* This view stresses the impossibility of objectivity and the way that the past is inevitably mediated or constructed through *present* sign systems again thought to be distinct from those of the past. Often this view is made to contribute to an anti-humanist argument which declares 'human nature', as a constant, to be dead. Difference is thus here inscribed as a *non-communicating* difference: the past cannot speak to us about the human because there is no such thing as human nature.
3. *The expressive–constructionist view.* This view shares much in common with the anti-humanist, constructionist perspective, but it retains a humanist dimension, either by conceiving of history simultaneously in terms of the discontinuity *and* continuity of human being, or by imagining history as a form of vital contact with difference and different voices that speak

to us in the present of lost and/or alternative ways of being. Difference is thus here a *communicative* difference.

Let me begin exploring these different discourses of difference by considering an example of what appears, at first, to be an anti-humanist discourse of difference. Here, history appears to be *only* thinkable in terms of radical differences which face each other in mutual misrecognition and which are prohibitive of any reference to the human. Of the distinction between traditional, humanist history and what he calls or called 'effective' history, Michel Foucault writes:

> 'Effective' history differs from traditional history in being without constants. Nothing in man – not even his body – is sufficiently stable to serve as the basis for self-recognition or for understanding other men. The traditional devices for constructing a comprehensive view of history and for retracing the past as a patient and continuous development must be systematically dismantled. Necessarily, we must dismiss those tendencies that encourage the consoling place of recognitions. Knowledge, even under the banner of history, does not depend on 'rediscovery', and it emphatically excludes the 'rediscovery of ourselves'. History becomes 'effective' to the degree that it introduces discontinuity into our very being – as it divides our emotions, dramatizes our instincts, multiplies our body and sets it against itself. 'Effective' history deprives the self of the reassuring stability of life and nature.[5]

Foucault is now dead. He is now, as we say, 'history'. But is it not possible to commune with the dead, especially when the dead have left writings behind them? Foucault's emphasis upon *radical discontinuity* would seem to forbid any such communing. Where I would normally respect the linguistic convention of referring to dead writers in the present tense – *as though their voices were recuperable in the present* – the fluctuation in my earlier use of tenses – 'calls or called', 'writes' – seems appropriate to Foucault's negation of continuity between past and present. I cannot communicate with Foucault because Foucault, by his own argument, is past: he is other, he is a stranger. In Foucault's conception of history there are no meeting places, howsoever precarious or short-lived, between past and present. There is no possibility of dialogue because the grounds upon which such a dialogue might take place – namely a shared sense of what it means to be human – do not exist. For the anti-humanist Foucault there is no such constant thing as human nature. Human beings are through and through mutable beings for whom 'nothing – not even [the] body – is sufficiently stable to serve as the basis for self-recognition or for understanding other men'.

But if Foucault's concept of history is anti-humanist in one respect, then it is nevertheless humanist in another, in that it imagines history as the site of what Fredric Jameson has referred to as an 'existential experience, a galvanic and electrifying event', which 'speaks to us about our own virtual and unrealized "human potentialities"'.[6] As language, within poststructuralism, is the site of a subject in process, so, likewise, history, according to this 'existential' or 'expressive' view, is the locus of human being and human possibility. Neither the object of disinterested contemplation nor a succession of non-communicative moments which have no bearing whatsoever on the human, history *matters* because it tells us what we were and what we might be. Referring, like Foucault, to Friedrich Nietzsche and Nietzsche's perspectives on history, Gilles Deleuze and Félix Guattari write that:

> There is no Nietzsche-the-self, professor of philology, who suddenly loses his mind and supposedly identifies with all sorts of strange people; rather, there is the Nietzschean subject who passes through a series of states and identifies these states with the names of history: '*every name in history is I*. . . .' The subject spreads itself out along the entire circumference of the circle, the center of which has been abandoned by the ego.[7]

Thus conceived, history is an expressive, communicative discourse of difference which offers us a means of transgressing the limitations of our own time and place. This understanding of difference contrasts with that other articulation of difference, also present in Foucault, which makes of the past a stranger who never speaks and who we cannot ever truly know.

Foucault's insistence upon radical discontinuity, communicative or otherwise, can be usefully placed against other forms of historicism which, in maintaining more of a dialectic between history as discontinuous and history as continuous, construct the difference of the past as more unambiguously communicative.

Here is the evocative beginning of Stephen Greenblatt's *Shake-spearean Negotiations*:

> I began with the desire to speak with the dead.
>
> This desire is a familiar, if unvoiced, motive in literary studies, a motive organized, professionalized, buried beneath thick layers of bureaucratic decorum: literature professors are salaried, middle-class shamans. If I never believed that the dead could hear me, and if I knew that the dead could not speak, I was nonetheless certain that I could re-create a conversation with them. Even when I came to understand that in my most intense moments of straining to listen all I could hear was my own voice, even then I did not abandon my desire. It was true that I could hear only my own voice, but my own voice was the voice of the dead, for the dead had contrived to leave textual traces of themselves, and these traces make themselves heard in the voice of the living.[8]

For Greenblatt, as for Foucault, the past is at several removes from the present, and therein lies its alluring strangeness. But for Greenblatt the voices of the past are not so completely estranged from the present as to be totally inaudible or incomprehensible. That a conversation between the living and the dead *is* just about possible speaks to the existence of some sort of continuous human being. Such continuity makes dialogue with the differences which also exist more feasible, for these differences are not so estranged as to be unrepeatable in the present.

Greenblatt's desire to animate the past bears comparison with what Raphael Samuel in *Theatres of Memory* calls 'living history'. By living history Samuel means theme parks, animations, historical reconstructions, interactive museums, and so forth. Samuel provocatively retrieves contemporary popular culture's enthusiasm for this kind of history from the condescension of the professional historian. Where the professional historian can only see the theme park and its analogues as a corruption of the 'proper' study of history, Samuel writes persuasively of the validity of this kind of memory-work:

> 'Living history' tells us as much about the present as it does about the past. In the spirit of the age – the here-and-now – it

is centrally involved not with politics and economics, the subjects of yesteryear's grand narratives, nor yet, except tangentially, with religion (typically absent in accounts of the recent past), but essentially with that great preoccupation of the 'Me' generation: lifestyles. It privileges the private over the public sphere. On stage, in Brian Friel's *Translations*, it turns the English conquest of Ireland into a love story gone wrong. At the cinema, in Kenneth Branagh's version of Shakespeare, it makes *Henry V* into a kind of *Hamlet*; a prince, in the manner of the current heir to the throne, wanting to be a private person even when he finds himself thrust into the role of king. At the Imperial War Museum, when it is not diverting us with 'Forces Sweethearts', it invites us to share the personal experience of shell-shock. Family fortunes rather than wars and diplomacy are the subject of its epics; when it seeks to reconstruct grand narrative it is through the medium of the history of the self.[9]

Samuel's living history is history which is as immediately relevant and involving as one's own life history. This is history conceived of *as* autobiography, history which abolishes distinctions between private and public by refusing the depersonalisation implied by the term 'public'. Samuel's enthusiasm for this kind of history is that, unlike those 'Dryasdust forms of scholarship' which deny history its human drama, living history animates the inanimate and resurrects the dead.[10]

Although living history may be in danger of narcissistically absorbing the otherness of the past into the 'me' and the 'here-and-now' of the present, the ironicising postmodern aspect of living history also considered by Samuel lays bare its self-conscious pretence:

In other aspects, 'living history', so far from representing a throw-back to the past, might be thought to have prefigured some of the favourite conceits – or genial tropes – of postmodernism. In place of facts it offers us images – 'hyperrealities' – in which the old is faked up to be more palpable than the here-and-now. It involves a quite conscious exercise in make-believe, not so much trading on our credulity as inviting us to connive at the subterfuge and give ourselves up to its pleasures. It eschews epic and grand narrative in favour of personal observation and local knowledge. It invites us to play games with the past and to pretend that we are at home in it, ignoring the limitations of time and space by reincarnating it in the here-and-now.[11]

If the illusionism of animated history makes us feel 'at home' in the past, then its simultaneous anti-illusionism exposes the illusion *as* an illusion and restores the past's difference from the present. Postmodern animations of the past are, for Samuel, this mixture of the present and the absent, the familiar and the estranged. Thus understood, living history recalls the similar tensions of Renaissance drama.

I intend Samuel and Greenblatt as a contrast to Foucault, whose more extreme insistence upon discontinuity forbids any sense of the continuity of the human. However, it is also instructive to consider briefly who Samuel thinks of as his and living history's antagonists. Samuel's targets in *Theatres of Memory* are not so much theorists of historical difference, like Foucault. Samuel's sparring partners are rather those 'Dryasdust forms of [historical] scholarship' which insist upon rendering the past as objectively and scientifically as possible:

> It [i.e. living history] was much more attentive to the small details of everyday life than those different versions of 'total history' which were all the rage in the 1950s – the abstracted empiricism of the social scientists, with their geometrically plotted histograms and their social structure; the cliometrics of the economic historians, reducing mighty social changes to the squiggles of a graph; or the *longue durée* of those *Annales* historians who boldly declared that without quantification no serious history was possible.[12]

To Samuel's distaste for such dehumanised history we can usefully add the voice of Paul Hamilton. In his exploration of eighteenth-century precursors to our own conceptions of history, Hamilton comments that for the philosophers Giambattista Vico and J. G. Herder, history 'had to be understood as something we are actively engaged in, like purposeful living, not external to, like the phenomena rationalized by scientific investigation'.[13] Samuel's examples of 'dryasdust' history continue the tradition of history conceived of on the model of science. Contrastingly, Samuel's living history and Vico's and Herder's purposeful human history constitute an alternative tradition of history conceived of on the model of autobiography and/or literature, literature being that seductively affective discourse which draws us in rather than shuts us out. What are the distinguishing textual characteristics of such history? Historians more committed to the notion of history-as-autobiography/literature rather than history-as-science are likely to make more use of the anecdote than the graph, to use literature and poetry as legitimate historical evidence, and to humanise history by calling it *remembrance* or *testimony* rather than *record* or *chronicle*. Which brings me conveniently back to the work of Stephen Greenblatt, and the widespread use, in his and other so-called New Historicist writing, of 'human' anecdote and novelistic discourse.[14] To conclude this section and by way of consolidating some of the above arguments, I want to look briefly at a passage – which takes the form of an anecdote – from his influential book, *Renaissance Self-Fashioning: From More to Shakespeare*:

A dinner party at Cardinal Wolsey's. Years later, in the Tower, More recalled the occasion and refashioned it in *A Dialogue of Comfort Against Tribulation* as a 'merry tale,' one of those sly jokes that interlace his most serious work. The story reaches back to a past that, in the gathering darkness of 1534, might well have seemed to More almost mythical, back before the collapse of his career, the collapse of his whole world. Perhaps as important, it reaches back to a time before More had decided to embark upon his career. He pictures himself as an ambitious, clever young man, eager to make a good impression, but at the same time an outsider: in his fictionalized version, he is a Hungarian visitor to Germany. The vainglorious prelate – transparently Wolsey – had that day made an oration so splendid in his own estimation that he sat as if on thorns until he could hear it commended by his guests. After casting about in vain for a discreet way of introducing the subject, the cardinal finally asked bluntly what the company thought of his oration. Eating and conversation came to an abrupt halt: 'Every man was fallen in so deep a study for the finding of some exquisite praise'. Then one by one in order, each guest brought forth his flattering speech.[15]

Greenblatt's skills at scene setting, characterisation and the creation of intrigue are those of the novelist. We are being invited to identify with More and More's experience of life as we might identify with a figure and his/her situation in a novel. The point of entry into history is, in other words, through the heart and mind of a particular individual who is at the same time sufficiently like anyone else (someone who enjoys a joke, who is also serious, who suffers misfortune, who plays the game of flattering someone in a position of power, and so on), to confer upon history a recognisably human dimension. This is animated history, history which, filtered as it is through the category of the (auto)biographical, understands public as private history and vice versa. The broadly human categories we might draw upon to describe an individual's life history are thought to be appropriate to the writing of the wider history which *Renaissance Self-Fashioning* will relate.

This does not mean that Greenblatt's book assumes the existence of a static human nature. Often the trick played by New Historicism is to draw us into a familiar-looking human narrative, only to estrange it by historicising concepts which we might have thought belonged to a generalisable humanity. An alternative strategy is to invoke timeless human categories and, at the same time, to describe particular historical manifestations of them. So Greenblatt uses both a humanist, transhistorical idiom when he speaks, for example, of such general human traits as 'man's longings, anxieties, and goals', while plotting a narrative of their specific mode of being and/or of their special relevance in the Renaissance.[16] Greenblatt thus maintains a sense of the continuity of the human even as he denies or complicates it. Located at the interface of human nature and culture, Greenblatt's brand of New Historicist writing tends to offer 'human interest' stories – about sexuality, power, role-playing, the self, the body, wonder, anxiety, fantasy, and so on – whose historical inflections are simultaneously traced. The past *is* a foreign country, but not so foreign as to prevent any kind of dialogue with the present. Enticingly within at the same time as beyond our grasp, the past is simultaneously continuous and discontinuous with the present, and speaks to both the sameness and diversity of the human.

It is worth finally comparing Greenblatt's style of history writing with a more scientific mode. Here is an excerpt from Lawrence Stone's *The Causes of the English Revolution 1529–1642*:

In attacking the problem of revolution, as most others of major significance in history, we historians should think twice before we spurn the help offered by our colleagues in the social sciences, who have, as it happens, been particularly active in the last few years in theorizing about the typology, causes, and evolutionary patterns of this particular phenomenon. The purpose of this chapter is not to advance any new hypothesis, but to provide a summary view and critical examination of the work that has been going on.[17]

Eschewing the 'antiquarian fact-grubbing to which [conventional] historians are so prone', Stone turns instead to sociological theories of revolution.[18] What characterises both these approaches, however, is their aspiration towards a hard scientific objectivity (one based on facts, the other on social scientific theory) removed from the *lived* history explored by Greenblatt. And where Stone will go on to think about the causes of the English Revolution by differentiating between long-term *'pre-conditions'* and short-term *'triggers'*,[19] Greenblatt will go on to speak of role-playing and fantasy. Greenblatt's history is psychic history. It is history which refuses the depersonalising idiom of both the social scientist and the positivist historian, thereby resisting oppositions between the public and private, the social and the psychological, and transforming history into, in Fredric Jameson's phrase, an 'existential experience'.

We can conclude this section by suggesting that, despite the differences in the way that they conceive of the human (as more or less variable), Greenblatt, Foucault and Samuel often share in common a view of the past as expressive of human experience, whereas Stone's scientific idiom tends to rid history of its experiential aspect.

HISTORICISM IN SUMMARY

• Modern historical consciousness is often based upon the consciousness of difference: differences *between* the past and present; and differences *within* the past and present.
• The various media through which history is filtered (autobiography, statistics, oral testimony, and so on) can be understood as different ways of conceiving of historical difference. These

different discourses of difference can be thought about under the headings of (a) *objectivist*; (b) *anti-humanist constructionist*; (c) *expressive–constructionist*.

- 'Expressive' history turns history and historical difference into a human experience. Anti-humanist history thinks of difference as non-communicating difference. Objective history understands history on the model of science.

THE WHITE DEVIL

Greenblatt's and Samuel's dialectical understanding of the past as simultaneously present and absent is particularly appropriate to some of the Renaissance's own conceptions of history, for these, too, attempt to overcome distinctions between past and present, even as they insist upon such distinctions. Writing of the Renaissance and medieval attitudes towards history drawn upon by Machiavelli in *The Prince*, and contrasting these with their modern objectivist counterparts, Janet Coleman has recently made the following claims:

> Machiavelli's historical analysis of ancient texts and the laws of human behaviour which he believes can be elicited from past writings about human action was part of a long tradition of reading texts that was elaborately developed during the Middle Ages. It was a method of reading that was not new in the Renaissance. Nor is it a method that resembles what modern historians are supposed to be doing when they read and interpret ancient historical texts to try to understand, in a disinterested way, what ancient authors meant within social contexts that were vastly different from those of the modern world and its values. Modern historians deal with an over-and-done-with past in and for itself, where the past-people's actions in the past may be understood but not imitated; Machiavelli's past is, for him, alive and capable of imitation. It is a past *for* the present.[20]

This perspective needs some qualification, for medieval and Renaissance concepts of history may well change according to which medieval and Renaissance texts are taken to be representative and how one reads them. English Renaissance drama, for example, is one place where a relationship between past and present is severely tested. In numerous Elizabethan and Jacobean plays, the sense of being exiled into an idiosyncratic secular time with its own distinctive behavioural codes puts pressure upon putatively universal values which are seen, from a presentist viewpoint, as anachronistic. The continuity which some of these plays nevertheless seek makes (partly) good Coleman's suggestion that the past, for medieval and Renaissance writers, was generally thought of as being '"usable" in the present'.[21]

The rest of this chapter will explore representations of history in three Renaissance plays: *The White Devil*, *As You Like It* and *Henry V*. Where the new and the old in *The White Devil* and *As You Like It* face one another as strangers and antagonists, the role which certain characters adopt as agents of mediation offers the endangered principle of continuity a slender lifeline. Although they struggle to do so, these plays preserve a dialectic between continuity and discontinuity. However, even when the principle of difference dominates, as it seems to in *Henry V*, difference is still anthropomorphised. History, whether continuous or discontinuous, is thus treated as a storehouse of human resources, providing actions which are imitable in the present.

The White Devil is a fast-moving, staccato play, full of abrupt transitions and stunted, stubbornly non-relating temporalities. Characters, as Alexander Leggatt points out, 'change suddenly before our eyes', making it difficult 'to get a fixed perspective on the action'.[22] Leggatt gives as one example Francisco's comment to Flamineo on Cornelia, Flamineo's mother: 'Your reverend mother/Is grown a very old woman in two hours' (V.iv.53–4). Time in this play thus seems to obey a principle of radical discontinuity. There seems to be no communication between one moment and the next. 'I remember nothing' (V.vi.204), says Flamineo as he nears his end, and as if in denial of the connective work of memory. Life for Flamineo is a succession of moments sealed off from one another and prohibitive of a sense of narrative. Moreover, difference in this play is not the expressive form of difference sometimes invoked by Foucault, and Deleuze and Guattari. It is not difference understood as human diversity. It is not difference which *communicates* to us the possibility of living otherwise. Difference is instead negatively inscribed, as the loss of fixed coordinates and the loss of communication.

Of all the characters Flamineo is the most destructive of a sense of a continuity and communication between past and present. As court lackey – 'Pursue your noble wishes', he tells Duke Bracciano, 'I am prompt/As lightning to your service' – and pander – 'The Fair Vittoria, my happy sister/Shall give you present audience' (I.i.4–7) – Flamineo consigns conventional morality to the past. The radical break with the conventional past which he advances and embodies is clarified early on in the play during Bracciano's first illicit assignation with Vittoria. Acting as independent and unseen commentators on the action, Flamineo and Cornelia (the mother of Flamineo and Vittoria) contribute wildly divergent perspectives. While Flamineo's asides are lewdly indulgent of the various transgressions which are taking place (including his own vicarious involvement in Bracciano's seduction of his sister), Cornelia's comments represent an endangered moral point of view:

> My fears are fall'n upon me, O my heart!
> My son the pandar: now I find our house
> Sinking to ruin. Earthquakes leave behind,
> Where they have tyrannized, iron, or lead, or stone,
> But – woe to ruin – violent lust leaves none.
>
> (I.ii.216–20)

Cornelia does not only condemn her children in asides but interrupts the action to speak out vociferously against them and against Bracciano. Castigating Vittoria and Flamineo for making of their present location a 'burial plot,/For both your honours' (I.ii.277–8), Cornelia also unceremoniously stops Duke Bracciano in mid-sentence to remind him of his forgotten responsibilities: 'The lives of princes should like dials move,/Whose regular example is so strong,/They make the times by them go right or wrong' (I.ii.287–9). Flamineo's response – 'So, have you done? (I.ii.290) – is partly that of the bored adolescent impatient with the trite parental morality of his mother, and partly that of the present-minded social realist. To Flamineo, Cornelia is an *anachronism*. She is the past. Her outmoded morality can have no purchase upon present reality. 'Are you out of your wits?' (I.ii.301), he asks her in disbelief that she could think of ruining his and his sister's chances of prosperity. 'I would fain know', he continues, 'where lies the mass of wealth/Which you have hoarded for my maintenance,/That I may bear my beard out of the level/

Of my lord's stirrup' (I.ii.311–13). To which Cornelia simply replies: 'What? because we are poor,/Shall we be vicious?' (I.ii.314). Flamineo's own lengthy response then takes the form of a potted history of his family's and his own diminishing fortunes. He ends his speech by reaffirming his mother as an anachronism from which he must and will sever contact:

> shall I,
> Having a path so open and so free
> To my preferment, still retain your milk
> In my pale forehead? no this face of mine
> I'll arm and fortify with lusty wine
> 'Gainst shame and blushing.
>
> (I.ii.327–32)

Past and present, as embodied respectively by Cornelia's conventional morality and Flamineo's pragmatism, thus seem utterly antagonistic. If Cornelia represents a pre-lapsarian or Platonic realm of essential moral principles, then Flamineo inhabits a fallen world of contingency and necessity, a world in which 'values' are dictated by – the lack of – money, power and position. If Cornelia represents the transcendent and the timeless, then Flamineo represents change and discontinuity. If Cornelia advances the importance of moral bases and foundations, then the relativist Flamineo cuts loose from such foundationalist thinking. Or if, reverting to the argument of Chapter 1, Cornelia's appropriation of moral authority re-presents the increasingly passé theatre of human judgement, then Flamineo's irony and disenchantment mark him as fashionable theatre sophisticate. Past and present are becoming strangers to one another. They are speaking different languages.

And yet the past in the shape of Cornelia is of course still making its presence felt *in the present*. This is not to suggest that Cornelia's morality, here and elsewhere in the play, is unquestionable. The play, as its title suggests, is itself far too relativistic and ambiguous to provide such an unassailable moral foundation. Nevertheless, there is a substantial difference between posing moral questions (as the play does via characters like Cornelia) and abandoning moral categories altogether (as Flamineo tends to). Cornelia's intervention contests stage space in such a way as to resituate it as a *moral* space which demands that the participants in the secular world of discontinuous history enter into dialogue with the 'timeless' moral discourses of the past. The past, in other words, still has to be fought off. The past still has to be consigned to the past. This is difficult because Flamineo is himself not totally in and of the present. He is, like other characters in other plays, the *knowing* lackey, the lackey who ventriloquises the role of the lackey because he seems to have no other option but to play along with the degraded discourses of the present. The ironic detachment of the ventriloquist from the corrupted discourses of contemporary court life means that the moral discourses of the past are not completely inaudible to him. Flamineo hears what Cornelia is saying. And possibly he is trying to persuade himself as much as Cornelia of the necessity of his present actions. Thus if the present-minded Flamineo promotes the idea of a radical break with the past, then that past still haunts Flamineo enough to cause him anguish in the face of transgression. Towards the end of his career as a corrupt courtier, his reflections at times draw close to the earlier perspectives of Cornelia:

> I have liv'd
> Riotously ill, like some that live at court;
> And sometimes, when my face was full of smiles
> Have felt the maze of conscience in my breast.
> Oft gay and honour'd robes those tortures try, –
> We think cag'd birds sing, when indeed they cry.
>
> (V.iv.118–23)

Flamineo's rupturing of time is here experienced as a severing of the self from the sources of well-being. Where Flamineo at first attempts to treat the past as an anachronism which has no bearing whatsoever on his present situation, he now treats history as an experiential encounter, an encounter, that is to say, with his other half or lost self. The past *is* Flamineo; it is that aspect of Flamineo which he has cast off but is now painfully attempting to retrieve.

I have so far discussed the scene of confrontation between Flamineo and Cornelia as though mother and son were its only protagonists or antagonists. While it is true that Flamineo and Cornelia mainly dominate the scene, Vittoria is also present. Vittoria's attitude to her mother is different from Flamineo's.

Whereas Flamineo seeks to render Cornelia's views anachronistic, to replace past with present, and to separate himself from his mother, Vittoria attempts – mostly without success because of the domination of other voices – to communicate with Cornelia as though Cornelia's moral perspectives were still valid. 'Dearest mother hear me' (I.ii.288), she pleads, as she tries to get past and present to listen to each other when others – not just Flamineo but also Bracciano – are doing the opposite: 'Come, come, I will not hear you', Bracciano tells Cornelia, in an attempt to cocoon himself in the decadent present.

Vittoria does not totally cohabit the prelapsarian world of her mother, for she is not the strict moralist that the mother is. At the same time, however, Vittoria brings something of her mother with her into the present. This is especially true during the scene of her trial, for she is as outspoken in this scene as her mother was earlier. Accusing her accusers of having 'ravish'd justice' (III.ii.274), Vittoria's outraged criticisms of authority also meet with the same response as her mother's previous condemnations: Bracciano's 'Fie, fie the woman's mad' (I.ii.297) is echoed in the later trial scene by Monticelso's 'Fie she's mad' (I.ii.270). Likewise, both women are described as Furies: Cornelia by Flamineo: 'What Fury rais'd thee up? (I.ii.270); and Vittoria by Monticelso: 'She's turn'd Fury' (III.ii.278).

Vittoria's re-enactment in the present of the maternal past can be construed as an example of living history. Where the past is in danger of dying, Vittoria revives it. Recent commentators have cast doubt upon the authenticity of Vittoria's performance during the trial scene. Rowland Wymer, for example, suggests that it is 'so perfect that, like Ford's Perkin Warbeck, it creates its own reality and leaves the audience with an unsolvable enigma to ponder rather than the satisfaction of penetrating a disguise'.[23] Such perspectives locate Vittoria as an adept ventriloquist who exists only in the play's present inauthentic world. They tend to ignore characters' albeit belated search for continuity with an otherwise estranged past. And so, although the play's represented past and present mainly face each other as antagonists in this play, there are moments when characters look to the past for resources lacking in the present. The past thus becomes usable in the present because of the principle of continuity which establishes communication between otherwise non-communicating differences.

AS YOU LIKE IT

As You Like It begins in the aftermath of a revolution in the state. The new order, headed by Duke Frederick and supported by Oliver, has displaced the old order, headed by Duke Frederick's brother Duke Senior, who is now living in exile in the Forest of Arden. The other principal casualties of the insurrection are Orlando, whose position has been usurped by his brother Oliver; Adam, loyal family retainer and servant of the old order; Rosalind, daughter to Duke Senior; and Duke Senior's courtiers, who are living in banishment with him. At the beginning of the play, then, past and present, old and new are utterly estranged from each other, with Duke Senior having literally been made a stranger of by his brother.

The play on several occasions insists upon the *radical break* which has taken place by emphasising the newness of the new and the oldness of the old: 'What's the new news at the new court?' (I.i.96–7) asks Oliver, to which Charles, Duke Frederick's wrestler, responds:

> There's no news at the court sir, but the old news. That is, the old Duke is banished by his younger brother the new Duke, and three or four loving lords have put themselves into voluntary exile with him, whose lands and revenues enrich the new Duke, therefore he gives them good leave to wander.
>
> (I.i.98–104)

The expectation of the new court is that by continually producing 'new' news it will be forever differentiating itself from 'old' news. The new court thus embodies the principle of radical discontinuity. Having broken with the past once, it is assumed that it will break any number of times with a 'past' which is barely passed. Therein lies the new order's dynamism.

The old order, by contrast, is identified – like Cornelia in *The White Devil* – with the ostensible timelessness of custom and tradition. The association of Adam and Arden with Eden identify the old usurped world as the stable prelapsarian opposite of the new world of fashion and change. As Orlando says nostalgically to and of Adam:

> O good old man, how well in thee appears
> The constant service of the antique world,
> When service sweat for duty, not for meed.
> Thou art not for the fashion of these times,
> Where none will sweat but for promotion,
> And having that, do choke their service up
> Even with the having; it is not so with thee.
> (II.iii.56–62)

There can be no points of contact, it seems, between old and new, for old and new, past and present are mutually exclusive. If the old has to do with loyalty, service, continuity, stasis and tradition, then the new is all about money, change, dynamism, aggressive careerism and innovation. The historical consciousness which informs *As You Like It* is once again consciousness of non-communicating differences.

However, the *key* difference between past and present has so far been passed over without much comment. This is the difference of attitudes towards family ties. It is upon this difference, the overcoming of it, and the relevance of family to the way the play itself treats history that I now want to focus.

The *coup d'état* which has taken place is an emphatically family affair, a matter of brothers displacing brothers. What the new order subverts and the old order reveres are the ostensibly sacrosanct bonds of kinship. At the beginning of the play, the displaced Orlando is bereft because he can only see himself in terms of the family – especially his father – and without a position in the family he is nothing. Orlando constantly reiterates the sacrosanct nature of the father/son bond and thinks of filiation as an almost sacred calling:

> I am more proud to be Sir Rowland's son,
> His youngest son, and would not change that calling
> To be adopted heir to Frederick.
> (I.ii.221–3)

Orlando on several occasions repeats this statement of his irreplaceable origins: 'I am the youngest son of Sir Rowland de Boys' (I.i.56); 'The spirit of my father grows strong in me' (I.i.70–1). Orlando, at least at the beginning of the play, is not the most mobile or flexible of thinkers. His tendency to repetition and reiteration identify him with the stasis, solidity and staunch family values of the 'antique world'.

Orlando's clear opposite is his brother Oliver. Oliver does not recognise his father's will (as in testament *and* desire), which was to make sure Orlando is well provided for by Oliver. And neither, as a consequence, does Oliver recognise his brother. As Orlando puts it, Oliver 'bars me the place of brother' (I.i.19). For Oliver as for the usurping Duke Frederick, kinship ties evidently do not signify. To Adam, therefore, who like Orlando can only think in terms of kinship, Oliver is indescribable. This is how he informs Orlando of Oliver's latest plot against him:

> O unhappy youth,
> Come not within these doors; within this roof
> The enemy of all your graces lives.
> Your brother, no, no brother, yet the son –
> Yet not the son, I will not call him son –
> Of him I was about to call his father,
> Hath heard your praises, and this night he means
> To burn the lodging where you use to lie.
>
> (II.iii.17–23)

Such is Oliver's breach of the bonds of kinship, and such is Adam's reverence for them, that Oliver is beyond Adam's capacity to name.

The play, then, seems polarised between what can be thought of as two radically incommensurable cultural formations, with the emergent formation, which is broadly identifiable as capitalist, in the process of consigning the residual feudal formation to the past. Most of the characters belong to either one or the other formation. That is to say, they are either ruthlessly acquisitive or loyal; destroyers of the bonds of kinship or guardians of them; dynamic or static; money-oriented or people-oriented; traditionalists or innovators. Needless to say, not all of the characters fit into this scheme, or if they do then they do not fit into it *all* of the time. These misfits suggest that the binary opposition between past and present may be transcended in the name of more expansive, all-encompassing humanity. The misfits are mainly Celia and Rosalind. The Nietzschean aphorism – '"*every name in history is I. . ."*' – suits Celia and Rosalind, for they do not fit perfectly into one or the other social formation. Their attitude towards family is especially worth considering as it straddles the divide between (feudal) reverence and (capitalist) transgression, traditional respect and energetic innovation.

At first Rosalind's position is similar to Orlando's: she is bereft because of her father Duke Senior's exile, and she is unable to replace the irreplaceable. 'Unless you could teach me to forget a banished father', she tells her friend Celia, 'you must not learn me how to remember any extraordinary pleasure' (I.ii.3–6). Celia's response to this is slightly convoluted because of the way it compactly imagines several analogies with Rosalind's situation and swiftly interchanges first- and second-person pronouns:

> Herein I see thou lov'st me not with the full weight that I love thee. If my uncle thy banished father had banished thy uncle the Duke my father, so thou hadst been still with me, I could have taught my love to take thy father for mine; so wouldst thou, if the truth of thy love to me were so righteously tempered as mine is to thee.
>
> (I.ii.7–13)

Celia's advice might be considered tactless: 'your father has been banished by mine, so why not adopt mine instead'. For Celia, signifiers of kinship are in other words interchangeable: one father can quite easily be replaced with another. Likewise, 'I' and 'thy', 'me' and 'thee' are not so firmly differentiated as to prevent fusion and confusion. This latter example of boundary negation probably compensates for Celia's tactlessness: Celia is not only offering her father as a surrogate for the real thing, she is also offering herself to Rosalind as a kind of surrogate family and term of endearment.

Family for Celia thus lacks the absoluteness which Orlando attaches to it. For Celia, kinship terms are transferable. They can be re-created, relocated, re-imagined. Celia *mobilises* Rosalind. She encourages Rosalind to think in terms of transfers of familial and other kinds of affection. And Rosalind is quick to learn from Celia, for she immediately mimics Celia's principle of transferring emotional focus from one object to another: 'Well, I will forget the condition of my estate, to rejoice in yours' (I.ii.14–15). It is possible that the final resting place which Celia imagines for Rosalind's *mobilised* affections is herself, for she mockingly discourages Rosalind from falling in love with a man (I.ii.25–8) and speaks several times of her love for Rosalind: 'Rosalind lacks then the love/Which teacheth thee that thou and I are one' (I.iii.92–3). But Celia does not openly avow sexual passion, for this would be to arrest the movements of affection which Celia catalyses.

In the mental and emotional mobility which she demonstrates, and in the disrespect which she shows for the 'natural' family, Celia is in many ways like her father. As Frederick has shown no respect for his natural brother, and has introduced the principles of radical instability and dynamic change into the 'new' court, so Celia is likewise irreverent and innovative. When Celia and Rosalind (on Celia's initiative) make plans to flee the new court *together*, Celia's flippant attitude towards the natural family only mirrors her father's casualness: 'Shall we be sunder'd? Shall we part, sweet girl?/No let my father seek another heir' (I.iii.94–5). She will be as apparently unconcerned to abandon her father as her father was to abandon his brother. There, though, the similarity ends, for whereas the 'tyrant Duke' (I.ii.278) seems intent on *destroying* the bonds of kinship, Celia *reconstructs* them. Her family – her adopted family – is Rosalind. Sharing love which is, as the new courtier Le Beau recognises, 'dearer than the natural bond of sisters' (I.ii.266), Celia and Rosalind create their own surrogate family.

Thus past and present, old and new meet in the figures of Celia and Rosalind. Rewriting the family without destroying it, Celia and Rosalind take the best from both worlds: the dynamism of the one, the loyalty of the other; the one's scope for innovation, the other's traditionalism, and so on. And these they combine to create what is arguably a richer and more authentic vision of the human than either social formation taken in isolation is able to produce. Only by overcoming the binary opposition of past *or* present, old *or* new is such a vision possible.

To conclude this section and to prepare for the next, I want briefly to consider history as form rather than theme. That is, I want to look at the way *As You Like It* mediates its historical themes. As the theoretical section of this chapter made clear, history can be mediated in a variety of ways: through statistics, graphs, economics, oral testimony, autobiography, re-enactments, theme parks, and so on. So how does *As You Like It* mediate its historical concerns? In terms of the history spectrum, which ranges from the 'objective' to the 'expressive', where does a dramatic text such as *As You Like It* lie? The question is, of course, loaded, for drama is hardly objective in the conventional sense of the word. It would be a mistake, therefore, to treat *As You Like It* as though it were a factual historical record. It would be foolish, for example, to take Orlando's representation of the feudal past as hard, objective scientific evidence of what that past was like. Orlando is being nostalgic, and nostalgia is not usually noted for its objectivity. Of course, this 'subjective' mediation of the past would be enough, in some (objective) historians' eyes, to disqualify it as history. But as the introductory section to this chapter suggested, history seen through the eyes of the subject may communicate its own kind of experiential truth.

History in *As You Like It* is more at the emotive than impersonal end of the spectrum because it also understands history to be mainly *family* history, and specifically *aristocratic* family history. The obvious reason for this is that aristocratic families were still hugely influential in Shakespeare's day. Because of this influence, familial terms and terms describing social institutions – such as kingship – are to a large extent interchangeable. *Kingship* and *kinship* are implied by one another. The king can be likened to a father, society to a family. King James himself affirmed the legitimacy of the often used analogy between family and state in a parliamentary speech of 1609:

In the Scriptures Kings are called Gods, and so their power after a certain relation compared to the Divine power. Kings are also compared to Fathers of families: for a King is truly *Parens Patriae* [father of his country], the politic father of his people.[24]

Society, on the basis of this analogy, is not something abstract and impersonal. Likewise, the history of society is neither abstract nor impersonal, for history is family history.

But families, as *As You Like It* shows, can be re-imagined by inventive individualists such as Celia. Affections can be transferred from father to surrogate father, from surrogate father to female friend, and so on. Family is less a 'natural', given phenomenon than a chosen allegiance. However, none of these qualifications change the central point which I have been making and with which I want to conclude, that historical themes in *As You Like It* are mediated through family saga, and through experiences – of mourning, desire, nostalgia and loss – normally associated with the affective life of the human subject. This is what makes the play an example of expressive, anthropomorphic history, even as its sense of the human is endangered by its simultaneous representation of the relationship between past and present as discontinuous and non-communicative.

HENRY V

Difference rules once again in *Henry V*, but this time explicitly at the level of form or genre. The history play is, in other words, about itself and the different ways in which history can be mediated.

An example of one of the play's genres of history is the interminable, 'dryasdust' chronicle presented by the Archbishop of Canterbury in justification of Henry's intended invasion of France. After over sixty of possibly the dullest lines in the entire Shakespearean canon, Henry asks: 'May I with right and conscience make this claim?'[25] Has Henry's attention wandered? It would hardly be surprising if it had. The Archbishop's careful cataloguing of examples of the Crown of France passing through female hands – examples which contravene the supposed Salic law which limited inheritance of the French monarchy to males – scarcely solicits attention. Although much is at stake here, not least the issue of sexual discrimination, the Archbishop's delivery deadens this as well as the other key question of Henry's legitimate or otherwise claim to France.

When the Archbishop, on Henry's impatient cue, is given a second opportunity to answer the question of legitimacy via a historical narrative, he takes what may have been Henry's more than gentle hint to adopt a racier style:

King Henry.
    May I with right and conscience make this claim?
Canterbury.
    The sin upon my head, dread sovereign!
    For in the Book of Numbers is it writ:
    'When the man dies, let the inheritance
    Descend unto the daughter.' Gracious lord,
    Stand for your own: unwind your bloody flag;
    Look back into your mighty ancestors:

Go, my dread lord, to your great-grandsire's tomb,
From whom you claim; invoke his warlike spirit,
And your great-uncle's, Edward the Black Prince,
Who on the French ground play'd a tragedy,
Making defeat on the full power of France;
Whiles his most mighty father on a hill
Stood smiling to behold his lion's whelp
Forage in blood of French nobility.

(I.ii.96–110)

Canterbury's provocation to Henry to reanimate the warlike spirit of his forebears constitutes a more inspired invocation of history. History is now *charismatic* aristocratic family history. It recalls what Jürgen Habermas refers to as aristocratic publicity (see Chapter 1). It is history as the narrative of potent aristocratic *subjects* of history. And so it is more affecting, especially, of course, for Henry. This is surely more what he wants to hear, because it offers him a seductive narrative about who he is and who he might be. However, if the Archbishop's second attempt at historical narrative brings history to life where previously it was dead, then it is thankfully not the only kind of 'living' or expressive history which the play presents. Aristocrats are, in other words, not the only subjects of history in the play. And other kinds of subjective experience – beyond that of the fantasy of the all-powerful agent – are available. Of which more anon.

The Archbishop's more upbeat narrative has much in common with another of the play's discourses of history which is supplied by the Chorus. History is imagined by the Chorus as a grand narrative in which England and King Harry are the glamorous heroes and Agincourt one of their finest hours. Although the Chorus keeps insisting that this momentous history cannot be animated by a few actors and a sparse stage (the wooden O referred to below), it can nevertheless be brought to life in our imagination:

O, for a muse of fire, that would ascend
The brightest heaven of invention;
A kingdom for a stage, princes to act
And monarchs to behold the swelling scene!
Then should the warlike Harry, like himself,
Assume the port of Mars; and at his heels,

> Leash'd in like hounds, should famine, sword, and fire
> Crouch for employment. But pardon, gentles all,
> The flat unraised spirits that hath dar'd
> On this unworthy scaffold to bring forth
> So great an object: can this cockpit hold
> The vasty fields of France? or may we cram
> Within this wooden O the very casques
> That did affright the air of Agincourt?
> O, pardon! since a crooked figure may
> Attest in little place a million;
> And let us, ciphers to this great accompt,
> On your imaginary forces work . . .
> . . . 'tis your thoughts now must deck our kings,
> Carry them here and there, jumping o'er times,
> Turning th'accomplishment of many years
> Into an hour-glass.
>
> ('Prologue', ll.1–18; 28–31)

History as a 'swelling scene' and 'great . . . object' is lost, because of the scant resources of the Renaissance stage, only to be found again in the imagination. Absent on stage, it will be made present – literally put into the present tense – if we imagine it: 'Suppose within the girdle of these walls/Are *now* [my emphasis] confin'd two mighty monarchies' (ll.19–20). The Chorus, like Bartholmew Cokes, like Giovanni and others, cannot abide a distance, cannot in this case tolerate the sense that the heroic historical moment might remain other or elusive to the present. And so the Chorus keeps on cajoling us to compensate for the misfit between the expansive past and the meagre theatrical present: 'Still be kind,/And eke out our performance with your mind' (III. 'Chorus', ll. 34–5). If the stage creates an anti-illusionist distance between past and present, then the imagining mind will create the full illusion of the presence of the past.

Inside the play itself, the Chorus's view of Agincourt in particular and history in general is sometimes – but only sometimes – corroborated. Henry's famous battle-speech, beginning 'Once more unto the breach' (III.i.1), arguably does what the Chorus wishes the play could *all* the time: vividly realise the glamour of war; celebrate England and the English; construct national history as an inspiring and heroic aristocratic family narrative:

On, on, you noblest English!
Whose blood is fet from fathers of war-proof;
Fathers that, like so many Alexanders,
Have in these parts from morn till even fought,
And sheath'd their swords for lack of argument.
Dishonour not your mothers; now attest
That those whom you call'd fathers did beget you.
Be copy now to men of grosser blood,
And teach them how to war.

(III.i.17–25)

Although this part of Henry's speech is explicitly directed to England's nobility, it is at the same time offered as a source of inspiration to 'men of grosser blood'. These men are invited to 'join' Henry's text of history as heroic aristocratic family narrative.

However, as I have already suggested, this way of making history 'live' does not dominate the play. 'Animations' of Agincourt multiply and in doing so call into question the extent to which the past can be resuscitated according to one or another *single* principle. The Chorus mistakenly thinks that history can be rendered *fully* present and *fully* unified in the minds of an audience who are asked to imagine Agincourt in one way and one way only, but in the play itself, diversity of perspective is progressively marked as 'truer' to historical experience. The view of Agincourt from 'below', for example, does not always conform to the Chorus's and sometimes Henry's view of war as heroic, glamorous and fulfilling. The 'Boy' wishes he 'were in an alehouse in London'. 'I would give all my fame', he says, 'for a pot of ale, and safety' (III.ii.12–13). Pistol concurs with this anti-war sentiment. Together, Pistol and the Boy imagine an elsewhere which is emphatically *not* that of the heroic war-zone to which the Chorus keeps attempting to co-opt our imagination:

Pistol. And I:
    If wishes would prevail with me,
    My purpose should not fail with me,
      But thither would I hie.
Boy.   As duly,
      But not as truly,
    As bird doth sing on bough.

(III.ii.14–20)

While the audience are repeatedly asked to imagine themselves *into* the field of battle, some of those already there are doing their best to imagine themselves *out* of it. Agincourt looks differently according to where one stands. History is not the same experience for everyone.

The Chorus would have us look past or through what happens on stage to the imagined glamour of the war-zone. It would have us treat the actors as mere 'ciphers to this great accompt' ('Prologue', l. 17), for what happens on stage is of small account by comparison with the heroic and expansive actuality. The Chorus thus deprives the theatre of its powers of representation, by pointing to the theatre's inability to represent the heroic reality. But we can give back to Shakespeare's play its representational power, by suggesting that the failure to represent heroic Agincourt is actually its success. *Henry V* takes us 'backstage', behind the scenes of heroic Agincourt, to forcefully present another reality. Discontent or so it seems with existing narratives of history, the temporarily uncrowned, incognito King Henry goes in search of this reality. 'I think the King is but a man', says the disguised Henry. 'His ceremonies laid by', he continues, 'in his nakedness he appears but a man' (IV.i.101–2, 105–6). Henry is writing his way *out* of history as a spectacular aristocratic family history and *into* an experience of history which will put him in touch with another self, the self beyond ceremony, the self beyond the signs and symbols of power. Henry becomes a *flâneur* of the battlefield, seeking out the diversity of historical experience which will enable him to transcend the limitations of his own circumscribed historical position.

'Living history', to revert by way of conclusion to Raphael Samuel, 'privileges the private over the public sphere.' 'At the cinema,' he continues, 'in Kenneth Branagh's version of Shakespeare, it makes *Henry V* into a kind of *Hamlet*; a prince, in the manner of the current heir to the throne, wanting to be a private person even when he finds himself thrust into the role of king.' Branagh's interpretation of the play is not unwarranted, for Henry does go in search of the private person. But 'private', in the context of the play, does not entail withdrawing from history (or attempting to), but a fuller involvement with it. Such is expressive history's assimilation of human to historical being.

6

Feminism
The Duchess of Malfi;
The Roaring Girl

There are now many different varieties of feminism as well as several different ways of making sense of this variety.[1] One useful way of plotting a narrative around contemporary feminisms, and one which synchronises well with the continuing concerns of this book, is suggested by Mary Eagleton. Eagleton points to the existence of a divide, which is sometimes crossed, between *anti*-theoretical and *pro*-theoretical feminisms. The anti-theoretical 'suspicion of theory', which Eagleton claims is 'widespread throughout feminism', is due to the hierarchical binary oppositions which theory is thought to reinforce:[2]

> Feminism would argue that the impersonality and disinterestedness of theory is fallacious, masking the needs and partiality of the theoretician and that it partakes of the hierarchical binary opposition to which Cixous refers in her essay 'Sorties: Out and Out: Attacks/Ways Out/Forays' (1986): theory is impersonal, public, objective, male; experience is personal, private, subjective, female. The anti-theorists undermine the primacy of theory by valorizing the subordinated term, variously styled as the experiential, the body, *jouissance*, the Mother.[3]

There are, of course, as many *pro*-theoretical feminists as there are those doubtful of theory. While this chapter cannot provide anything like a comprehensive account of all contemporary feminisms, it will be able to explore this main line of division, suggested by Eagleton, between feminist theory and feminist antitheory. This tension in feminism is also often the tension between anti-foundationalist and foundationalist conceptions of gender, and relates, as well, to conflicts between anti-humanism and humanism, rationalism and neo-Romanticism.

161

If the anti-humanism of modern literary theory can be characterised, as I suggested in the Introduction, in terms of its scepticism,
critical distance and refusal to identify with one or another image
of the human, then certain strands of feminism have taken and
indeed have often led this anti-humanist turn by emphasising
the always and everywhere *constructed* nature of the human and
human beings in general, and of female and male identity in
particular. It is easy to see why the insistence upon the social
construction of reality and consciousness should appeal to many
feminist thinkers. Once social constructions of gender are recognised *as* constructions, once it is recognised that notions of
'Woman' as 'naturally' or 'essentially' intuitive, irrational or
emotional, and so forth, are social stereotypes which have no
grounding whatsoever in nature, then those social constructions
may be changed. The 'loss' of universals, metaphysical absolutes
and transcendent categories which accompanies the insistence
upon the social construction of reality is from this perspective
more of a gain, for if there is no such essential thing as woman
or man, then these concepts can be contested and redefined.

The other side to feminism which this chapter will explore is
a form of foundationalism which, like other strands of modern
theory, might be seen as having at least *one* of its origins in
Romanticism. Drawing on the work of Philippe Lacoue-Labarthe
and Jean-Luc Nancy, Niall Lucy provocatively suggests that
'today everyone is still a 'romantic'.[4] It may be that Romanticism, as the still often unacknowledged precursor of much modern
literary theory, informs, not just poststructuralism, as was
suggested in Chapter 3, but certain varieties of feminist – as well
as Marxist, historicist and psychoanalytic – writing.[5] Lucy defines
Romanticism thus:

> For romanticism . . . the world as experienced through the faculty
> of the imagination is full of wondrous enigmatic things that
> can in no way be reduced to objects but which are what they
> are, like a poem or some other work of literature, only as the
> sublime *question* of what they are. Their true nature is that
> their true nature, like the true nature of literature, remains
> forever out of reach of rational, scientific or pragmatic systems
> of calculation and knowledge.[6]

In the context of the human, Romanticism widens the gap, discussed in previous chapters in the context of the Renaissance, between 'inner' and 'outer' realities by pointing, Hamlet-like, to a mysterious interiority which cannot adequately be brought to language, and which suggests the existence of an untapped well of human being and human possibility residing beyond ordinary, mundane existence. It is the Romantic in Hamlet that says to Horatio, 'There are more things in heaven and earth, Horatio,/ Than are dreamt of in your philosophy' (I.v.174–5), as it is arguably the Romantic in the feminist thinker Hélène Cixous that writes: 'I, too, overflow; my desires have invented new desires, my body knows unheard-of songs.'[7] Although the human according to such a Romantic conception of it, is, to quote Iago out of context again, 'an essence that's not seen' (*Othello*, IV.i.16), it is still a foundationalist conception in that it posits an authentic truth about human and/or specifically feminine being. The 'and/or' is vital here, as it is possible to have an idea of what human being essentially is, *without* having an essentialist or foundationalist concept of gender. Whether or not feminists embrace the idea of a distinctively and essentially 'feminine' consciousness, they may still be locatable, as I shall argue later, within a foundationalist paradigm with regard to human being, by virtue of their albeit different emphases upon the idea of life being, to borrow Lucy's phrase, 'forever out of reach of rational, scientific or pragmatic systems of calculation and knowledge'. Feminism's variation upon such a foundationalist conception is, like many psychoanalytic critics, to locate one or another form of pre-discursive or extra-discursive multiplicity as the 'natural' state from which we are separated by language and culture.

ANTI-FOUNDATIONALIST FEMINISMS

First let me offer an example of an anti-foundationalist form of feminism which steers well clear of any Romantic/humanist reference to the self and/or to life and their mysterious depths, and concentrates instead upon identity as a purely linguistic, 'external' and largely *un*mysterious phenomenon. Judith Butler's *Gender Trouble* is a persuasive and influential example of a rigorously theoretical, relentlessly constructionist form of feminism which argues strenuously against what she refers to as the 'foundational illusions of identity'.[8] Identity, for Butler, has no being or basis outside the cultural domain which constructs it. Thus sexual identity is not something we should think of as belonging to some inner core of our personality. 'Being' lesbian, straight or gay is not, for Butler, a matter of *being*, but of 'performing' a culturally constructed gender identity which, via explicit performance, can be made visible precisely as one of several possible performances or constructions:

> No longer believable as an interior 'truth' of dispositions and identity, sex will be shown to be a performatively enacted signification (and hence not 'to be'), one that, released from its naturalized interiority and surface, can occasion the parodic proliferation and subversive play of gendered meanings.[9]

Interiority, frequently the mark of a complexly recessed subjectivity, is here understood by Butler as nothing more and nothing less than the means whereby an externally imposed, socially constructed identity becomes successfully ingrained, internalised and (mis)taken as natural. Thus Butler does not so much return the psyche to language – as I argued poststructuralism and psychoanalysis do by investing language with emotional intensity and 'depth' – as undermine the capacity of signs to have anything other than a superficial effect upon a subject who is thereby enabled to manipulate them.

Parody comes to play an especially important role in Butler's detailed and challenging discussion, for the parodying of gender identity which she sees at work in 'the cultural practices of drag, cross-dressing, and the sexual stylization of butch/femme identities' has the effect of externalising and so denaturalising sex and gender.[10] 'The notion of gender parody defended here', writes Butler, 'does not assume that there is an original which such parodic identities imitate. Indeed, the parody is *of* the very notion of an original.'[11] In releasing us from understanding identity in terms of origins, foundations and essences (terms which encourage us to think about who we 'really' are), parody enables us to play with roles none of which definitively identify us. Through parody, identity is theatricalised, made visible as a cultural role rather than an intrinsic attribute of self.

Butler's argument thus resembles the anti-illusionist dimension of Renaissance drama discussed in Chapters 1 and 3. It will be worthwhile briefly rehearsing the main points of this discussion in order to situate Butler's anti-humanist anti-illusionism more precisely. The drama's anti-illusionism, I have previously argued, can take one of (at least) two different forms. It can either fuel a healthy scepticism towards roles which might otherwise be natu-ralised by conflating 'role' with 'self', the qualification being, however, that this scepticism is never so 'cool' or so complete as to totally prohibit emotional investment in one or another performance. Alternatively, anti-illusionism can, when exploited by the likes of Iago, generate 'humanist' anxiety about the total alienation of roles from a self who refuses to be in any way affected by them. I would argue that both these types of anti-illusionism invite us to think about their effects from within a humanist paradigm. Is scepticism a form of denial of human emotion? Does total identification with a role consume the human capacity for self-consciousness? These questions invite us to consider what human consciousness 'essentially' is.

Butler does not participate in the 'old' humanist paradigm which promotes questions about human consciousness and human experience. Neither does she contribute to a revised humanism which sees language as the locus of the human. The questions which Butler explores are instead questions about language and language's mode of functioning. Thus agency and creativity, for example, are not understood to be the actual or potential prop-erty of 'people', but as mere effects of language, based upon language's capacity to exceed its own rules. Attributes that might once have been thought of as actual or potential human attributes are in this way 'exported' by Butler from the human to the linguistic, and in the process emptied of much of the psychic and emotional baggage that comes with them:

As a process, signification harbors within itself what the epis-temological discourse refers to as 'agency'. The rules that govern intelligible identity, i.e., that enable and restrict the intelligible assertion of an 'I', rules that are partially structured around matrices of gender hierarchy and compulsory heterosexuality, operate through *repetition*. Indeed, when the subject is said to be constituted, that means simply that the subject is a conse-quence of certain rule-governed discourses that govern the intelligible invocation of identity. The subject is not *determined* by the rules through which it is generated because signification is *not a founding act, but rather a regulated process of repetition* that both conceals itself and enforces its rules precisely through the production of substantializing effects. In a sense, all signification takes place within the orbit of the compulsion to repeat; 'agency', then, is to be located within the possibility of a variation on that repetition.[12]

These fruitful insights into the nature of language feed the idea that gender identity is never something that can be established once and for all. It is constantly being repeated – or varied – through linguistic performance. The idea that language is always variable – or at least potentially variable – closely resembles the poststructuralist/Derridean view of language as continually undoing settled meanings and concepts, but unlike other varieties of poststructuralism which rehabilitate subjectivity as process, Butler's use of an impersonal quasi-structuralist vocabulary distances her from subjective categories. Thus the question of why language should vary in one way rather than another is not answered by Butler, because that surely would entail the existence of an 'outside' agency ('people' who want life and language to change in one way rather than another). Butler, however, dismantles concepts of outside and inside by intensively interrogating the idea that there are any realities 'external' to language. This applies even to the seemingly incontrovertible fact of anatomical differences between the sexes. Paraphrasing some of the ideas of Monique Wittig, Butler writes that 'there is no reason to divide up human bodies into male and female sexes except that such a division suits the economic needs of heterosexuality and lends a naturalistic gloss to the institution of heterosexuality'.[13] Where many feminists differentiate between the concepts of sex and gender (on the basis that sex is biologically given whereas gender is the cultural interpretation, the social construction of biological difference), Butler, via Wittig, questions even this supposedly fundamental external reality.

The anti-foundationalist feminism which I have taken Butler's *Gender Trouble* to represent would look somewhat different had another 'representative' example been selected. I chose to discuss Butler's book because it argues its position in a very direct, explicit and exhaustive way. In doing so, it both lays bare and thoroughly explores the premises upon which other feminisms, such as recent 'materialist' feminisms, rest. Materialist feminism develops from

Marxist philosophy an emphasis upon our material conditions of existence (upon capitalism, for example, as the economic and social system which currently organises human life); but it also takes as an important aspect of our material conditions of existence the material of language. Butler's book can therefore help to illuminate and deepen such claims as Valerie Wayne's that: 'our bodies [are] sites for the inscriptions of ideology and power, since we cannot "know" them in any unmediated form and they, as we, are products of the cultural meanings ascribed to them'.[14] Like Butler, Wayne repudiates the idea that the body precedes – is external to – language. But unlike Butler, she takes this semiotic/textualist perspective as something of a given.

BEYOND LANGUAGE

Butler's style of theorising is rationalist and quasi-scientific. Discourse is something that can be analysed, and likewise, identity, as an effect of discourse, can be rendered unmysterious and knowable. While Butler's feminism shares in common with the other feminisms to be examined in this section an emphasis upon the power of language to mediate reality, the difference between them is the way that these other varieties of feminisms have more time than Butler has for the *extra*-discursive – for that which is ostensibly and sometimes mysteriously beyond language. We are linguistic beings but we are not just linguistic beings – this is often the emphasis of the other versions of feminism I shall now explore.

For Butler, appeals to supposedly extra-linguistic realities are *constraining*: appeals to biology, for example, are made by heterosexual culture to legitimate and restrict us to heterosexual identities. This view of putatively external realties is compelling, especially in the context of feminism, for women have undoubtedly been constrained by appeals to biology or nature (such as 'a woman's natural place is in the home'). However, constraint is not the *only* way of thinking about realities which are actually or ostensibly external to language.

Biology is, of course, only one of several putatively 'external' realities which may *challenge* as much as *consolidate* a social and sexual status quo. As I argued in Chapter 2 (and elsewhere), appeals to the extra-discursivity of concepts such as justice may challenge their cultural and/or 'private' appropriation. If justice was as any culture or American president wanted it to be, then its survival as any kind of yardstick for measuring injustice and oppression would be seriously threatened. All I am wanting to establish, here, is the idea that appeals to one or another extra-discursive entity – whether body, libido, consciousness, self, justice, need, affective experience, and so on – are not exclusively the preserve of those seeking to maintain the sexual and social order of things. They can equally be of use to the disenfranchised.

The extra-discursive realities invoked by French feminists, for example, are mainly expressive of the idea of a subversive *excess* which undermines the man-made linguistic order. Excess is variously conceived as pre-cultural libidinal energy (Julia Kristeva/ Hélène Cixous), the untapped resources/unrealised possibilities of the self (Hélène Cixous), or that which transcends and transgresses masculinist systems of representation organised around repressive binary oppositions (Luce Irigaray). There are important differences between these writers, as well as different ways of locating each one of them: Kristeva, for example, is considered to be essentialist by some feminist commentators and anti-essentialist by others.[15] However, the difficulty of subsuming them under one or another heading is partly the subversive point of their writing, especially in the case of Cixous and Irigaray, for it points to the uncontainable excess and multiplicity identified above as the basis of their foundationalism.

There is thus something of a paradox in identifying these feminists in terms of their foundationalism, since foundations and identity are simultaneously what they resist. Hélène Cixous, for example, writes that 'You can't talk about *a* female sexuality, uniform, homogenous, classifiable into codes – any more than you can talk about one unconscious resembling another. Women's imaginary is inexhaustible, like music, painting, writing: their stream of phantasms is incredible.' She continues:

I have been amazed more than once by a description a woman gave me of a world all her own which she had been secretly haunting since early childhood. A world of searching, the elaboration of a knowledge, on the basis of a systematic experimentation with the bodily functions, a passionate and precise interrogation of her erotogeneity. This practice, extraordinarily rich and inventive, in particular as concerns masturbation, is prolonged or accompanied by a production of forms, a veritable aesthetic activity, each stage of rapture inscribing a resonant vision, a composition, something beautiful. Beauty will no longer be forbidden.

I wished that that woman would write and proclaim this unique empire so that other women, other unacknowledged sovereigns, might exclaim: I, too, overflow; my desires have invented new desires, my body knows unheard-of songs.[16]

Cixous practices what she preaches here by writing this fluid, 'inexhaustible' prose. This type of writing, which is mainly associated with Cixous and Luce Irigaray and which is often referred to as *l'écriture féminine*, is designed to counteract what Cixous sees as 'the pervasive masculine urge to judge, diagnose, digest, name'.[17] In eschewing the philosophical exactness and rectitude that, say, Butler's writing possesses, Cixous's free-flowing, lyrical writing makes it difficult to locate the nature of its 'excess' with any degree of precision. Is it the plural nature of female sexuality which, as Luce Irigaray also suggests, naturally exceeds patriarchal boundaries and definitions? Or is this too literal an interpretation? Should we instead think of excess in terms of an infinitely imaginative and expressive female 'self' who is laying claim to the right to signify and interpret *her* body in her own way? In the first instance, it is the female *libido* which is the source of the energy and creativity which are in *excess* of patriarchal language. In the second instance, it is the expressive female *self* which places itself beyond all stultifying confines.

Whichever interpretation we choose, one point seems clear: the female body and/or self are being located somewhere outside or beyond language as creative, transforming agencies. This is very different from Judith Butler's position, for, as we have seen, she understands agency and excess as *linguistic* phenomena, and the body, likewise, as a 'signifying practice within a cultural field'.[18] Cixous, Irigaray and Butler all draw upon language-based theories: they all make use, for instance, of the poststructuralist emphasis upon the creativity of language, but, unlike Butler, Cixous and Irigaray retain a notion of *human* and specifically *feminine* creativity which transgresses and transcends available languages. In some of Irigaray's writing, 'woman' is thought of as being so far beyond the confines of male-dominated forms of representation that she becomes, like an object of the Romantic imagination, sublime. In a masculine culture that 'claims to enumerate everything, cipher everything by units, inventory everything by individualities', woman, writes Irigaray, 'renders any definition inadequate . . . she has no "proper" name'.[19]

In the case of Irigaray and Cixous, a foundationalist concept of the human as multiple and heterogeneous feeds their arguably essentialist concepts of Woman. It is 'Woman' who perpetuates a Romantic vision by embodying a fuller, richer and more authentic humanity than her robotic, technocratic, and spiritually atrophied counterpart, 'Man'. Although Irigaray and Cixous both leave themselves vulnerable to the criticism that their essentialist appeals to what Woman 'really' is (fecund, enigmatic, multiple, creative, and so on) are themselves derived from masculine constructions of gender, they nevertheless pose a challenge to those constructionist, language-based theories which are developed at the expense of subjective categories.[20] For Cixous especially, writing is criticism, is theorising, is conceptualising, and so on – but writing is also a form of self-expression, which constructs the self as a site of resistance to the cultural construction of femininity and a sign of what culture has excluded.

In Cixous's writing, theory and the concept-centredness of theory are also placed in opposition to 'life' – and to poetry as a simulacrum of life – because concepts interrupt the natural rhythm and flow of existence:

> What is most true is poetic because it is not stopped-stoppable. All that is stopped, grasped, all that is subjugated, easily transmitted, easily picked up, all that comes under the word concept, which is to say all that is taken, caged, is *less* true. Has lost what is life itself, which is always in the process of seething, of emitting, of transmitting itself. Each object is in reality a small virtual volcano. There is a continuity in the living; whereas theory entails a discontinuity, a cut, which is altogether the opposite of life. I am not anathematizing all theory. It is indispensable, at times, to make progress, but alone it is false.[21]

For language, via poetry, to come into sensuous contact with 'life' is for language to become mimetic of something which is presumed to reside *outside* language. Such is the appeal, once again, to the extra-discursive – here, 'life' – as a site of energy, plenitude, flux and creativity. For Cixous, experience of life is

always excessive to the concept and it is the mark of any sufficiently rounded human being to recognise that one cannot live
by concepts alone.

A variation on the foundationalism of Cixous and Irigaray is
Julia Kristeva's concept of the *semiotic* (not to be confused with
semiotics). Again, it is important to identify what I mean by
Kristeva's foundationalism here, because, unlike Irigaray and
Cixous, Kristeva can be seen as essentialist with respect to the
human, but anti-essentialist with respect to gender identity. Drawing on psychoanalysis, Kristeva identifies the semiotic as the
unstructured, unregulated and amorphous state of existence in
which the infant lives prior to his/her initiation into the more
ordered world of language, referred to by Kristeva as the *symbolic*.
The symbolic and the semiotic could be seen as roughly anal-
ogous with structuralist and poststructuralist accounts of language:
language as a *system* of oppositions and differences characterises its symbolic aspect, whilst language at play and in flux
approximates the semiotic state. The semiotic also bears comparison
to Cixous's image of 'life' which is 'always in the process of
seething, of emitting, of transmitting itself'. And just as Cixous
finds poetry mimetic of 'life', so Kristeva sees poetry as an
approximation of the creative and disorderly energies at work
in the semiotic. Poetry, writes Kristeva, 'transgresses grammatical rules', and 'puts the subject in process/on trial', one effect of
which is to undermine the presumed naturalness of our culturally
and linguistically constructed subjectivities.[22]

Kristeva's semiotic generates an image of the human which is
thus once again based upon a conception of excess and inexhaust-
ibility. French feminisms may take the linguistic turn that other
movements, like structuralism and poststructuralism, have taken.
They may fruitfully utilise those language-based theories which
say that the subject is culturally constructed. But they do not
'take to language' completely. There is 'something else', a something else which (patriarchal) language as currently constituted
does not accommodate. This excess, this 'something else' goes
by different names – body, libido, interiority, the feminine, the
unconscious, the semiotic, life, creativity. These beyonds – not
yet fully part of the here and now – are potentially healing and
redeeming of the defects of culture and language. The *difference*
between Kristeva, on the one hand, and Cixous and Irigaray, on
the other, is that Kristeva arguably does not identify women

exclusively with the vibrant life forces of the semiotic. As Toril Moi suggests, Kristeva's feminism is premised upon concepts of *'positionality'* rather than 'essences', meaning that Kristeva conceives of male and female identity, from a constructionist perspective, in terms of the way men and women are allocated subjectivities.[23] Although it may be the case that men have traditionally been assigned 'symbolic' and women something approximating 'semiotic' identities (or non-identities), these assignments do not reflect the supposedly innate character of women and men. Where Kristeva *is* essentialist is in her conception of the human subject as a multi-layered, multi-levelled being whose social self masks the unknown reserves and energies of the semiotic.

To conclude this section, I shall glance briefly at one further example of feminist work, that of Elaine Showalter. Showalter is often taken to be representative of certain influential tendencies within American or Anglo-American feminism, and differentiated from French feminisms on the basis that the latter are more pro-theoretical and constructionist than the former.[24] As ever, there is the problem of who is taken to be representative of what tendencies and how one interprets texts. My own angle is that Showalter shares in common with Cixous and Irigaray a distrust of theory and with Cixous, Irigaray and Kristeva, a preoccupation with the extra-discursive.

A key word in Showalter's essay 'Towards a Feminist Poetics' of 1979 is *experience*. For Showalter, experience has to be central to any feminist project because associated as it is with the 'feminine' realm of the personal and the subjective, it combats the dehumanisation which is rife in the masculine world:

> While scientific criticism struggles to purge itself of the subjective, feminist criticism is willing to assert (in the title of a recent anthology) *The Authority of Experience.* The experience of women can easily disappear, become mute, invalid, and invisible, lost in the diagrams of the structuralist or the class conflict of the Marxists. Experience is not emotion; we must protest now as in the nineteenth century against the equation of the feminine with the irrational. But we must also recognize that the questions we most need to ask go beyond those that science can answer.[25]

Showalter's emphasis upon experience suggests a kind of defiance by the individual to instant sociological and historical categorisation. Experience suggests that life *lived* by an individual is different from life as it might be subsequently theorised, and that the contingent, singular experience of individuals is not immediately available to the schematisations of those forms of historicism which take science as their model. Experience implicitly privileges the idea of the singularity of individual life-histories which thereby resist instant assimilation to social and macro-historical concepts and categories. The insistence, via the appeal to experience, upon the subjective and personal assumes that the subjective and the personal are *always to some extent* in excess of those social categories and linguistic codes which would comprehend them.

'Experience' thus suggests that history might fruitfully begin, not by explaining one or another social system or linguistic code, but at the concrete level of an individual's life-history. Women, associated as they often have been with the private sphere, are seen by Showalter as offering a special vantage point in this respect, for they have not been subject to the depersonalising effects of the public sphere.

FEMINISM IN SUMMARY

- One way of plotting a narrative around the several varieties of feminism which have been influential upon modern literary theory (and upon other disciplines and practices) in recent years is by exploring such main lines of division between them as humanism versus anti-humanism, foundationalism versus anti-foundationalism and theoreticism versus anti-theoreticism.
- The rigorously theoretical, anti-foundationalist and anti-humanist feminism of Judith Butler emphasises the cultural/ linguistic construction of gender, subjectivity and consciousness, and – using poststructuralist insights – the instability and impermanence of these constructions. Feminist theories of this kind understand appeals to extra-linguistic realities (such as self, consciousness, libido, body, 'life', and so on) to be mere *illusions* designed to ground and naturalise cultural identity.
- Anglo-American and French feminisms have more sympathy for the putatively extra-linguistic. The emphases of these

feminisms upon personal experience, the female body, the female imaginary, female consciousness, *l'écriture féminine* and the semiotic variously appeal to the principle of excess: to that which is excessive to (patriarchal) language. Thus while Anglo-American and especially French feminisms emphasise the subject as a linguistic/socially constructed being, they simultaneously look beyond language to an unconstrained, expressive self and/ or body unlimited by social constructions of gender. These appeals make it possible to locate French and Anglo-American feminisms within the paradigm of Romanticism.

• Essentialism with respect to the human does not necessarily entail an essentialist conception of gender identity. In Kristeva's work, these essentialisms arguably do not coincide, whereas, in Cixous and Irigaray, they arguably do coincide.

THE DUCHESS OF MALFI

I have argued that French and Anglo-American feminisms maintain a regard for the extra-discursive, a regard which sometimes manifests itself as a valorisation of the self as the site of unrealised possibility. The regard is emphatically not for the fixed, mono-lithic self often imagined by theorists to be the only way of being a self, but for the female self as untapped resource and as process. The female self conceived by Irigaray and Cixous is the site – not of a closure – but of a fuller, richer, more authentic way of being than social constructions of the subject allow.

The Duchess of Malfi likewise maintains or creates a regard for the possibility of authentic selfhood. The duchess may not be Cixous's or Irigaray's 'sublime' female self, fluid and inexhaust-ible, but she is nevertheless something of a free spirit who attempts to live beyond existing discourses of gender and existing constructions of identity.

Like *Hamlet*, the play depicts a world of corrupted authority, a world in which patriarchs and princes no longer command respect, and in which the link between secular and sacred auth-ority is once again severed. The Italian court in which the characters move is patently not like the French state which the returning Antonio invokes at the beginning of the play:

In seeking to reduce both State and people
To a fix'd order, their judicious King
Begins at home. Quits first his royal palace
Of flatt'ring sycophants, of dissolute,
And infamous persons, which he sweetly terms
His Master's master's-piece, the work of Heaven,
Consid'ring duly, that a Prince's court
Is like a common fountain, whence should flow
Pure silver-drops in general. But if't chance
Some curs'd example poison't near the head,
Death and diseases through the whole land spread.

(I.i.5–15)

A poisoned body politic, such as Malfi's, means that authority, value and meaning are devolved. The place to which they are devolved is the individual. In the absence of a just and meaningful distribution of morality and identity from 'on high', value has to be resurrected and redeemed at the level of the self-authenticating individual. The play, in effect, puts the individual 'on trial'. It tests the extent to which the 'poison' emanating from the head of the body politic will be resisted by individuals who are required to take fuller responsibility for the maintenance of value.

The character who 'passes' the play's test where others miserably fail is the Duchess of Malfi, for she maintains a sense of a multiple though still integrated self in the face of various assaults upon it. Where her lover and eventual husband, Antonio, seeks along with the other leading male characters to enclose her either verbally or physically within an imprisoning frame, the duchess cuts loose and will not be so 'cas'd up' (III.ii.138). Prior to her first appearance Antonio has already attempted to confine the duchess to the realm of pure, disembodied spirit. 'Her days', says Antonio, 'are practis'd in such noble virtue,/That, sure her nights, nay more, her very sleeps,/Are more in heaven, than other ladies' shrifts' (I.ii.123–5). He proceeds to encapsulate her statuesque perfection in the formula: 'All her particular worth grows to this sum:/She stains [i.e. eclipses] the time past: lights the time to come' (I.ii.129–30).

Verbal portraits which approximate the stasis of religious iconography are demolished, Protestant-style, by a duchess who refuses to be simply allocated identities from elsewhere, even when – or especially when – the allocation is from her lover. Antonio will have to learn to see the duchess anew, with fresh eyes, as a 'flesh, and blood' rather than 'alabaster' duchess (I.ii.369–70). Requiring him to see *her* rather than that single image of her which his overly decorous and deferential attitude only allows him to see, the duchess initiates Antonio into the art of the self, the art of living and thinking beyond conventions and socially ascribed identities.

The duchess has paradoxically to *order* her dependent to become independent. 'Awake, awake, man', she commands Antonio, using her superior social status to encourage Antonio to think beyond status and to 'put off', as she herself does, 'all vain ceremony' (I.ii.371–2). At the beginning of the play Antonio seems to think he is still at the French court, where hierarchy and social convention are deemed to have religious foundations. In the different, delegitimised state of Malfi, however, social custom is questionable and reorientations of meaning, value and morality are possible. The individual is therefore faced with the problem as well as the possibility of giving meaning to her/his own life. Antonio thus cannot live the protected existence of someone whose beliefs have been determined elsewhere, by God or the godly prince or an admired social superior. These beliefs – in deference and hierarchy, for example – will have to be adjusted and perhaps even abandoned in the light of his 'own' experience (such as falling for the duchess), which does not conform to the rules. The set speeches which he delivers at the beginning of the play on the ideal court and later on ambition – 'Ambition, Madam, is a great man's madness' (I.ii.337–8) – could be seen as examples of cultural constructed values speaking *through* Antonio as though Antonio were merely their conduit. This lends him a certain impersonal authority as the spokesman for ostensibly universal values which do not depend upon the person for their validity, but such is the questionability of values in the 'fallen' world of Malfi that the self will need to become more active in accepting or negating such values. Self-confidence is what the duchess teaches Antonio, meaning confidence in the capacity of the self to lay claim to itself as a source of value. When the duchess decides to defy her brothers in marrying her servant Antonio she describes herself as venturing forth 'into a wilderness,/Where I shall find no path, nor friendly clew/To be my guide' (I.ii.278–9). Casting herself in the role of heroic individual is one example of the self-authentication which becomes necessary and/or possible in a world which has lost *its* authenticity.

Antonio is not the only one who learns the art of the self from the duchess. Directly affected by the 'poison' emanating from the head of the body politic, Bosola increasingly looks to the duchess as a model. Bosola is in danger of becoming a total cipher, a mere tool of the court, a vacuous and vacant space which the 'system' – no longer legitimisable as a body politic that has a care for its members – may use as it will. Although Bosola *performs* the role of the murderous servant in the parodic way that Judith Butler thinks of as subversive of status quos – 'Whose throat must I cut' (I.ii.170), he prematurely asks Ferdinand, in mockery of his role as the villainous tool – the performative identities acted out by Bosola create in him a need for authentic identity. Is it possible for him to keep on selling out to a system which has lost all credibility without experiencing bad faith and without wishing to compensate for that bad faith?

This question is couched in terms which the play itself encourages. That is to say, we are invited to ponder the effects of power upon the individual psyche and consider the care of the self which has become a personal responsibility due to the utter indifference of those in power. Ferdinand has long since abandoned any kind of positive paternal role. He is therefore indifferent to the state of Bosola's soul. To Ferdinand, Bosola is a mere object, a means to an end, a vehicle. Care of the self – like everything else – thus devolves upon the individual. Bosola is for most of the play careless of a self which comes under increasing under scrutiny. When he gives himself to Ferdinand with the words 'I am your creature' (I.ii.208), the trial of the self begins. What is on trial is the extent of the self's corruptibility by power, the extent to which the self may be moulded, constructed and hollowed out. At this point in the play Bosola does not fully recognise the nature of the trial because he is selfless and absent.

Such is the play's (qualified) optimism, and such is the presence of the duchess within the play, that Bosola is afforded the means of overcoming the self-loathing produced by what he comes to recognise as his alienation from a better self. Discarding his inauthentic existence and 'painted honour' (IV.ii.330), Bosola belatedly discovers himself as subject rather than object. Over the dead body of the duchess he gives up that parodically performative mode which has allowed him to disavow personal responsibility, and instead displays emotion which he can lay claim to as authentically his:

> Oh, she's gone again: there the cords of life broke.
> Oh sacred innocence, that sweetly sleeps
> On turtles' feathers: whilst a guilty conscience
> Is a black register, wherein is writ
> All our good deeds and bad; a perspective
> That shows us hell; that we cannot be suffer'd
> To do good when we have a mind to it!
> This is manly sorrow:
> These tears, I am very certain, never grew
> In my mother's milk. My estate is sunk
> Below the degree of fear: where were
> These penitent fountains while she was living?
> Oh, they were frozen up: here is a sight
> As direful to my soul as is the sword
> Unto a wretch hath slain his father.
>
> (IV.ii.348–62)

Bosola moves in this speech from the relative anonymity of the first-person plural (*'our* good deeds', 'a perspective that shows *us* hell' *'we* cannot be suffer'd', and so on) to the greater self-ownership of the first-person singular (*'My* estate', *my* soul', 'I'll bear thee hence'). He also wants to claim the 'manly tears' he weeps as his rather than the inheritance of his mother. The attempt to differentiate between 'we' and 'me', between what is inalienably his and what has been imposed upon him from without contributes to Bosola's discovery of a self that has at least *some* say in what gets taken in or cast out. The servant's claim that s/he was only acting under orders is the claim of the selfless dependant, whereas admission of responsibility is a self-affirming act. Bosola's confession signals the beginning of the end of his days as an insentient, unthinking 'creature' of power.

It is important – in the face of less nuanced expressions of self within *The Duchess of Malfi* and elsewhere (see Chapter 3) – to stress that the play's ideal self seems to be a self whose boundaries are at once firm yet negotiable. The duchess is again the model here, for she crosses the boundaries of class by marrying Antonio, at the same time as she makes of herself an inviolable boundary which resists the attempts of her brothers to repossess her. Her inviolability is manifested in the way that she refuses to recognise her brother Ferdinand's 'justice' and authority, calling him instead an 'oppressor' (III.v.142) – an act which insists upon her *own* authority and moral autonomy. It is also manifested in the way that she determines – or affects – not to be affected by the physical and mental tortures devised by Ferdinand: 'methinks,/The manner of your death should much afflict you?/ This cord should terrify you?', taunts Bosola, to which she stoically replies 'Not a whit' (IV.ii.211–12). If she elsewhere insists upon being 'flesh, and blood', then during the scenes of torture she becomes inviolable 'alabaster' and disembodied spirit placed beyond the reach of the brother who tries, time and again, to invade her space.

However, the duchess is implacable some but not all of the time. When the autonomy for which she has struggled is threatened she responds with yet more adamant displays of her independence. Yet elsewhere her independence manifests itself not as a defensive closure or cloistering of the self but as a freedom from social constraints. Neither is she so solemnly earnest about her independence and autonomy as to be unable to perform otherwise for her own and Antonio's pleasure. The private realm which they create maintains momentum through its use of a flirtatiously performative mode whereby the duchess and Antonio can play out different roles to each other. 'To what use will you put me?' (III.ii.8), asks the usually dominant duchess, temporarily discarding her independence in order to become or rather to pretend to be a sexual object. The duchess, is in other words, neither the fixed self which has often been imagined by theory nor the sovereign ego which appears in this (via Ferdinand) and other plays. However, for those who survive her the duchess becomes a shrine worshipped by Bosola for her 'sacred innocence' (IV.ii.349) or, as Delio implies at the end of the play, by everyone for the 'integrity' of her life (V.v.119). This is the work of selective memory, for she is not asexual and she is not simply or solely the austere voice of integrity. To suggest, however, that the duchess's art of the self is more subtle and complex than the adulation allows is not to suggest that it is so esoteric (or sublime) that it cannot be learned. Her struggle for independence is available to Antonio and Bosola as an imitable model and they both become more independent as a result of their emulation of her.

The democratising tendency suggested by men following the lead of a woman who also instigates a cross-class marriage is perceived as such a serious threat to the status quo that Ferdinand's patriarchal imagination begins to work overtime. A woman with a voice of her own who encourages others to find their own voices cannot be tolerated because it thoroughly undermines the aristocratic/patriarchal monopoly on individualism which Ferdinand seeks to establish. That *he* alone should be a law unto himself in a court populated by the creatures of his creation is a narcissistic fantasy which joins Ferdinand to the largely male-dominated Renaissance tradition of spectacular individualists. 'Do not you ask the reason', Ferdinand orders Bosola, for his decision not to have the duchess remarry, 'but be satisfied, I say I would not' (I.ii.178). This arrogant and patronising refusal to make himself accountable is the basis of Ferdinand's total and arbitrary privatisation of power. Within such a capriciously personal regime, the court, the duchess, and the members of the body politic are not his responsibility but his playthings.

Ferdinand, like most egotists, is also paranoid. This paranoia, the paranoia that prompts him to employ spies, can be seen as being based upon the fear that his subjects may not be entirely his, and that he may indeed be creating the conditions for their independence/disillusionment through the example of his own tyrannical personal rule and the delegitimisation of authority which accompanies it.

Ferdinand's paranoid inability to recognise the duchess's authority and independence fuels a succession of misogynist diatribes. In the scene where he discovers the duchess's pregnancy, Ferdinand works himself up into such a frenzy that even his similarly minded brother the cardinal is alarmed at the 'wild . . . tempest' that Ferdinand is turning himself into (II.v.17). The duchess, according to Ferdinand (and sometimes the cardinal), is 'grown a notorious strumpet' (II.v.4); she has brought the family into disrepute (II.v.22–9); her 'blood' is 'infected' (II.v.26); and she exemplifies the 'slight, weak bulrush' that is 'woman' (II.v.26). Ignorant, at this stage, of the identity of her lover, Ferdinand also fantasises about the nature of the cross-class hybridisation which he thinks must have occurred as a result of the duchess looking beyond aristocracy for a lover:

Ferdinand. Methinks I see her laughing,
Excellent hyena! Talk to me somewhat, quickly,
Or my imagination will carry me
To see her in the shameful act of sin.
Cardinal. With whom?
Ferdinand. Happily, with some strong thigh'd bargeman;
Or one o'th' wood-yard, that can quoit the sledge
Or toss the bar, or else some lovely squire
That carries coals up to her privy lodging
Cardinal. You fly beyond your reason.

(II.v.38–47)

Ferdinand is probably the most transgressive and imaginatively fertile of all the play's characters. Figuring the duchess as a sexual libertine in a range of erotic situations which cut across the barriers of class and whose protagonists exude vitality, Ferdinand vicariously experiences several sexual possibilities here. Indeed, throughout the play Ferdinand gives himself permission to exceed boundaries of all kinds: of reason, morality and justice; of class and sexual identity (in his imagination, at least); and of the private world established by the duchess and Antonio. But although Ferdinand, like the duchess, supplies a model for transgression, secrecy and individualism, he makes it clear that these are *not* to be imitated by his subjects. When his 'creatures' look as though they might be developing lives of their own, Ferdinand establishes himself as the physician who will cleanse the body politic of its pollution, 'purge infected blood' (II.v.26) and restore those boundaries which have been transcended and/or redrawn by erring individuals. And so the private space colonised by the duchess is recolonised by Ferdinand. An example of such recolonisation occurs during a bedroom scene between the duchess and Antonio. Ferdinand first observes the scene in secret and then equally furtively takes the place of Antonio during Antonio's temporary absence (III.ii.62). At first the voyeur, Ferdinand's subsequent usurpation of the place of the lover is accompanied by his wielding of the 'vulgar' Freudian phallic symbol of '*a poniard*' (III.ii.68). This menacing sexual threat re-establishes his 'right' to penetrate any boundary which is ostensibly closed off from him and thereby undermines attempts by others to create their own independent spaces. The scene also highlights once again the precariousness of individualism as an unequivocal source of authentic meaning and value, for Ferdinand's giving of the law to himself is here and elsewhere morally and socially catastrophic. Thankfully, however, Ferdinand does not have the last word as far as practices of self are concerned.

Ferdinand's brutal policing of semi-autonomous spaces which are creative rather than destructive of value becomes ever more menacing and macabre. In IV.i he accompanies the gift he gives to his sister of a *'dead man's hand'* with the words 'I come to seal my peace with you: here's a hand' (l.43). He then presents a tableau showing *'the artificial figures of* ANTONIO *and his children; appearing as if they were dead'* (ll.56–7). Ferdinand's appearances in the play are frequently accompanied by such more or less legible icons and tableaux. Where there was life Ferdinand freezes it, frames it, purges it of its infected blood. Or else, in an appropriation of religious iconography similar to the appropriations discussed in Chapter 1, he makes a tableau of himself and his turbulent and tyrannical personal rule. Attempting to disseminate himself into the minds of his disaffected subjects, Ferdinand leaves behind him a succession of nightmarish mnemonics of his potency. That it is the duchess's voice that survives, and her practice of self that is remembered, are the sources of the play's optimism.

The reading I have offered of the play is no doubt in danger of idealising the individual and the individual's capacity for heroic struggle against the forces of oppression. Is individualism always and everywhere so positively heroic? The play itself answers this question in the negative, for it does not flinch from portraying the 'downside' of individualism in the shape of Ferdinand. The negative of the positive shows individualism to be a politically ambivalent, volatile phenomenon, one which can be appropriated to different class and gender agendas (see Chapter 3). My reading of the play suggests that concepts of self and self-naming are too important and potentially liberating to be discarded as part of an outmoded humanist paradigm. To jettison concepts of human autonomy and agency in the name of the more decidedly 'textual' notions of agency and liberation advocated by Judith Butler may therefore be a mistake.

The further criticism that a feminism insistent upon the cultural/ linguistic construction of reality might make is that my interpretation *only* succeeds in legitimating another kind of socially and historically specific status quo based upon the heterosexual and monogamous nuclear family. To read the duchess as an expressive, unconstrained self is from this point of view to ignore the specific social and sexual ideals which she represents. I would answer this valid criticism by claiming that the private bourgeois familial space cleared by the duchess is significantly freer in terms of the self-expression that it encourages than the public world presided over by Ferdinand. In other words, the devolution of power and authority to the individual may be seen as being accommodated by the formation of a private space set apart from the public. That the nuclear family happens to occupy this private space does not mean that it will always occupy it. The duchess's 'example' is itself much more expansive and available for resignification and recontextualisation than a narrowly ideological interpretation might suggest.

Another way of putting this is to suggest that the voice and immortal spirit which, in the last act, survive the duchess's body and specific location in the world have the effect of making of the duchess's self/soul a memorable and world-transcending principle. This simultaneous contextualisation and decontextualisation of the duchess accords with the play's generic status as tragedy. I argued from the structuralist perspective of Chapter 2 that such is tragedy's aspiration towards universality that tragic protagonists not only represent themselves but some larger principle(s). *The Duchess of Malfi* is one of a handful of Renaissance tragedies in which a female protagonist insists upon her own particularity at the same time as the play makes of her practice of self an example. The duchess thus accesses both the particularising and universalising axes of tragedy.

THE ROARING GIRL

The central, female protagonist in *The Duchess of Malfi* empowers herself and others by constituting the 'I' as an alternative foundation of meaning and value. Interpretable as independent 'self' rather than social construct, a free spirit who attempts to live life beyond the way it has been programmed for her by men, she is amenable to a foundationalist concept of the human as transgressive of existing categories and discourses. In the following section I want to shift the focus of the discussion somewhat by reconsidering the value for feminism of the *refusal* of appeals to such putatively extra-discursive, foundational concepts as 'spirit', 'self', 'life', and so forth. As we move from tragedy back to comedy, so the liberating possibilities of the parodic performance of gender identity come back into view and the language of foundations and authentic selfhood are made to seem leaden and constraining. The prologue to Thomas Dekker's and Thomas Middleton's comedy *The Roaring Girl* importunes the audience to 'think our scene/Cannot speak high, the subject being but mean'.[26] However, the modesty which comedy often assumes in relation to its supposedly more prestigious and elevated counterpart, tragedy, is in this instance false, for the prologue proceeds to mock the outdated grandeur of tragedy: 'tragic passion,/And such grave stuff, is this day out of fashion' (ll.11–12). Tragedy's large, universalising ambitions, ambitions which frequently manifest themselves in the tragic protagonist's quest for meaning and authenticity in a fallen world, are to be displaced by the altogether more irreverent mode of comedy. Comedy is, in other words, less metaphysical than tragedy. It is less intensely concerned with the grounds, origins and foundations of existence. Comedy instead mocks foundations. Thus where tragedy is more liable to demonise inauthentic performers and role-players such as Iago because they threaten values which are ostensibly 'basic' to human life, comedy is more liable to celebrate the performer's subversion of all things supposedly essential and basic.

Moll Cutpurse, the 'roaring girl' of the play's title, based upon the real-life figure known in seventeenth-century London as Moll or Mary Frith, is the flamboyantly performative figure who shows identity to be no more and no less than a manipulation of signs and appearances. As a woman who cross-dresses and *acts* like a man (often more effectively than the men in the play who are supposed to *really be* men), Moll makes a mockery of the idea that gender identity is innate. For if she can act like a man without being one, then being a man – or woman – must surely be an act? As a result of this conception of gender identity as an act that can be put on or put off, the question of who Moll *really* is cannot be answered because she subverts the foundationalist premises of such a question. Thus to a foundationalist like Sir Alexander Wengrave, Moll's ambivalent gender identity is, as we shall see, monstrous and beyond comprehension.

For most of the play Alexander Wengrave's son Sebastian pretends to be enamoured of Moll so that his real love for Mary

Fitzgerald (also known as Moll) may seem more acceptable to his father. The ruse, which Moll agrees to maintain, works straightaway. In the first act Sir Alexander's anxiety and confusion are evident in the anecdote he tells about a father, son and woman who turn out, of course, to be himself, Sebastian and Moll. The woman who is supposed to represent Moll is described thus:

> A scurvy woman,
> On whom the passionate old man swore he [his son] doted.
> 'A creature' saith he, 'nature hath brought forth
> To mock the sex of woman'. It is a thing
> One knows not how to name: her birth began
> Ere she was all made. 'Tis woman more than man,
> Man more than woman, and, – which to none can hap–
> The sun gives her two shadows to one shape;
> Nay, more, let this strange thing, walk, stand or sit,
> No blazing star draws more eyes after it.
>
> (I.ii.125–34)

This 'thing' has no proper identity. It is a hybrid thing born before it/she 'was all made'. It is a thing which is in excess of the single name of man or woman and beyond the natural, God-given order of gender differences. To Sir Alexander, who can only think of gender difference at the beginning of the play as a basic, natural, God-given difference, Moll is a freak show.

The confusion that Moll visits upon the likes of Sir Alexander is the greater because her cross-dressed identity is not temporary, as it is in numerous other comedies of the period, but permanent. In *As You Like It*, for example, the foreknowledge that Rosalind's disguise as a man will be temporary makes it possible to read her as 'really' a woman underneath. But such is Moll's always already crossed identity that – to Sir Alexander again – she 'strays so from her kind,/Nature repents she made her' (I.ii.213–14). Let me try to be as clear as possible about what is happening here by recalling the distinction referred to earlier between sex (meaning anatomy) and gender (meaning the culturally constructed 'masculine' or 'feminine' attributes which are assigned to male and female bodies). The persistence of Moll's culturally constructed masculine persona means that her culturally constructed femininity is difficult to recuperate. Yet her female anatomy – which should for a foundationalist like Sir Alexander give rise to feminine behaviour – belies her masculinity.

As I have already suggested, one of the conclusions about gender identity that Moll invites is that gender identity is a fiction, a matter of performance, a question of manipulating a set of culturally constructed *signs*. In this respect Moll resembles Tamburlaine or Iago, characters who also construe identity – though not specifically *gender* identity – in terms of performance. The further, yet more radical conclusion is that the body is itself a matter of performance and interpretation. However, both conclusions are resisted by most of the characters in the play in favour of another perspective entirely, which is that Moll's indeterminate gender must have a biological basis. The ribald curiosity that surfaces at regular intervals about Moll's anatomy implies that Moll's crossed attire arises from a crossed body. However, these changing-room jokes do not totally allay the suspicion aroused by Moll that life and particularly gender identity are a masquerade.

Moll thus makes it difficult to think foundationally in terms of one or another supposedly authentic grounding of identity. She causes, in Judith Butler's phrase, gender trouble. The pretence that Sebastian is in love with Moll and is set upon marrying her is sustained right until the end of the play. In the final act the marriage between the two conspirators looks imminent. Moll's appearance *'dressed as a man'* elicits the nervous question from Sir Alexander, 'Is this your wedding gown?' (V.ii.99). Goshawk tries to alleviate Alexander's worries by assuring him that 'No Priest will marry her, sir, for a woman/Whiles that shape's on, and it was never known,/Two men were married and conjoined in one!' (V.ii.104–6). Sebastian and Moll, of course, know what Sir Alexander as yet does not, that they have no intention of marrying. Or do they? Certainly Moll is adamant in her determination not to marry anyone, for as she tells Sebastian in an earlier scene:

> I have the head now of myself, and am man enough for a woman; marriage is but a chopping and changing, where a maiden loses one head, and has a worse i'th' place

> (II.ii.42–5)

But what of Sebastian? Does Sebastian know that his love for Moll has always been and is still a pretence? Can the pretence to be in love with someone turn into reality? What kind of foundational or foundationless thing is love? Is it not, as Chapter 3 suggested, an absent presence, an invisible essence which promises to be a foundation – *true* love – at the same time as it withholds certainty and knowledge? The conspiracy which develops between Sebastian and Moll creates a bond which is far more intimate than anything that takes place between Sebastian and his supposedly true love Mary. So is Moll the true object of his desire?

Love trouble breeds more gender trouble. For if Sebastian's love for Moll is more real than he cares to admit, then what is the nature of his desire? Heterosexual? Homosexual? Both? Or is it the enticing erotic *possibilities* which Moll as neither/nor or both/and suggests? From this last perspective Moll can be seen as representing a release from fixed gender identity and sexual orientation, a dismantling of all things supposedly true, authentic, foundational or essential in the name of, again, the comic *performance* of sexual identities, none of which is 'truer' than any other.

Let me return, by way of concluding this part of my reading of the play, to the questions of genre and gender. Judith Butler's insistence that gender and sexuality are or should be understood as performative *discourses*, rather than affirmations of personal identity, is conducive to the anti-foundational character of comedy. Comedy's mockery of foundations would seem to make of comedy a natural ally to anti-foundationalist feminist discourses seeking to challenge the supposed foundations of gender identity.

However, there are two problems with this kind of conclusion about the relationship of genre to gender. One is that Renaissance comedies are hardly ever pure (tragedy is, in other words, never entirely absent). The other is that it implicitly makes of foundationalist discourses a masculine phenomenon from which women either are excluded or should exclude themselves. As far as *The Roaring Girl* is concerned, the outcome of such a cemented alliance between feminism and comedy would be to treat the proto-feminist Moll *exclusively* as a comic character who will, as the prologue puts it, 'fill with laughter our vast theatre' (l.10) and refuse (again as the prologue does) to grant her any tragic status. But Moll, I want to argue, is not only a comic – in the sense of anti-foundationalist – figure. She is also concerned

– like the duchess of Malfi and Hamlet and Hieronimo – with foundational categories such as truth, self and authenticity. If the comedy, via Moll, mocks the foundationalist thinking of characters such as Sir Alexander, then it also seeks to *replace* it with a better form of foundationalism. This better foundationalism locates the self as a source of authority and a much more active and astute perceiver of the world than Sir Alexander's foundationalism allows it or requires it to be. The concluding part of this section will attempt to substantiate this claim.

Moll is the catalyst for the several changes of perception which occur – or which are at least given the opportunity to occur – during the course of the play. The most striking of these is Sir Alexander's transition from blinkered to enlightened or at least semi-enlightened perception. At the end of the play he makes two apologies, one to Mary and one to Moll, in which he confesses to the perceptual mistakes he has made. To Mary, his son's original love whom he first rejected as an unsuitable match, he admits that:

Forgive me, worthy gentlewoman, 'twas my blindness:
When I rejected thee, I saw thee not;
Sorrow and wilful rashness grew like films
Over the eyes of judgement, now so clear
I see the brightness of thy worth appear.

(V.ii.191–5)

And to Moll herself he offers the following slightly more equivocal apology:

In troth thou'rt a good wench; I'm sorry now
The opinion was so hard I conceived of thee:

(V.ii.227–8)

Sir Alexander has only been able to see Mary through capitalist perception as a 'beggar's heir' (I.i.87) and Moll, similarly, through the world's eyes, as titillating freak show, whore and monstrous aberration of nature. The world's foundationalist assumptions about the nature of gender identity are slavishly and unthinkingly accepted by Sir Alexander. Foundations have become axioms – automatic grounds for action and belief.

These grounds will have to be transcended if characters who are set in their ways are to have at least a chance of seeing others outside the social and linguistic frames upon which they have become lazily *dependent*. Moll's flamboyant and persistent *independence* offers characters the possibility of refreshed vision and contact, such that when they see Moll they will not automatically see whore or aberration but new possibility. There are infinitely more ways of knowing people, implies Moll in one of the several choric speeches the play gives to her, than the ready made categories to which they are consigned:

> . . . must you have
> A black ill name because ill things you know?
> Good troth, my lord, I am made Moll Cutpurse so.
> How many are whores, in small ruff and still looks?
> How many chaste, whose names fill slander's books?
> Were all men cuckolds, whom gallants in their scorns
> Call so, we should not walk for goring horns.
> Perhaps for my mad going, some reprove me;
> I please myself, and care not else who loves me.
>
> (V.i.341–9)

'Good my lord,' she continues, 'let not my name condemn me to you or to the world' (V.i.353–4). Getting an instant fix on people may be the aim of the schematising urban gallant looking to reduce people to the convenient sound-bites of gossip. It may equally be the tired habit of those who exist entirely within the bounds of unquestioned convention. However, the play's value-system, which has Moll at its centre, credits those who make a greater perceptual effort than to rely upon the hand-me-down mediations of hearsay and received opinion. This value-system is already in evidence in the prologue. Having defined various types of 'roaring girl' and contrasted them unfavourably with Moll, who 'flies/With wings more lofty' (ll. 25–6), the Prologue asks the audience to ignore this convenient characterisation of Moll and think more speculatively and imaginatively about her:[27]

> Thus her character lies –
> Yet what need characters, when to give a guess
> Is better than the person to express?
> But would you know who 'tis? Would you hear her name? –
> She is called Mad Moll; her life our acts proclaim!
>
> (ll.26–30)

The perceiver who depends too much upon 'external' sources – such as the Prologue, or later Sir Alexander – for his/her judgement of Moll's character will not be making a sufficiently attentive and imaginative effort of understanding and will thereby be doing violence to his/her object of perception.

Within the play itself, Moll takes revenge on those who do not bother to find out who she is and instead come to quick conclusions about her character. Laxton, for example, is attracted to Moll and, as Mary Beth Rose suggests, 'automatically assumes from her unconventional sexual behaviour that she is a whore'.[28] When she arrives at their rendezvous dressed as a man Laxton significantly fails to recognise her straightaway – 'I'll swear I knew thee not' (III.i.57), he tells Moll – because he is looking for Moll the whore. When Moll then says that he will be required to recognise, as in understand, who she is ('you shall know me now!' III.i.58), Laxton again automatically takes this to mean sexual knowledge ('No, not here: we shall be spied i'faith! – The coach is better', III.i.59–60). Moll then proceeds to initiate Laxton in the art of not making assumptions, of not framing people according to predetermined criteria:

why, good fisherman,
Am I thought meat for you, that never yet
Had angling rod cast towards me? – 'Cause you'll say
I'm given to sport, I'm often merry, jest;
Had mirth no kindred in the world but lust?
O shame take all her friends then! But howe'er
Thou and the baser world censure my life,
I'll send 'em word by thee, and write so much
Upon thy breast, 'cause thou shalt bear't in mind:
Tell them 'twere base to yield, where I have conquered.
I scorn to prostitute myself to a man,
I that can prostitute a man to me!

(III.i.101–12)

Like the Duchess of Malfi, Moll teaches those around her to practice an art of the self which would make them less dependent upon received wisdom, less protected by societal codes and conventions, and enable them to see what they keep seeing through or past.

The two plays which I have discussed suggest that feminism

need not choose between foundationalist and anti-foundationalist discourses, that the languages of tragedy and comedy, authentic selfhood and performative identity are both recuperable for feminism. If the paradigm of foundationalist humanism enables feminism to locate women as actual or potential agents whose independent subjectivity exceeds and resists cultural constructions of gender identity, then the paradigm of constructionism/performative identity supplies feminism with the equally useful means of contesting the complacency of absolute foundations. It seems to me that Moll herself straddles binary oppositions not only between the masculine and the feminine, but between the authentic and the performative, the grounded and the groundless, the search for self and the deferral of self which takes place in the name of experimentation.

7

Marxism
The Shoemakers' Holiday; Macbeth

The contribution that Marxism can make to an understanding of some of the key tensions which I see existing in modern literary theory between humanist, anti-humanist and neo-humanist tendencies is immense. I would also go so far as to say that Marxism itself cannot be fully understood without taking account of the debate which has taken place within Marxism between these tendencies. This chapter will therefore examine the humanisms and anti-humanisms which exist within different strains of Marxist thought, and the attempt, within still further varieties of Marxist theory, to reconcile them. It should come as no surprise by now to find that the place of their reconciliation is that traditionally humanist discourse, literature.[1]

HUMANIST MARXISMS

The related concepts of alienation and reification are vital to the humanist concerns of Marxism, and so it will be useful to begin by exploring these two key Marxist categories. In *Capital* Marx writes of the way capitalism renders human values and processes indecipherable because of the way the capitalist system reifies value by attaching value to *things* rather than people. I buy a jar of coffee from a supermarket, but such is the distance between the point of production and the point of consumption that I have no immediate knowledge of the human conditions under which the coffee was produced. *Things* thus appear to exist independently of the human beings who labour to create them. Such is the reification of human processes and human value that both become invisible. 'Value', writes Marx, 'does not have its description branded on its forehead; it rather transforms every product of labour into a social hieroglyphic.' He continues:

> Later on, men try to decipher the hieroglyphic, to get behind the secret of their own social product: for the characteristic which objects of utility have of being values is as much men's social product as is their language. The belated scientific discovery that the products of labour, in so far as they are values, are merely the material expressions of the human labour expended to produce them, marks an epoch in the history of mankind's development, but by no means banishes the semblance of objectivity possessed by the social characteristics of labour.[2]

We belatedly discover that commodities are the product of human labour and human arrangements even as the capitalist system still feels precisely like an impersonal system which is alien and impervious to human projects and realities. Capitalism still appears, to use Marx's term, 'objective' (meaning, in this instance, reified or thing-like), rather than subjective (meaning something to do with human values and choices – including choices about what we make of ourselves). Creations are thus alienated from their creators. Products are indecipherable as *human* products. Objects are set over against subjects.

Reification and alienation also work in more devastatingly obvious ways by turning people into appendages of machines, and forcing them to trade in their bodies, and some would say their souls as well, for money, money being that utterly indiscriminate medium of exchange which renders unlike things, including people-as-things, anonymously alike. The fact that my twelve pounds can buy me either several pints of lager, or a copy of Marx's *Capital*, or a garden rake, suggests that these objects, their usefulness, and the time and trouble it took to produce them, are somehow equivalent.

The concepts of *alienation* and *reification* are therefore central to Marx's writing because they attach to various moments within the capitalist cycle of production and consumption. At the point of production, alienation manifests itself in the expropriation by the capitalist of the product of the worker's time, and in the alienation of the human body and soul into wage labour. At the point of consumption, alienation can refer to the alienation of the consumer from knowledge of the means and conditions of production, the alienation of value from human processes to the commodity and the alienation of *use* values into *exchange* values. There are two aspects to this last example of alienation: first, the system of exchange of money for goods means that the intrinsic usefulness of things such as bread is overwhelmed by their status as commodities which are useful only insofar as they can be sold; and second, use values are alienated into exchange values through the homogenisation, within the exchange system, of the uniqueness and variety of labour expended to produce useful things. Of the anonymity of the exchange system, which is epitomised by the total facelessness of money, Marx writes:

> . . . commodities strip off every trace of their natural and original use-value, and of the particular kind of useful labour to which they owe their creation, in order to pupate into the homogeneous social materialization of undifferentiated human labour. From the mere look of a piece of money, we cannot tell what breed of commodity has been transformed into it. In their money-form all commodities look alike. Hence money may be dirt, although dirt is not money.[3]

The centrality of the concepts of alienation and reification in Marx and subsequent Marxist writing thus make of Marxism a humanism. The conclusion which seems naturally to suggest itself from the specific instances of alienation outlined above is that, under capitalism, the uniqueness of particular human beings is eroded, and the human 'spirit', in general, is stultified and unfulfilled. The more expansive statements which Marx himself makes in *Capital* and elsewhere on the subject of fulfilment underscore the humanist conclusion that capitalism alienates humanity while socialism promises to bring humanity to itself. *The Communist Manifesto*, for example, looks forward to the future enrichment, within communism, of human beings both in general and as individuals: 'In place of the old bourgeois society, with its classes and class antagonisms, we shall have an association in which the free development of each is the condition for the free development of all.'[4] They also speak of that false individualism of bourgeois society – 'In bourgeois society capital is independent and has individuality, while the living person is dependent and has no individuality' – which will be replaced

with the more authentic individuality released by communism.[5]
The appeal to the individual and to the human as rich, but
currently untapped, resources points to the importance of the
human subject to that strain of Marxism which seeks to create a
society in the image of the human.

Thus conceived, Marxism can be joined to – as well as differentiated from – some of the other movements and theories
examined in previous chapters. The notion, for example, that
human beings are thoroughly historical beings who will eventually find themselves through, rather than be repressed by, history,
connects Marx and Marxism to the expressive theories of history
described in Chapter 5. The implication that there is such a thing
as a human essence or spirit, currently alienated under capitalism,
echoes the essentialism of certain forms of feminism. The vital
experiential encounter which Marxism makes of the individual's
relationship to history and society mirrors poststructuralism's
conception of language as the place where the subject encoun-
ters itself – as process. Meanwhile, Marx's essentialist concept
of humanity is clearly at odds with poststructuralism's anti-
essentialist view that all signifiers – including 'humanity' – are
never fully present to themselves.

ANTI-HUMANIST MARXISMS

So much, then, for one side of the story about Marxism which
this chapter will tell and for one way of thinking about Marxism's
alignment and non-alignment with other theories. There are
numerous other aspects of Marx and Marxism, and so it is to
the *anti*-humanism of Marxism to which I now want briefly to
turn. This will be examined via Marxist concepts of ideology.

In *The German Ideology*, ideology is mainly used by Marx to
refer to the ruling ideas of a dominating class.[6] Because it is in
the interests of a ruling class to put the best possible face upon
the unequal and exploitative system over which it presides, by
renaming, say, war as chivalry, or colonialism as civilisation, or
greed as enterprise culture, these ruling ideas are illusory. They
are designed to make us complicit and even happy with a system
against which we might otherwise rebel. If ideology thus
encourages 'false consciousness' and distorted appearances of the
way things are, then Marxism is that quasi-structuralist conceptual

science which penetrates to the underlying laws of any given system of exploitation and exposes the true nature of social reality. In *The German Ideology* Marx himself pours scorn on the way the historiography of his own time fails to penetrate beneath appearances: 'Whilst in ordinary life every shopkeeper is very well able to distinguish between what somebody professes to be and what he really is, our historiography has not yet won this trivial insight.'[7]

However, under the influence of those styles of theorising – such as semiotics and poststructuralism – which question science's claims to truth by treating science as just another discourse, just one other way of mediating reality, Marxist theorists have tended to revise or withdraw the confident assertion of clear-cut oppositions between truth and illusion, Marxist science and bourgeois ideology. For doesn't poststructuralism teach us that science is itself ideological in its privileging of the seemingly transparent and self-identical concept which pretends simply to *reflect* rather than to *mediate* reality? And doesn't poststructuralism also show us that the discipline of tight conceptual thinking is disciplinarian in the way that it inhibits the natural playfulness and *jouissance* of language? Despite the problem as to whether 'objectivity' is possible or even desirable, and despite, also, the embrace by some Marxist thinkers of the revolutionary potential of poststructuralist ideas, most Marxists still have something critical to say about ideology. The criticism might not be presented as unassailable scientific 'truth', but it nevertheless retains a demystificatory ambition.

More often than not, the demystification of ideology is targeted at the subject and at categories associated with the subject. *This is because ideology works at the level of the subject and 'subjective' experience.* It tells us what it thinks we want to hear: that we are free, autonomous individuals, that society is the voluntary choice of those individuals, that we live in a humane world, and so on. Writing of the difference between (Marxist) science, on the one hand, and (bourgeois) art and ideology, on the other, Terry Eagleton produces the following, usefully neat formulae:

> Ideology signifies the imaginary ways in which men experience the real world, which is, of course, the kind of experience literature gives us too – what it feels like to live in particular conditions, rather than a conceptual analysis of those conditions.

However, art does more than just passively reflect that experience. It is held within ideology, but also manages to distance itself from it, to the point where it permits us to 'feel' and 'perceive' the ideology from which it springs. In doing this, art does not enable us to *know* the truth which ideology conceals, since for Althusser 'knowledge' in the strict sense means *scientific* knowledge – the kind of knowledge of, say, capitalism which Marx's *Capital* rather than Dickens's *Hard Times* allows us. The difference between science and art is not that they deal with different objects, but that they deal with the same objects in different ways. Science gives us conceptual knowledge of a situation: art gives us the experience of that situation, which is equivalent to ideology.[8]

This passage bears out the previous point that 'post-scientific' Marxism, represented here by Eagleton, is not so securely based upon an illusion/truth opposition that it treats ideology as merely illusory. And yet there is still an appeal being made here (via Althusser) to a hierarchy of knowledges which locates science as the truth that art *almost* attains. It is as if Eagleton is ceding ground to that humanist strain of Marxism which is on the side of the subject but is at the same time unwilling to give up entirely on Marxism's claim to objectivity. Eagleton has been a key player in Marxist debates in recent times, and what is often impressive about his work is a suppleness of thought which entails a continual shuttling back and forth between the rival claims of art and science, subject and object, experience and concept. In this respect Eagleton follows in a line of Marxist thinkers who, in straddling the divide within Marxism (and culture more generally) between humanism and science, attempt to heal the rift that capitalism is itself partly responsible for having created between subjective and objective modes of knowledge. The rest of this introductory section will explore the work of Marxists who, like Eagleton, look to literature as the place where the antagonism between subject and object is mended.

SUBJECTS AND OBJECTS IN MARXIST THOUGHT

First let us identify the range of meaning which these two terms, 'subject' and 'object', contain within Marxist discourse. *Subject* and *subjectivity* can be variously associated with such putatively human, but nonetheless alienable, attributes as feeling, need, desire, sensuousness, spontaneity, individuality, agency, consciousness, experience, and so forth. Meanwhile, the *object* may refer literally to a thing or commodity, but beyond this to any phenomenon which approximates the status of a thing because of its tangibility and/or solidity and/or inanimate nature. Thus a concept can be referred to as an object or as object-like because a concept pins down what might otherwise remain elusive to thought. The social and material conditions of our existence are likewise 'objective' in that they suggest an 'external', given state of affairs which we may not be able to change. Other human beings can be 'objects' either in the neutral and mundane sense of being distinct from the subject (we can speak of someone being an object of someone's affection), or in the less neutral sense of being treated like an object (as in sex object). Technical or specialist knowledge could likewise be thought of as 'objective' in two senses: positively, because we would on the whole think it a good thing that someone mending our car had some solid knowledge of how engines work; negatively, because specialist knowledge shuts the non-specialist out and can appear, in the case of specialised legal language, for example, alienating and impersonal.

It is clear from this brief outline, then, that just as there are, as previous chapters have shown, different kinds of *subject*, so there are different kinds of *object*. However, although subject and object have a range of meanings within Marxist and other types of discourse, they are not *so* mutable within Marxism as to become totally insubstantial, for there is a kind of essentialism or 'bottom line' within Marxism which insists that it is ultimately possible to tell the difference between a human being and a lump of lard. *Objectivism* or *reification* or *objectification* are the terms which Marxism uses to describe that state of affairs in which an inanimate and immutable world of things subsumes the animate, human world of subjects. Conversely, the term *subjectivism* is sometimes used to describe the narcissistic absorption of the object world by the subject.

The work of the mid-twentieth-century Hungarian Marxist thinker, Georg Lukács, is one example of Marxism's persistent attempt to reconcile the categories of subject and object. Lukács sternly defended realist literature against modernism because, for Lukács, realism, unlike modernism, achieves an ideal balance between subject and object, inner and outer, individual and social:

Achilles and Werther, Oedipus and Tom Jones, Antigone and Anna Karenina: their individual existence – their *Sein an sich*, in the Hegelian terminology; their 'ontological being', as a more fashionable terminology has it – cannot be distinguished from their social and historical environment. Their human significance, their specific individuality cannot be separated from the context in which they were created.[9]

The objectively given social world into which human beings are born speaks to what Lukács sees as our innate sociability, for 'man', he claims, following Aristotle, is *'zoon politikon*, a social animal'.[10] Society, as represented in realist literature, is not something imposed upon us from without, but comes instead from within. The external and the internal are thus reconciled. So, too, is the closely related other pair of potential opposites, the individual and the social, for society within realist literature accommodates rather than effaces our uniqueness and specificity. Modernism, by contrast, disregards the 'dialectic between the individual's subjectivity and objective reality' by privileging one side only of this equation through its indulgent use of, for example, stream-of-consciousness techniques which champion subjective impressionism and sensory data.[11]

Lukács thus turns to literature, and specifically realist literature, to find an image of a non-alienated human consciousness able to express itself through the object world. Rather than finding the external world antipathetic towards or negligent of the human subject, society as represented in the realist novel nurtures subjectivity. As Theodor Adorno, a critic of Lukács, succinctly puts it: Lukács opposes to the 'official objectivism' of the Stalinist era an 'aesthetic concept of objectivity which is altogether more in tune with the dignity of man'.[12] Subsequent Marxist thinkers, such as Adorno himself, will work further variations upon the subject/object dialectic and as a result arrive at very different reasons for valuing one kind of literature over another. So whereas Lukács is the champion of realism, Adorno himself is the champion of modernism. What both share in common, however, is the conviction that literature is redemptive of an endangered dialectic.

Adorno, who with Herbert Marcuse, Max Horkheimer and Walter Benjamin was a member of the Frankfurt School, established in the 1930s, appears on first impression to privilege the subject over the object, for he values modernist art for the very same reason – namely its subjectivism – for which Lukács castigates it. For Adorno, the increasingly ubiquitous and invasive 'organized culture' of commodity capitalism prohibits the possibility of authentic subjective experience. In *Minima Moralia*, Adorno gives as one example of the commodification of contemporary life the popularisation of Freudian 'depth-psychology':

> Now that depth-psychology, with the help of films, soap operas and Horney, has delved into the deepest recesses, people's last possibility of experiencing themselves has been cut off by organized culture. Ready-made enlightenment turns not only spontaneous reflection but also analytical insights – whose power equals the energy and suffering that it cost to gain them – into mass-produced articles and the painful secrets of the individual history, which the orthodox method is already inclined to reduce to formulae, into commonplace conventions. Dispelling rationalizations becomes itself rationalization. Instead of working to gain self-awareness, the initiates become adept at subsuming all instinctual conflicts under such concepts as inferiority complex, mother-fixation, extroversion and introversion, to which they are in reality inaccessible. Terror before the abyss of the self is removed by the consciousness of being concerned with nothing so very different from arthritis or sinus trouble. Thus conflicts lose their menace. They are accepted, but by no means cured, being merely fitted as an unavoidable component into the surface of standardized life.[13]

One of the few places where subjective experience does survive is in the modernist – but not only the modernist – artwork. The modernist text is sufficiently removed from social reality, by virtue of its difficulty, that it cannot easily be absorbed by and into 'standardized life'. Thus where the actual world of commodities reduces the human subject to the status of yet another object (as in the example of depth-psychology), art is the place where we may begin to know and experience a better, richer kind of subjectivity. What prevents art from being merely consolatory, however, is that we are made painfully aware of the rift between art and social reality. 'Art' writes Adorno, speaking now of art in general rather than modernist art in particular 'is the negative knowledge of the actual world', meaning that art makes us acutely aware of the shortcomings of commodification through its difference from it.[14] If in actual capitalist society we stand helpless before economic and social forces whose *object-like* existence seems far beyond our capacity to alter, then art is that *subjectively* oriented, human-friendly playground which does allow us to intervene in a more malleable world. In Adorno's terms, art allows the 'object' to be 'spontaneously absorbed into the subject':

> In the form of an [aesthetic] image the object is absorbed into the subject instead of following the bidding of the alienated world and persisting obdurately in a state of reification. The contradiction between the object reconciled in the subject, i.e. spontaneously absorbed into the subject, and the actual unreconciled object in the outside world, confers on the work of art a vantage-point from which it can criticize actuality.[15]

As for Lukács, so also for Adorno – though in a different way – the aesthetic is the place where beleaguered human values survive.

However, although Adorno, like Lukács, Herbert Marcuse and others, look towards art to recuperate a non-alienated form of human being, they do not *only* locate themselves in this way. Lukács, as we have seen, is suspicious of that abstract, solipsistic form of subjectivity which sets itself apart from all tangible objects, concrete social settings, and so forth, while Adorno, in *Aesthetic Theory*, affirms in typically dialectical fashion that the work of art is itself both a tangible, irreducible object set apart from the subject *and* the occasion for less tangible – because difficult to express – subjective responses:

> If it is essential to artworks that they be things, it is no less essential that they negate their own status as things, and thus art turns against art. The totally objectivated artwork would congeal into a mere thing, whereas if it altogether evaded objectivation it would regress to an impotently powerless subjective impulse and flounder in the empirical world.[16]

I take this to mean that if a work of art were such a subjective phenomenon that nothing definite or objective could be said about it, then art would be incapable of taking its place within – and changing – the empirical world of objects. At the same time, if the work of art were to become a static, immovable, fully known quantity then it would lose its fascination for, and openness to interpretation by, the subject. The balance between the subjective and the objective sought after here recalls the similar equilibrium advanced by Lukács. Art for Lukács and for the Adorno of *Aesthetic Theory* thus again works towards a reconciliation of principles which, in real capitalist or Stalinist life, are torn apart from one another.

Where Adorno (in some of his work) and Lukács (in most of it) attempt in different ways to preserve a dialogue between subject and object, there are plenty of other Marxist thinkers who seem less inclined towards such dialogues and reconciliations. For the anti-humanist Bertolt Brecht, for example, in 'A Short Organum for the Theatre' (published in 1949), the subject is bourgeois Enemy and ideological Illusion. If bourgeois art and the bourgeois theatre have traditionally been the places to which the individual escapes to restore his or her wounded human sensibility after a hard day's utilitarian, alienated labour, then Brecht's theatre further alienates the subject. Instead of salvaging the human in the face of dehumanisation, Brecht's theatre estranges its audiences from 'what they think of as "the" human experience' in order to make them aware of change, history-as-difference, and the objective social conditions of their existence:[17]

> This technique [i.e. of alienating the familiar] allows the theatre to make use in its representations of the new social-scientific method known as dialectical materialism. In order to unearth society's laws of motion this method treats social situations as processes, and traces out their inconsistencies. It regards nothing as existing except in so far as it changes, in other words is in disharmony with itself. This also goes for those human feelings, opinions and attitudes through which at any time the form of men's life together finds its expression.[18]

Instead of humanism and subjective experience, the Brechtian theatre offers its audiences science and objective knowledge. Brecht's 'theatre of the scientific age' will also be an *anti-illusionist* theatre.[19] Such a theatre will undermine the infantile longing, satisfied by the pre-Brechtian, bourgeois theatre, for illusionist identification and indivisibility of experience:

> the spectator wants to be put in possession of quite definite sensations, just as a child does when it climbs on to one of the horses on a roundabout: the sensation of pride that it can ride, and has a horse; the pleasure of being carried, and whirled past other children; the adventurous daydreams in which it pursues others or is pursued, etc. In leading the child to experience all this the degree to which its wooden seat resembles a horse counts little, nor does it matter that the ride is confined to a small circle. The one important point for the spectators in these houses is that they should be able to swap a contradictory world for a consistent one, one that that they scarcely know for one of which they can dream . . . That is the sort of theatre which we face in our operations, and so far it has been fully able to transmute out optimistic friends, whom we have called the children of the scientific era, into a cowed, credulous, hypnotized mass.[20]

This might very easily stand as a comment upon the behaviour of Cokes at the fair in *Bartholmew Fair* or else upon the attitude of the citizens towards the play they are watching in *The Knight of the Burning Pestle*. Such total emotional identification is based upon the supposed universality of human feelings and constitutes, for Brecht, a 'bad' kind of humanism which in its emphasis upon the *sameness* of human emotion eradicates the *differences* between social classes, character and actor, past and present and the reality of stage objects and their subjective transformation in the audience's imagination.

However, if Brecht's emphasis upon social science, anti-illusionism and critical distance places him on the side of objects and objectivity (Brechtian theatre being the place where one can acquire objective knowledge of social reality), then this objectivity is not totally deprived of subjective content. Contrasting old types of alienation effects or 'A-effects' with their new Brechtian counterparts, Brecht writes:

> The old A-effects quite remove the object represented from the spectator's grasp, turning it into something that cannot be

altered . . . The new alienations are only designed to free socially-conditioned phenomena from that stamp of familiarity which protects them against our grasp today.[21]

To see a supposedly objective, predetermined state of affairs as changeable is to release human creativity. Brecht is not simply eradicating the human subject but replacing a static with a more dynamic version of it:

> Our own period, which is transforming nature in so many and different ways, takes pleasure in understanding things so that we can interfere. There is a great deal to man, we say; so a great deal can be made out of him. He does not have to stay the way he is now, nor does he have to be seen only as he is now, but also as he might become.[22]

As with nature so, too, with human nature. Both are pliable. Art is still, after all, humanist, in that it shows us the many different selves that lie buried or repressed within us, but now the human is an altogether more open-ended signifier. Thus Brecht's theatre is at once anti-humanist and humanist, 'scientific' and expressive, suspicious of the subjectivist categories of experience and emotion yet calling upon his audiences to become subjects rather than objects of history.

Finally, we can return to Terry Eagleton and Eagleton's own distinctive variation on the subject/object dialectic which is, in *The Ideology of the Aesthetic*, simultaneously to engage with and treat as illusory (as ideological) the kind of subjectivity which art, from the eighteenth century onwards, has been taken to embody. 'What emerges . . . in the late eighteenth century', writes Eagleton, 'is the curious idea of the work of art as a kind of *subject*.'[23] This conception of the aesthetic coincides with the development of bourgeois society which, according to Eagleton, is a society of *consent* rather than *coercion*. Within such a society, claims Eagleton, 'the aesthetic moves into the foreground', since the mysterious individuality or genius of the work of art provides bourgeois society with a model for the way it should ideally express the individuality of its members:

> Like the work of art as defined by the discourse of aesthetics, the bourgeois subject is autonomous and self-determining,

acknowledges no merely extrinsic law but instead, in some mysterious fashion, gives the law to itself. In doing so, the law becomes the form which shapes into harmonious unity the turbulent content of the subject's appetites and inclinations. The compulsion of the autocratic power is replaced by the more gratifying compulsion of the subject's self-identity.[24]

It is typical of Eagleton to write highly persuasively of ideas from which we are simultaneously asked to keep a critical distance. If Eagleton's characterisation of the subject looks temptingly usable (as a personal and political idea) and also seems genuinely to reflect the way subjectivity 'really' is, then he keeps reminding us that the subject is nevertheless an ideological construction.

MARXISM IN SUMMARY

- The humanist and anti-humanist tendencies of Marxism often go their separate ways. Where the emphasis on reification and alienation makes of Marxism a humanism, the concept of ideology fuels a more 'objective', scientific, anti-humanist Marxism. Some Marxist thinkers, however, attempt to reconcile, or at least maintain a dialogue between, these humanist and anti-humanist traditions. Literature is often looked to as the place where such a dialogue takes place.
- 'Subject' and 'object' within Marxist thought and elsewhere have a range of meanings, but Marxism retains a notion of each term's own substantial content and therefore difference from its opposite. This difference makes it possible to identify the extent of the subject's 'good' or 'bad' objectification.
- The reconciliation which some Marxist thinkers look to effect between subject and object takes different forms. For Lukács, realist literature achieves an ideal balance between subject and object. For Adorno, the subjectivism of modernist literature in particular and art in general redeems the subject from its objectification by the culture industry, at the same time as the concept of objectivity as it applies to art allows for a Lukácsian reconciliation of subject and object. Brecht seems more suspicious of the subject, but nevertheless his concept of objectivity is not totally deprived of subjective content. Eagleton writes persuasively of the subject, to the extent of encouraging us to

identify with his characterisation of it, but simultaneously reminds us that it is an ideological construct.

THE SHOEMAKERS' HOLIDAY

This and the section which follows will present two very different kinds of Marxist criticism. The first will be broadly anti-humanist and treat humanism, with suspicion, as an ideological illusion which masks from people their 'real', objective conditions of existence. The psychologism and subjectivity associated with humanist discourse will therefore be viewed as the enemies of 'objective', conceptual understanding. The second, contrasting reading will be broadly humanist, and make use of the Marxist categories of reification and alienation to explore the way Shakespeare's Macbeth lives an alienated existence. The second reading will also show how the play attempts to reconcile, in quasi-Marxist fashion, inner and outer, subjective and objective, worlds.

Thomas Dekker's *The Shoemakers' Holiday* can be seen as appealing to seemingly timeless human values as a way of masking the reality that cash values are, in fact, eradicating each and every supposedly 'essential' human thing. Unable to cope with the emerging harsh realities of capitalism and commerce, the play mobilises a humanist rhetoric by way of reassuring its audience that human(e) values will always survive. As David Scott Kastan suggests, 'Dekker confronts the increasingly complex social and economic organization of pre-industrialized England but converts it into a comforting fiction of reciprocity and respect.'[25]

There are, to be sure, challenges to the play's anthropomorphic design. The key to Simon Eyre's financial success, for example, is the deal he strikes with the Dutch merchant ship owner who is obliged to sell off his cargo cheaply to Eyre because, as Eyre's foreman Hodge reports, the merchant 'dares not show his head' in London.[26] We are not given the reason for the merchant's reluctance to trade openly, but, as the recent editor of the play D. J. Palmer suggests, it may have been the result of the 'Elizabethan trade policy that discriminated against foreigners' (p. 34n.). This is Hodge's account of the deal:

The truth is, Firk, that the merchant owner of the ship dares not show his head, and therefore this skipper that deals for him, for the love he bears to Hans, offers my master Eyre a bargain in the commodities. He shall have a reasonable day of payment; he may sell the wares by that time, and be an huge gainer himself.

(II.iii.16–21)

Where the commercial transaction locates the relationship between Eyre and the Dutch captain who acts on behalf of the merchant as a purely and impersonally contractual relationship, the language of affective bonds – operative in the 'love [the skipper] bears to Hans' – rehumanises it. As Kastan puts it, 'the availability of the Dutch cargo is determined by an emotional rather than economic bond'.[27] 'Bonds' thus displace 'contracts', and love makes its present felt in areas where its existence seems threatened.[28] The world looks as though it might be exceeding the terms of a humanist rhetoric, but the play's romantic discourse intervenes to redeem history and place it once again under its confidently humanist auspices.

A similar defeat of the language of contracts by the language of affective bonds takes place within the workplace. To speak of Eyre as an employer and the shoemakers who work for him as employees is rendered largely inappropriate by the play's characterisation of Eyre as a genial father figure who professes to 'love [his] men as [his] life' (I.iv.69–70). Eyre may have an eye on profit margins (II.iii.71–7) and output ('O haste to work, my fine foreman, haste to work', I.iv.23), but capitalist man is assimilated into the prior role of caring father. Eyre, it seems, is running a commercial enterprise as though it were a family. It is, in this sense, a 'family business'. As for his employees, Hodge, Firk, Ralph and the disguised Lacy, these act less like impersonally contracted employees than as Eyre's occasionally unruly and petulant children. When Eyre's wife, Margery, for example, makes a fairly innocuous comment about Firk's holiday-mood singing – 'You sing, Sir Sauce, but I beshrew my heart;/I fear for this your singing we shall smart' (II.iii.29–30) – Firk, and Hodge on Firk's behalf, take offence and threaten to down tools and leave. When Margery then exacerbates the situation by implying that one anonymous workforce may easily be replaced by another – 'I pray, let them go; there be mo maids than Mawkin, more men

than Hodge, and more fools than Firk' (II.iii.55–6) – Eyre is obliged
to intervene with words of reassurance:

> Stay, my fine knaves, you arms of my trade, you pillars of my
> profession. What, shall a tittle-tattle's words make you forsake
> Simon Eyre? Avaunt, kitchen-stuff! Rip, you brown-bread
> tannikin! Out of my sight, move me not! Have not I ta'en you
> from selling tripes in Eastcheap, and set you in my shop, and
> made you hail-fellow with Simon Eyre the shoemaker? And
> now do you deal thus with my journeymen? Look, you powder-
> beef-quean, on the face of Hodge: here's a face for a lord!
>
> (II.iii.61–9)

The scene is like an inverted Oedipal triangle with the children
(Hodge and Firk) resenting the interference of a third party/
father-figure (Margery) in the dyadic union which exists between
children and mother-figure (Eyre). This gesture towards a psychoanalytic reading is only intended to show how the workplace is
represented in the play on the model of a family. Work is not
continuous in Eyre's shop because there is always the possibility of tensions or squabbles erupting between 'workers' who are
not required to leave their emotions at home. For most of Eyre's
employees, of course, work *is* home, though a home which Margery
would redefine as a workplace, a place of contractual exchange.

The language of bonds thus once again defeats the language
of contracts, even as the latter makes its impact felt through
Margery's hard-headed approach to her husband's employees.
In other words, just as the language of affective bonds reaches
outwards, to embrace and redefine the language of contracts and
commercial transactions, so the opposite also occurs: the language
of commerce reaches 'inwards', in an attempt to infiltrate and
commodify the affairs of the heart. Thinking that love can be
bought and quantified, the city gentleman Hammon, for example,
offers money to shoemaker Rafe in exchange for Rafe's wife Jane:
'here in fair gold/Is twenty pound, I'll give it for thy Jane./If
this content thee not, thou shalt have more' (V.ii.78–80). Love,
however, in the shape of Rafe, remains solidly resistant to this
attempt to hijack it on behalf of the dehumanising discourse of
monetary exchange: 'dost thou think a shoemaker is so base, to
be a bawd to his own wife for commodity? Take thy gold, choke
with it!' (V.ii.84–6).

Affective ties thus not only stand firm in the play in the face of their threatened dissolution by cash values, they also continue to exert an influence upon a public sphere which would at the very least exile them from its orbit. Values which *we* conventionally associate with the private sphere still impact upon a public sphere which has not yet totally cast aside its conceptions of society as a human organism, a body politic, and/or an extended family. If Henry V is the king to whom Dekker's play refers, then it is decidedly not the Hal who in Shakespeare's plays promises to banish the body (in the shape of Falstaff) from the body politic, who nurtures *a*ffective relationships as long as they serve the purpose of achieving *e*ffective government, and who, as a result, in *Henry V* feels himself to be alienated from the ordinary emotions of 'private men' (*Henry V*. IV.i.230). Dekker's Henry is a Henry who instead places affective humanism at the centre of public life, castigating those who would 'offend Love's laws' (V.v.77) either by defending class differences against the power of love to transgress them, or by attempting to commodify emotions. And nowhere in the play is there any suggestion – as there is in *I Henry IV* that Hal might be appealing to affective humanism merely as a political strategy.

Simon Eyre can also be brought into juxtaposition with Hal, for where Hal alienates moral attributes so as to make them available as strategies, Eyre's catchphrase 'Prince am I none, yet am I princely born' (III.ii.145–6) locates nobility as an innate and inalienable attribute of character. This vision of human being as intrinsically noble forms the basis of the play's celebration of the triumph of a benevolent and loving human nature over the forces of dehumanisation and/or corruption.

MACBETH

Examination of the ideology of a text places us at a critical distance from it. This section will get on more intimate terms with the text. It will accordingly treat 'humanist' categories less as illusory and ideological than 'real'. It will also explore the way in which *Macbeth* attempts to reconcile subject and object, inner and outer worlds.

The world of *Macbeth* is traumatic. Killer soldiers are rewarded for their acts of bloody execution in the war-zone.[29] Because the war-zone will not stay within its prescribed boundaries, a child is stabbed and murdered on stage in the presence of the child's mother, and men – one of whom happens to be the king – are butchered in their sleep. I am made complicit with the murder of the king. I want it to happen. Thus another boundary – the moral boundary separating me from a transgression – is eroded. The woman partly responsible for the murders is subsequently traumatised. The man partly responsible for the murders is himself murdered.

Recent theoretically informed criticism – *some* of it at any rate, and some of it Marxist – has tended to avoid the play's emotional impact in favour of a more distanced location of the (variously understood) ideology of the play. Peter Stallybrass, for instance, thinks that the concepts of 'witchcraft, sovereignty, the family . . . map out the ideological terrain of *Macbeth*';[30] Malcolm Evans explores the 'instances of disruption to the harmonious, univocal discourse of Tudor and Stuart absolutism' which 'proliferate in the early scenes';[31] Alan Sinfield suggests that modern theoretical approaches to *Macbeth* in particular and to literature in general question the assumption of older criticism that 'the characters are actual people' by treating them instead as 'textual arrangements which involve ideas about people'.[32]

Modern theoretical criticism, as represented here at least, thus tells us not to get too *involved*. It tells us to keep our distance, to be dispassionate, lest we make the humanist error of mistaking ideology (that which societies construct and naturalise as the 'truth' about human being) for the thing – human being – itself. Characteristically the insistence is upon the social construction of reality, the importance of realising that the social construction of reality is not 'reality' itself (which does not exist in any ontological sense because it is only ever socially constructed) and the priority of 'textual arrangements' over people ('textual arrangements' – social constructions – come *first* and 'people' *second* because people are the effect of social constructions). I do not want to deny the importance and necessity of locating texts in their ideological contexts. However, if we are to countenance the notion that literature is a non-prescriptive humanist discourse, then the hierarchical relationship between 'textual arrangements' and 'people' needs to be reversed, or equalised or, ideally, considered more *dialectically*. For what if 'textual arrangements' were the product of 'people' who then somehow lost sight of the fact that these textual arrangements were originally their own creations? One of the outcomes of this loss of symbiotic relationship between creator and creation, producer and produced, would be to call the alienated creation something like a 'textual arrangement'. We create, but we forget why we created, and thus our creations seem alien and inhuman. Let me briefly recall Marx – the humanist Marx, that is – to consolidate this point. 'Value', writes Marx, 'does not have its description branded on its forehead; it rather transforms every product of labour into a social hieroglyphic.' Marx has in mind here the principle of reification. As already explained, reification makes it difficult to read off human values and processes from the things which human beings produce.

We can adapt Marx's insights to *Macbeth*, for *Macbeth* can be seen as an attempt to recover the putatively inner, human, experiential dimension of otherwise external and alien phenomena. The dagger, for instance, is the *thing* whose origin in human processes the play seeks to disclose even as Macbeth contributes towards its reification:

> Is this a dagger, which I see before me,
> The handle toward my hand? Come, let me clutch thee: –
> I have thee not, and yet I see thee still.
> Art thou not, fatal vision, sensible
> To feeling, as to sight? or art thou but
> A dagger of the mind, a false creation,
> Proceeding from the heat-oppressed brain?
> I see thee yet, in form as palpable
> As this which now I draw.
> Thou marshall'st me the way I was going;
>
> (II.i.33–42)

It is all too tempting for Macbeth to alienate the murder which he is about to commit from himself and treat the dagger as though it represented a purely external compulsion. 'Thou marshall'st me', Macbeth says to the dagger, as though it has nothing to do with him only to admit in the next breath that it is signposting 'the way that I was going'.

Murder cannot be disowned by Macbeth because the play eroticises it. Murder of the king and father figure is taboo and what is taboo becomes the site in the play of awe, fear and fascination. Taboos forbid, but in forbidding they excite interest in what lies beyond the limits which they impose. This is what I take Georges Bataille to mean when he suggests that '*transgression does not deny the taboo but transcends it and completes it*'.[33] Taboo and transgression, in other words, *imply* as much as they *oppose* one another, for the taboo creates the desire to transgress it. In Bataille's words again: the 'taboo would forbid the transgression but the fascination compels it'.[34] What, then, could excite more fear and erotic fascination than the prospect of murdering the king?

The eroticism of taboos and transgressions is more fully realised by Lady Macbeth than it is by Macbeth. This is because Macbeth, prone as he is to the externalisation of internal phenomena, cannot immediately see the erotic implications of the taboo. The name that he initially gives to his murderous impulse is ambition – 'vaulting ambition' (I.vii.27). This seems a fairly reserved, alienated way of thinking about the taboo he is contemplating breaking. Does the idea of ambition really speak to what is going on 'inside' Macbeth? The appeal to ambition functions like the dagger, as a way of avoiding personal confrontation with murder's inner erotic implications.

Macbeth is schooled in the art of the erotic by the better-versed Lady Macbeth. It is she who sees more clearly the erotic potential of the taboo. It is she who more daringly relates murder to the senses. Perhaps this is because, as a female outsider to a male-dominated society, she is less given to the externalisations and displacements of that masculine culture. Compared with Lady Macbeth's imaginative foreplay, Macbeth's seems dull and inhibited. In response to Macbeth's worry that their enterprise might fail, Lady Macbeth imagines for him and for herself the sexual scene of the murder:

> We fail?
> But screw your courage to the sticking place,
> And we'll not fail. When Duncan is asleep
> (Whereto the rather shall his day's hard journey
> Soundly invite him), his two chamberlains
> Will I with wine and wassail so convince,
> That memory, the warder of the brain,
> Shall be a fume, and the receipt of reason
> A limbeck only: when in swinish sleep
> Their drenched natures lie, as in a death,

What cannot you and I perform upon
Th'unguarded Duncan?

(I.vii.60–71)

The place of murder will be exotic, sensual, decadent. It will be
a scene of carnivalesque excess to which drunken chamberlains
with fumed memories will be made to contribute. In such a
situation of unfastened boundaries what are the limits of the possible? 'What are the limits of the self'? What cannot 'you and
I' perform? That 'you and I' becomes an irresistible prospect of
potent indivisibility.

   Macbeth may thus be understood as an attempt to overcome
the alienation of a culture which has forgotten or which only
half remembers its own subjective erotic investment in the creation of taboos. 'There's no art', says Duncan of the deceitful
Macdonwald, 'To find the mind's construction in the face' (I.iv.12–
13). Duncan's words testify to the rift which exists in the play
between surfaces and depths, outer and inner worlds. Men cannot
be trusted or known in *Macbeth* because most of them do not
know or *recognise* themselves. Shakespeare's tragic protagonists
are nevertheless sufficiently agitated and disquieted to want to
at least try to decipher the 'social hieroglyphic'. Insofar as we
identify with them, their disquiet becomes ours and we are
encouraged to discover the human creators whose physiognomy
cannot be immediately recognised in their alienated creations.
Duncan is therefore wrong. There is a (Shakespearean) art which
at least tries to find 'the mind's construction in the face' and
restore inner to outer, private to public, creator to created.

   I do not want to overstate the idea that taboo and transgression are implied by one another and that failure to recognise
this truth constitutes a failure to acknowledge the inner erotic
component of such seemingly outer phenomena as social taboos.
Alongside the notion that taboos incite transgression, another
perspective should be added. This is that taboos and boundaries
are as necessary to the individual in their moral and prohibitive
aspect as they are integral to his/her erotic life. This is emphatically not to suggest that morality is always and everywhere the
spontaneous expression of individuals who freely choose to, say,
honour their country or the institution of marriage as though
such socially constructed moral agendas were natural. Because
morality, like virtually everything else in Shakespeare's tragedies,

is on trial, such obvious social constructions of morality are severely tested. The illusion of morality – that which passes for morality in the form of the ostensibly just war represented in the first act of the play, for example – does not survive tragedy's search for more authentic values.

Tragedy's drive towards authenticity involves placing people in such extreme situations that they – and we – are forced to confront the question of what ultimately matters. The notion of *subjective experience* is once again all-important here, for only by seriously contemplating the breaking of a taboo is the taboo experienced as an *internal* rather than simply *external* necessity. Here is Georges Bataille again:

> We must know, we can know that prohibitions are not imposed from without. This is clear to us in the anguish we feel when we are violating the taboo, especially at that moment when our feelings hang in the balance, when the taboo still holds good and yet we are yielding to the impulsion it forbids. If we observe the taboo, if we submit to it, we are no longer conscious of it. But in the act of violating it we feel the anguish of mind without which the taboo could not exist: that is the experience of sin . . . The inner experience of eroticism demands from the subject a sensitiveness to the anguish at the heart of the taboo no less great than the desire which leads him to infringe it.[35]

This seems perfectly to capture *Macbeth*'s intense evocation of pain and pleasure, anguish and fascination. That these emotions have to be felt on the pulse by the tragic protagonist and through him/her by the audience constitutes a privileging of the human witness, a privileging of the idea of subjective testimony. It is through this insistence upon human testimony that tragedy in particular and literature in general attempt to 'get behind the secret' of the alienated social products of men and women.

It would not do to be dogmatic about such matters. I cannot know *for certain* the human impulses which underlie the social hieroglyphic. Perhaps there *is* only the hieroglyphic. Perhaps there is nothing beneath it. Perhaps the human is, after all, too indeterminate and ambiguous a thing to be located? At the close of *King Lear* Edgar says to the surviving characters of the tragedy:

The weight of this sad time we must obey;
Speak what we feel, not what we ought to say.

(V.iii.322)

These words from the closing speech of *King Lear* resonate across the Shakespearean canon. Tongues and hearts are so often alienated from one another that the task of putting them back together seems as urgent as it seems monumental. For to quote another Shakespearean *locus classicus*, if the self has that 'within which passes show' (*Hamlet* I.ii.85), then how can that recessed interiority ever be brought to language? How can the heart and tongue, the private and the public come together? The difficulty of answering these questions does not stop Shakespeare from asking them.

Conclusion

Giovanni in *'Tis Pity She's a Whore* cannot abide the gap separating himself from his sister; he cannot tolerate the externality of the world. In this he contrasts with the Friar, who insists upon a remote and alien God. Like Giovanni, Cokes in *Bartholmew Fair* displays an infantile desire for oneness and indivisibility and so disqualifies himself time and again from the adult separateness which the play endorses, though not without qualification. Bottom and company in *A Midsummer Night's Dream* live divided lives – as actors and the characters whom the actors play – but attempt at the same time to overcome this division. Similarly, Tamburlaine tries to sink himself into his desired role and avoid recognition of any alienating distance between self and role, actor and character. The citizens in *The Knight of the Burning Pestle* over-identify with 'their' Rafe and try to make of the theatre a surrogate home and family. The point of contrast here is with the implied sophistication of the actual Blackfriars audience who are identified with irony, distance and anti-illusionism. In *Othello* the outsider tries to make of Venice a home and in doing so helps to overcome the Venetians' own various senses of displacement. The glaring exception here is Iago, who turns exile into an art.

These motifs have their parallels in the theories discussed in this book. For example, in rendering concepts simultaneously knowable and unknowable, present and absent, familiar and strange, poststructuralism resembles those numerous figures in Renaissance drama who experience a kind of homelessness, or more positively a sense of release – but who may also long for somewhere to be. As for psychoanalysis, it *to some extent* mirrors the likes of Giovanni and Cokes in the way that it uses categories associated with the private realm (desire, affect, trauma, pleasure, sexuality, love) to challenge the potentially external, public phenomena of history, language and society. *Like* Giovanni and Cokes, psychoanalysis, in other words, denies the notion that 'outside' phenomena have nothing to do with the subject. *Unlike* Cokes and Giovanni, however, psychoanalysis – or some of it at any rate – implies that we need to learn to live with loss.

216

Structuralism, poststructuralism and psychoanalysis, informed as they are by semiotics, *all* insist upon the externality of language – in other words, upon the idea that language precedes us – but they each supply antidotes to this sense of language's externality: structuralism by affirming that we are *naturally* linguistic beings; poststructuralism by the implication that language's lack of definitive signifieds opens us up to new meaning and possibility; and psychoanalysis, as already suggested, by its 'heating up' of language, its understanding of language as the site of human desire and trauma.

So what is the story? What is it that both modern theory and Renaissance drama – at least in these *selected* aspects – share in common? What is the long history which they both possibly share? It seems to me that the significant antinomy here is between a sense of the remote or the removed, on the one hand, and, on the other, a desire – which is never unequivocal in the case of theory – to bring the remote or the strange back into the orbit of the known. Whether the removed or estranged phenomenon in question is a concept (such as love), or a sister (like Annabella), or a culture (as Venice is to Othello), or language (seen as that which speaks us from elsewhere), or theatrical conventions in a fast-flowing commercial environment, the alien object is partially salvaged so that its externality does not become *total*. Love placed beyond all comprehension. A sister completely unmoved by a brother. A Venetian culture which there was no possibility of adopting. A language removed from all desire and subjectivity. Theatrical conventions which were completely unrecognisable to each other. These extreme examples of alienated objects would be utterly beyond retrieval, utterly beyond the ken and affective experience of the subject. It is the productive tension between the present and the absent, the near and the far, the familiar and the strange, the continuous and the discontinuous which these highlighted aspects of the drama and of theory maintain.

I argued in the Introduction that the *anti*-humanism of modern literary theory performs a kind of estrangement effect. We are asked to become strangers to our own sign-systems and look at them as an outsider might. As far as literature is concerned, this estrangement effect involves refusing the identifications with one or another form of 'life' that a literary text might offer us in order to focus upon the historical, linguistic and unconscious determinations of life. The emphasis of modern literary theory upon the textual, social and/or ideological construction of human experience makes detached critics of us.

The other side of theory which this book has been at pains to unearth is the kind of humanism or neo-humanism which says that language and history *matter* in the same way that literary texts were once thought to matter, or, in Helen Gardner's phrase, to 'reveal us to ourselves'.[1] In the case of history, this means that we encounter a distant historical phenomenon less as an 'object' of contemplation than as another 'self'. It is 'us' that we are experiencing, or another or lost part of ourselves. This is what I take Fredric Jameson to mean when he refers to the 'existential view' of history as a 'galvanic and electrifying event' which 'speaks to us about our own virtual and unrealized possibilities'.[2] Likewise, language, within neo-humanist stands of contemporary criticism, is an affectively charged experience, and at several removes from the bloodless register of the more technocratic and scientific wings of modern literary theory.

Notes

Introduction

1. Hélène Cixous *et al.*, 'Conversations with Hélène Cixous and members of the Centre d'Etudes Féminines', in Susan Sellers (ed.), *Writing Differences: Readings from the Seminar of Hélène Cixous* (New York: St. Martin's Press, 1988), p. 147.
2. For a discussion of the humanist assumptions of traditional literary criticism, see Catherine Belsey, *Critical Practice* (London: Methuen, 1980), pp. 7–14. For discussion of the history of the term 'humanism', see Tony Davies, *Humanism* (London: Routledge, 1997). For a useful account of the anti-humanism of recent French thought and the kinds of humanism which preceded it, see Kate Soper, *Humanism and Anti-Humanism* (London: Hutchinson, 1986).
3. William Shakespeare, *Twelfth Night*, The Arden Shakespeare, ed. J. M. Lothian and T. W. Craik (London: Methuen, 1975), II.v.106–27. Further references to this edition are given within the text.
4. F. R. Leavis, *The Common Pursuit* (London: Chatto and Windus, 1952), p. 292.
5. Helen Gardner, 'The Argument about "The Ecstasy"', in Julian Lovelock (ed.), *Donne: Songs and Sonets* (Basingstoke: Macmillan, 1973), p. 242.
6. A. E. Dyson, 'General Editor's Preface', in Lovelock (ed.), *Donne*, p. 9.
7. Leavis, *Common Pursuit*, p. 287.
8. For further discussion of the origins and implications for literary study of the term 'canon', see John Guillory, 'Canon', in Frank Lentricchia and Thomas McLaughlin (eds), *Critical Terms for Literary Study* (Chicago: University of Chicago Press, 1990), pp. 233–49. See also Frank Kermode's defence of the concept of a literary canon in *An Appetite for Poetry* (London: Collins, 1989), p. 15.
9. For further definitions and discussions of intertextuality, see Andrew Bennett and Nicholas Royle, *An Introduction to Literature, Criticism and Theory* (London: Prentice Hall/Harvester Wheatsheaf), pp. 70–1; Brenda Marshall, *Teaching the Postmodern* (New York: Routledge, 1992), pp. 121–46; and Martin Montgomery, Alan Durant, Nigel Fabb, Tom Furniss and Sara Mills, *Ways of Reading* (London: Routledge, 1992), pp. 157–66.
10. For discussion of similar oppositions, in literary criticism, between science and art, the technocratic and the spiritual, see Terry Eagleton, *Literary Theory: An Introduction* (Oxford: Blackwell, 1983), p. 199.
11. Michel Foucault, *The Order of Things*, trans. Alan Sheridan (London: Tavistock, 1970), p. 385.
12. Claude Lévi-Strauss, *The Savage Mind* (London: Weidenfeld and Nicolson, 1966), p. 247.

13. Roland Barthes, *Image–Music–Text*, trans. Stephen Heath (London: Fontana, 1977), p. 145.
14. Belsey, *Critical Practice*, p. 7.
15. William Shakespeare, *Hamlet*, The Arden Shakespeare, ed. Harold Jenkins (London: Methuen, 1982), I.ii.77–86. Further references to this edition are given within the text.

Chapter 1

1. David Lodge, *Nice Work* (London: Penguin, 1989), p. 39.
2. Ibid., pp. 292–3.
3. Ibid., p. 40.
4. Ferdinand de Saussure, *Course in General Linguistics*, trans. Roy Harris (London: Duckworth, 1983), p. 97. For useful, introductory accounts of semiotics, see Terence Hawkes, *Structuralism and Semiotics* (London: Methuen, 1977), pp. 19–28; David Robey, 'Modern Linguistics and the Language of Literature', in Ann Jefferson and David Robey (eds), *Modern Literary Theory*, 2nd ed. (London: Batsford, 1986), pp. 46–51; and Graeme Turner, *British Cultural Studies* (London: Unwin Hyman, 1990), pp. 11–23. For criticism of the way Saussure has been interpreted, see Brian Vickers, *Appropriating Shakespeare* (New Haven: Yale University Press, 1993), pp. 4–14.
5. Saussure, *Course in General Linguistics*, pp. 65–6.
6. Ibid., p. 115.
7. Jacques Derrida, *Of Grammatology*, trans. Gayatri Spivak (Baltimore: Johns Hopkins University Press, 1976), p. 158.
8. Jean Baudrillard, *Simulations*, trans. Paul Foss, Paul Patton and Philip Beitchman (New York: Semiotext(e), 1983), p. 25.
9. Ibid., p. 26.
10. For further discussion of Renaissance players and playhouses seen as symbols of protean mutability, see Steven Mullaney, *The Place of the Stage* (Chicago: Chicago University Press, 1988), pp. 50–1; and Louis Adrian Montrose, 'The Purpose of Playing: Reflections on a Shakespearean Anthropology', *Helios*, n. s., 7 (1980), 51–74. For further accounts of playing, playhouses and the social contexts of Renaissance drama, see A. R. Braunmuller and Michael Hattaway (eds), *The Cambridge Companion to English Renaissance Drama* (Cambridge: Cambridge University Press, 1990); Michael Bristol, *Carnival and Theater* (New York: Methuen, 1985); Douglas Bruster, *Drama and the Market in the Age of Shakespeare* (Cambridge: Cambridge University Press, 1992); Andrew Gurr, *Playgoing in Shakespeare's London*, 2nd ed (Cambridge: Cambridge University Press, 1987); Andrew Gurr, *The Shakespearean Stage 1574–1642*, 3rd ed. (Cambridge: Cambridge University Press, 1992); Annabel Patterson, *Shakespeare and the Popular Voice* (Cambridge, MA: Blackwell, 1989); Robert Weimann, *Shakespeare and the Popular Tradition in the Theater* (Baltimore: Johns Hopkins University Press, 1978); Stanley Wells (ed.), *The Cambridge Companion to Shakespeare Studies* (Cambridge: Cambridge University

Press, 1986); Glynne Wickham, *Early English Stages, 1300–1600*, vol. 2 (London: Routledge and Kegan Paul, 1963).

11. William Shakespeare, *A Midsummer Night's Dream*, The Arden Shakespeare, ed. Harold F. Brooks (London: Methuen, 1979), V.i.26–7.

12. For an account of the history of playhouse building, see Gurr, *Shakespearean Stage*, pp. 119–21.

13. For a detailed account of the rise and fall of the various boy and adult companies, see ibid., pp. 33–67. For distinctions between boy and adult styles of acting, see Gurr, *Playgoing*, pp. 158–64 and Alexander Leggatt, *English Drama: Shakespeare to the Restoration 1590–1660* (London: Longman, 1988), pp. 10–11.

14. These headings are adapted from the distinction made between a 'theatre of enchantment' and a 'theatre of estrangement' in Neil Carson, 'John Webster: The Apprentice Years', *Elizabethan Theatre*, 6 (1978), 76–87 (80).

15. Richard Halpern's similar point about *Julius Caesar* in relation to The Globe was the inspiration for my own point about *Tamburlaine Part I* performing a commemorative function. See Richard Halpern, *Shakespeare Among the Moderns* (Ithaca: Cornell University Press, 1997), p. 77.

16. Christopher Marlowe, *The Complete Plays*, ed. J. B. Steane (Penguin: Harmondsworth, 1969), I.ii.34–51. Further references to this edition are given within the text.

17. For similar points, see Gurr, *Playgoing*, p. 105.

18. Bristol, *Carnival and Theater*, p. 65. For further discussion of role-playing and impersonation in the Renaissance, see Stephen Greenblatt's influential *Renaissance Self-Fashioning* (Chicago: University of Chicago Press, 1980).

19. Jürgen Habermas, *The Structural Transformation of the Public Sphere*, trans. Thomas Burger (Cambridge: Polity Press, 1989), p. 9. I am also indebted to Richard Halpern's interesting discussion of Habermas in relation to Shakespeare in Halpern, *Shakespeare Among the Moderns*, pp. 69–78.

20. Leonard Tennenhouse, *Power on Display* (New York: Methuen, 1986), p. 103.

21. See Desiderius Erasmus, *Praise of Folly*, trans. Betty Radice (Harmondsworth: Penguin, 1971), pp. 175–8.

22. The contradictory implications of the theatricalisation of authority on the Renaissance stage are also discussed in Stephen Greenblatt, 'Invisible bullets: Renaissance authority and its subversion, *Henry IV* and *Henry V*', in Jonathan Dollimore and Alan Sinfield (eds), *Political Shakespeare* (Manchester: Manchester University Press, 1985), pp. 43–5.

23. Edward Burns, *Character: Acting and Being on the Pre-Modern Stage* (London: Macmillan, 1990), p. 128.

24. Simon Shepherd and Peter Womack, *English Drama: A Cultural History* (Oxford: Blackwell, 1996), p. 63. Shepherd and Womack's discussion of the play was the stimulus for my own interpretation of it.

25. Francis Beaumont, *The Knight of the Burning Pestle*, ed. John Doebler

Notes to pp. 32–44

(London: Edward Arnold, 1967), 'Induction', ll. 34–5, 43. Further references to this edition are given within the text.

26. This point is made in Shepherd and Womack, *English Drama*, p. 62.
27. Ibid., p. 63.
28. For further discussion of Othello's inscription/self-inscription as honorary white, see Ania Loomba, *Gender, Race, Renaissance Drama* (Manchester: Manchester University Press, 1989), pp. 48–64. Issues of race and racism are also dealt with in Emily Bartels, 'Making More of the Moor: Aaron, Othello, and Renaissance Refashionings of Race', *Shakespeare Quarterly*, 41 (1990), 433–54; Arthur Little, Jr., '"An essence that's not seen": The Primal Scene of Racism in *Othello*', *Shakespeare Quarterly*, 44 (1993), 304–24; Michael Neill, 'Unproper Beds: Race, Adultery, and the Hideous in *Othello*', *Shakespeare Quarterly*, 40 (1989), 383–412; and Karen Newman, '"And wash the Ethiop white": femininity and the monstrous in *Othello*', in Jean Howard and Marion O'Connor (eds), *Shakespeare Reproduced: The Text in History and Ideology* (New York: Methuen, 1987), pp. 141–62.
29. William Shakespeare, *Othello*, The Arden Shakespeare, ed. M. R. Ridley (London: Methuen, 1958). Further references to this edition are given within the text.
30. For an interesting, differently focused discussion of displacement in *Othello*, see Julia Genster, 'Lieutenancy, Standing In, and *Othello*', *English Literary History*, 57 (1990), 785–809.
31. For further discussion of Machiavellian and other types of efficiency in the play, see Andrew Mousley, 'Language as Cultural Capital and Identity as Appropriation: Shakespeare's *Othello* and Renaissance Commonplace Books', in Suzanne Stern-Gillet, Tadeusz Slawek, Tadeusz Rachval and Roger Whitehouse (eds), *Culture and Identity: Selected Aspects and Approaches* (Katowice: University of Silesia Press, 1996), pp. 287–93.
32. For further discussion of Iago as improviser, see Greenblatt, *Renaissance Self-Fashioning*, pp. 232–7.

Chapter 2

1. Quoted in Shakespeare, *The Sonnets and A Lover's Complaint*, ed. John Kerrigan (London: Penguin, 1986), p. 19.
2. Jonathan Culler, *Structuralist Poetics* (London: Routledge and Kegan Paul, 1975), p. 5. For other accounts of structuralism, see Hawkes, *Structuralism and Semiotics*, pp. 11–18; Ann Jefferson, 'Structuralism and post-structuralism' in Jefferson and Robey (eds), *Modern Literary Theory*, pp. 92–121; David Robey (ed.), *Structuralism: An Introduction* (Oxford: Clarendon, 1973); Robert Scholes, *Structuralism in Literature* (New Haven: Yale University Press, 1974), pp. 1–12; Raman Selden and Peter Widdowson, *A Reader's Guide to Contemporary Literary Theory*, 3rd ed. (New York: Harvester Wheatsheaf, 1993), pp. 103–24; John Sturrock, *Structuralism* (London: Paladin, 1986).
3. Culler, *Structuralist Poetics*, p. 5.

4. Saussure, *Course in General Linguistics*, pp. 13–14.
5. Hawkes, *Structuralism and Semiotics*, p. 119.
6. Barthes, *Image–Music–Text*, p. 146.
7. Thomas Hardy, *Chosen Poems*, ed. James Gibson (London: Macmillan Education, 1975), p. 81.
8. Ibid., p. 81.
9. Tzvetan Todorov, *The Poetics of Prose*, trans. Richard Howard (Oxford: Blackwell, 1977), p. 43.
10. Ibid., pp. 42–52; Franco Moretti, *Signs Taken for Wonders*, trans. Susan Fischer, David Forgacs and David Miller (London: Verso, 1983), pp. 130–56; Vladimir Propp, *Morphology of the Folktale*, 2nd ed., trans. Laurence Scott (Austin: University of Texas Press); A. J. Greimas, *Structural Semantics*, trans. Daniele McDowell, Ronald Schleifer and Alan Velie (Lincoln: University of Nebraska Press, 1983).
11. Foucault, *Order of Things*, p. xiv.
12. Ibid., p. xi.
13. Ibid.
14. Roland Barthes, *Mythologies*, trans. Annette Lavers (London: Granada, 1973), p. 11.
15. Ibid., p. 60.
16. Saussure, *Course in General Linguistics*, p. 115.
17. Culler, *Structuralist Poetics*, pp. 225–6.
18. Philip Sidney, *A Defence of Poetry*, ed. Jan Van Dorsten (Oxford: Oxford University Press, 1966), p. 45.
19. For further discussion of tragedy and travesty, see Naomi Conn Liebler, *Shakespeare's Festive Tragedy* (London: Routledge, 1995).
20. William Shakespeare, *As You Like It*, The Arden Shakespeare, ed. Agnes Latham (London: Methuen, 1975), V.iv.107–14. Further references to this edition are given within the text.
21. William Shakespeare, *King Lear*, The Arden Shakespeare, ed. Kenneth Muir (London: Methuen, 1972), I.i..35. Further references to this edition are given within the text.
22. For other attempts to theorise tragedy/Shakespearean tragedy, see Walter Benjamin, *The Origins of German Tragic Drama*, trans. John Osborne (London: Verso, 1985); A. C. Bradley, *Shakespearean Tragedy* (London: Macmillan & Co., 1904); René Girard, *Violence and the Sacred*, trans. Patrick Gregory (Baltimore: Johns Hopkins University Press, 1977); Lucien Goldmann, *The Hidden God*, trans. Philip Thody (London: Routledge and Kegan Paul, 1976); John Kerrigan, *Revenge Tragedy* (Oxford: Clarendon, 1997); Liebler, *Shakespeare's Festive Tragedy*; Friedrich Nietzsche, *The Birth of Tragedy*, trans. Walter Kaufmann (New York: Vintage Books, 1967); A. D. Nuttall, *Why Does Tragedy Give Pleasure?* (Oxford: Clarendon, 1996); Timothy Reiss, *Tragedy and Truth* (New Haven: Yale University Press, 1980); M. S. Silk (ed.), *Tragedy and the Tragic* (Oxford: Clarendon, 1996); George Steiner, *The Death of Tragedy* (London: Faber and Faber, 1961); Raymond Williams, *Modern Tragedy* (London: Chatto and Windus, 1966). For useful surveys of theories of tragedy, see John Drakakis (ed.), *Shakespearean Tragedy* (London: Longman, 1992), pp. 1–44; John

Drakakis and Naomi Conn Liebler (eds), *Tragedy* (London: Longman, 1998), pp. 1–20; and Clifford Leech, *Tragedy* (London: Methuen, 1969). See also Drakakis and Liebler (eds), *Tragedy*, for a useful anthology of writings on tragedy.

23. John Webster, *The Duchess of Malfi*, New Mermaids, ed. Elizabeth Brennan (London: Ernest Benn, 1964), I.ii.171–7. Further references to this edition are given within the text.
24. Sigmund Freud, *The Interpretation of Dreams*, The Penguin Freud Library, vol. 4, trans. James Strachey (London: Penguin, 1976), p. 367.
25. John Webster, *The White Devil*, The Revels Plays, ed. John Russell Brown (London: Methuen, 1960), V.iv.118–21. Further references to this edition are given within the text.
26. Aristotle, *The Poetics*, trans. Stephen Halliwell (London: Duckworth, 1987), p. 37.
27. Ibid., p. 43.
28. Ibid.
29. Reiss, *Tragedy and Truth*, p. 14.
30. Ibid., pp. 16–17.
31. Aristotle, *Poetics*, p. 42.
32. Thomas Norton and Thomas Sackville, *Gorbuduc*, in T. W. Craik (ed.), *Minor Elizabethan Tragedies* (London: J. M. Dent, 1974).
33. Thomas Kyd, *The Spanish Tragedy*, New Mermaids, 2nd ed., ed. J. R. Mulryne (London: A. and C. Black, 1989), III.ii.7. Further references to this edition are given within the text.
34. Aristotle, *Poetics*, p. 41.
35. Sidney, *Defence of Poetry*, pp. 31–2.

Chapter 3

1. Jean-François Lyotard, *The Postmodern Condition*, trans. G. Bennington and B. Massumi (Manchester: Manchester University Press, 1984), p. 82.
2. For an extensive discussion of the connection of literary theory in general to Romanticism, see Andrew Bowie, *From Romanticism to Critical Theory* (London: Routledge, 1997). For more general discussion of the continuities and discontinuities between poststructuralism and earlier types of criticism, see Ann Jefferson, 'Structuralism and Poststructuralism', in Jefferson and Robey (eds), *Modern Literary Theory*, pp. 116–19. For introductory accounts of poststructuralism, see Christopher Norris, *Deconstruction: Theory and Practice*, 2nd ed. (London: Routledge, 1991); Selden and Widdowson, *Reader's Guide to Contemporary Literary Theory*, pp. 125–73; Jonathan Culler, 'Derrida', in John Sturrock (ed.), *Structuralism and Since: From Lévi-Strauss to Derrida* (Oxford: Oxford University Press, 1979), pp. 154–80.
3. Cleanth Brooks, *The Well Wrought Urn*, revised ed. (London: Methuen, 1968), p. 13.
4. See Selden and Widdowson, *Reader's Guide to Contemporary Literary Theory*, for a similar point, p. 127.

5. Barthes, *Image–Music–Text*, p. 142.
6. Jacques Derrida, *Writing and Difference*, trans. Alan Bass (London: Routledge and Kegan Paul, 1978), pp. 29–30.
7. Roland Barthes, *The Pleasure of the Text*, trans. Richard Miller (Oxford: Blackwell, 1990), p. 14.
8. Derrida, *Writing and Difference*, p. 6.
9. Ibid., p. 6.
10. Derrida, *Of Grammatology*, p. 144.
11. Ibid., p. 145.
12. Ibid.
13. Derrida, *Writing and Difference*, p. 280; Jacques Derrida, *Positions*, trans. Alan Bass (London: The Athlone Press, 1987), p. 26.
14. Derrida, *Positions*, p. 20.
15. Emmanuel Kant, *The Critique of Judgement*, trans. James Creed Meredith (Oxford: Clarendon, 1952), pp. 104, 92.
16. William Wordsworth, *The Prelude of 1805* in *The Prelude, 1799, 1805, 1850*, ed. Jonathan Wordsworth, M. H. Abrams and Stephen Gill (New York: W. W. Norton, 1979), V.595–605.
17. For a useful discussion of this conception of literary discourse, see Derek Attridge, *Peculiar Language: Literature as Difference from the Renaissance to James Joyce* (London: Methuen, 1988), pp. 3–7.
18. For a succinct as well as provocative account of the errancy and ambiguity of love in the play, see Terry Eagleton, *William Shakespeare* (Oxford: Blackwell, 1986), pp. 21–6.
19. Barthes, *Pleasure of the Text*, pp. 9–10.
20. See the similar points made about love in Terry Eagleton, *Shakespeare*, pp. 18–19.
21. Catherine Belsey, *The Subject of Tragedy* (London: Methuen, 1985), p. 42. For other discussions of individualism/inwardness in *Hamlet*, see Francis Barker, *The Tremulous Private Body* (London: Methuen, 1984), pp. 25–40; Katharine Eisaman Maus, *Inwardness and Theater in the English Renaissance* (Chicago: University of Chicago Press, 1995), pp. 1–6; and Andrew Mousley, '*Hamlet* and the Politics of Individualism', in Mark Thornton Burnett and John Manning (eds), *New Essays on Hamlet* (New York: AMS Press, 1994), pp. 67–82. For further discussion of concepts of self in the Renaissance see Andrew Mousley, 'Renaissance Selves and Life Writing: *The Autobiography* of Thomas Whythorne', *Forum for Modern Language Studies*, 26 (1990), 222–30; and Andrew Mousley, 'Self, State, and Seventeenth-Century News', *The Seventeenth Century*, 6 (1991), 149–68.
22. Some of these points are made in Mousley, '*Hamlet* and the Politics of Individualism', pp. 68–9.
23. Robert Watson, 'Tragedy' in Braunmuller and Hattaway (eds), *Cambridge Companion to English Renaissance Drama*, p. 318.
24. Ben Jonson, *The Alchemist*, Methuen English Texts, ed. Peter Bement (London: Methuen, 1987), I.ii.198. Further references to this edition are given within the text.
25. Vickers, *Appropriating Shakespeare*, p. 39.

Chapter 4

1. Useful discussions of the use of psychoanalytic categories in modern literary theory include: Maud Ellman (ed.), *Psychoanalytic Literary Criticism* (London: Longman, 1994), pp. 1–34; Shoshana Felman (ed.), *Literature and Psychoanalysis* (Baltimore: Johns Hopkins University Press), pp. 5–10; Elizabeth Wright, *Psychoanalytic Criticism* (London: Methuen, 1984).
2. Jacques Lacan, *The Four Fundamental Concepts of Psycho-Analysis*, trans. Alan Sheridan (London: Hogarth Press, 1977), p. 197.
3. Ellman (ed.), *Psychoanalytic Literary Criticism*, p. 16.
4. Sigmund Freud, *On Sexuality*, The Penguin Freud Library, vol. 7, trans. James Strachey (London: Penguin, 1977), p. 109.
5. Ibid., p. 157.
6. Ibid., p. 144.
7. Jean Laplanche, *Life and Death in Psychoanalysis*, trans. Jeffrey Mehlman (Baltimore: Johns Hopkins University Press, 1976), p. 20.
8. For a discussion of metaphor and metonymy in relation to the Freudian concepts of condensation and displacement, see Wright, *Psychoanalytic Criticism*, pp. 23–4.
9. Julia Kristeva, *Black Sun: Depression and Melancholia*, trans. Leon S. Roudiez (New York: Columbia University Press, 1989), p. 43.
10. Laplanche, *Life and Death*, p. 20.
11. Jacques Lacan, *Écrits: A Selection*, trans. Alan Sheridan (London: Tavistock, 1977), p. 297.
12. Ben Jonson, *Bartholmew Fair*, New Mermaids, ed. G. R. Hibbard (London: Ernest Benn, 1977), 'Induction', ll. 62–5. Further references to this edition are given within the text.
13. Ben Jonson, *Timber: or Discoveries*, in *The Complete Poems*, ed. George Parfitt (Harmondsworth: Penguin, 1975), p. 417.
14. For an interesting discussion of the links between Bakhtin's work on carnival and the psychoanalytically oriented work of Julia Kristeva, see Pam Morris, 'Re-routing Kristeva: from pessimism to parody', *Textual Practice*, 6 (1992), 31–46.
15. Mikhail Bakhtin, *Rabelais and his World*, trans. Helene Iswolsky (Bloomington: Indiana University Press, 1984), p. 10.
16. Ibid., p. 11.
17. Ibid., pp. 18, 81.
18. Ibid., p. 19.
19. For further discussion of carnival in *Bartholmew Fair*, see Jonathan Haynes, 'Festivity and the Dramatic Economy of *Bartholomew Fair*', *English Literary History*, 51 (1984), 645–68; and Peter Womack, *Ben Jonson* (Oxford: Blackwell, 1986), pp. 144–59.
20. John Ford, *'Tis pity She's a Whore*, New Mermaids, ed. Brian Morris (London: Ernest Benn, 1968), I.i. passim. Further references to this edition are given within the text.
21. Michael Neill, '"What Strange Riddle's This?": Deciphering *'Tis Pity She's a Whore*', in Michael Neill (ed.), *John Ford: Critical Re-Visions* (Cambridge: Cambridge University Press, 1988), p. 163.
22. Ibid., p. 163.

Chapter 5

1. For challenging and wide-ranging discussions of history and historicism, see Paul Hamilton, *Historicism* (London: Routledge, 1996); and David Simpson, 'Literary Criticism and the Return to "History"', *Critical Inquiry*, 14 (1988), 721–47. For discussions of history and forms of historicism in specific relation to the Renaissance, see Albert Cook, 'Historiography and/or Historicism: Context and Theoretical (De)-Integration of Renaissance Drama', *Centennial Review*, 40 (1996), 31–47; Lisa Jardine, 'Strains of Renaissance Reading', *English Literary Renaissance*, 25 (1995), 289–306; Katharine E. Maus, 'Renaissance Studies Today', *English Literary Renaissance*, 25 (1995), 402–14; and Kathleen E. McLuskie '"Old Mouse-Eaten Records": The Anxiety of History', *English Literary Renaissance*, 25 (1995), 415–31. All of the above make some reference to New Historicism, but for further discussions of New Historicism, see note 14, below.
2. Debora Shuger, *Habits of Thought in the English Renaissance* (Berkeley: University of California Press, 1990), p. 6.
3. Niccolò Machiavelli, *The Prince*, trans. George Bull (Harmondsworth: Penguin, 1961). See especially Chapter XVIII, 'How Princes should honour their word'. For further discussion of the emergent discourse of politics in *The Prince*, see Thomas Greene, 'The End of Discourse in Machiavelli's *The Prince*', in Patricia Parker and David Quint (eds), *Literary Theory/Renaissance Texts* (Baltimore: Johns Hopkins University Press, 1986), pp. 372–96; and Andrew Mousley, 'The Prince and Textual Politics', in Martin Coyle (ed.), *Niccolò Machiavelli's The Prince: New Interdisciplinary Essays* (Manchester and New York: Manchester University Press, 1995), pp. 151–73.
4. R. M. Rayner, *A Short History of Britain*, 3rd ed. (London: Longman, 1957), p. 1.
5. Michel Foucault, 'Nietzsche, Genealogy, History', in Paul Rabinow (ed.), *The Foucault Reader* (New York: Pantheon, 1984), pp. 87–8.
6. Fredric Jameson, *The Ideologies of Theory: Essays 1971–1986*, vol. 2 (London: Routledge, 1988), p. 175.
7. Quoted in Gilles Deleuze and Félix Guattari, *Anti-Oedipus*, trans. Robert Hurley, Mark Seem and Helen Lane (London: Athlone Press, 1984), p. 21.
8. Stephen Greenblatt, *Shakespearean Negotiations* (Oxford: Clarendon, 1988), p. 1.
9. Raphael Samuel, *Theatres of Memory*, vol. 1 (London: Verso, 1994), pp. 196–7.
10. Ibid., p. 198.
11. Ibid., pp. 195–6.
12. Ibid., p. 198.
13. Hamilton, *Historicism*, p. 41.
14. This chapter does not engage with debates surrounding New Historicism, as I see New Historicism, or at least some of it, as continuous with what I have been referring to as an 'expressive' view of history. For discussions of New Historicism, see Jean E. Howard, 'The New

Historicism in Renaissance Studies', *English Literary Renaissance*, 16 (1986), 13–43; Edward Pechter, 'The New Historicism and its Discontents: Politicizing Renaissance Drama', *Proceedings of the Modern Language Association*, 102 (1987), 292–303; Richard Strier, Leah Marcus, Richard Helgerson and James G. Turner, 'Historicism, New and Old: Excerpts from a Panel Discussion', in Claude J. Summers and Ted-Larry Pebworth (eds), *'The Muses Common-Weale': Poetry and Politics in the Seventeenth Century* (Columbia: University of Missouri Press, 1988), pp. 207–17; Harold Veeser (ed.), *The New Historicism* (New York: Routledge, 1994).

15. Greenblatt, *Renaissance Self-Fashioning*, p. 11.
16. Ibid., p. 13.
17. Lawrence Stone, *The Causes of the English Revolution 1529–1642* (London: Routledge and Kegan Paul, 1972), p. 3.
18. Ibid., p. 22.
19. Ibid., p. 37.
20. Janet Coleman, 'Machiavelli's *via moderna*: medieval and Renaissance attitudes to history', in Coyle (ed.), *Niccolò Machiavelli's The Prince*, pp. 41–2.
21. Ibid., p. 42.
22. Leggatt, *English Drama*, p. 154.
23. Rowland Wymer, *Webster and Ford* (Basingstoke: Macmillan, 1995), p. 41.
24. James I, 'A Speech to the Lords and Commons of the Parliament at White-hall', in James I, *The Workes 1616* (Hildesheim: Georg Olms, 1971), p. 529. The spelling from this facsimile edition has been modernised.
25. William Shakespeare, *Henry V*, The Arden Shakespeare, ed. J. H. Walter (London: Methuen, 1954), I.ii.96. Further references to this edition are given within the text.

Chapter 6

1. Julia Kristeva distinguishes three different aspects of feminist struggle in Julia Kristeva, 'Women's Time', *Signs*, 7 (1981), 13–35 (33–4); Selden and Widdowson summarise three historical waves of feminism in Selden and Widdowson, *Reader's Guide to Contemporary Literary Theory*, pp. 206–32; Toril Moi divides feminist criticism into 'female' criticism and 'feminine' theory in Toril Moi, 'Feminist Literary Criticism', in Jefferson and Robey (eds), *Modern Literary Theory*, pp. 215–20. Both Moi and Selden and Widdowson offer good introductions to feminist criticism. For other useful introductions/discussions, see Catherine Belsey and Jane Moore (eds), *The Feminist Reader: Essays in Gender and the Politics of Literary Criticism* (Basingstoke: Macmillan, 1989); Mary Eagleton (ed.), *Feminist Literary Criticism* (London: Longman, 1991), pp. 1–23; Myra Jehlen, 'Gender', in Lentricchia and McLaughlin (eds), *Critical Terms for Literary Study*, pp. 263–73; Toril Moi, *Sexual/Textual Politics* (London: Methuen, 1985); and Elaine Showalter (ed.), *The New Feminist Criticism* (New York: Pantheon,

1985). For an especially wide ranging collection of essays on feminism, see Linda Nicholson (ed.), *Feminism/Postmodernism* (New York: Routledge, 1990).
2. Eagleton (ed.), *Feminist Literary Criticism*, p. 5.
3. Ibid., p. 6.
4. Niall Lucy, *Postmodern Literary Theory* (Oxford: Blackwell, 1997), p. 32. See also Bowie, *From Romanticism to Critical Theory.*
5. 'The romantic "poem"', writes Lucy, 'becomes the psychoanalytic "dream"' (p. 36). The expressive theory of history discussed in Chapter 5 has arguably Romantic affiliations. The connection of Marxism to Romanticism will be glanced at in the next chapter.
6. Lucy, *Postmodern Literary Theory*, p. 37.
7. Hélène Cixous, 'The Laugh of the Medusa', in Elaine Marks and Isabelle de Courtivron (eds), *New French Feminisms* (Brighton: Harvester, 1981), p. 246.
8. Judith Butler, *Gender Trouble* (New York: Routledge, 1990), p. 34.
9. Ibid., p. 33.
10. Ibid., p. 137.
11. Ibid., p. 138.
12. Ibid., p. 145.
13. Ibid., p. 112.
14. Valerie Wayne (ed.), *The Matter of Difference: Materialist Feminist Criticism of Shakespeare* (Ithaca: Cornell University Press, 1991), p. 8.
15. For these contrasting perspectives, see Butler, *Gender Trouble*, pp. 90–1 and Moi, 'Feminist Literary Criticism', in Jefferson and Robey (eds), *Modern Literary Theory*, p. 213.
16. Cixous, 'The Laugh of the Medusa', in Marks and de Courtivron, *New French Feminisms*, p. 246.
17. Hélène Cixous, 'Castration or Decapitation?', in Mary Eagleton (ed.), *Feminist Literary Theory: A Reader*, 2nd ed. (Oxford: Blackwell, 1996), p. 323.
18. Butler, *Gender Trouble*, p. 139.
19. Luce Irigaray, 'This Sex Which is Not One', in Marks and de Courtivron, *New French Feminisms*, p. 101.
20. For criticism of Cixous and Irigarary's essentialist conceptions of gender, see Kadiatu Kanneh, 'Love, mourning and metaphor: terms of identity', in Isobel Armstrong (ed.), *New Feminist Discourses* (London: Routledge, 1992), pp. 135–53; and Ann Rosalind Jones, 'Writing the Body: Toward an Understanding of l'Écriture féminine', in Showalter (ed.), *New Feminist Criticism*, pp. 361–77.
21. Hélène Cixous, *Rootprints*, trans. Eric Prenowitz (London: Routledge, 1997), p. 4.
22. Julia Kristeva, *Revolution in Poetic Language*, trans. Margaret Waller (New York: Columbia University Press, 1984), pp. 57, 58.
23. Moi, 'Feminist Literary Criticism', in Jefferson and Robey (eds), *Modern Literary Theory*, p. 213.
24. See, for example, Eagleton (ed.), *Feminist Literary Criticism*, pp. 8–11; and Selden and Widdowson, *Reader's Guide to Contemporary Literary Theory*, p. 213.

25. Elaine Showalter, 'Toward a Feminist Poetics', in Showalter (ed.), *New Feminist Criticism*, p. 141.
26. Thomas Middleton and Thomas Dekker, *The Roaring Girl*, The Revels Plays, ed. Paul Mulholland (Manchester: Manchester University Press, 1987), 'Prologue', ll. 7–8. Further references to this edition are given within the text.
27. Mary Beth Rose makes the similar point that the play 'calls for a joint creative effort by audience and playwrights to assess her identity' in Mary Beth Rose, *The Expense of Spirit: Love and Sexuality in English Renaissance Drama* (Ithaca: Cornell University Press, 1988), p. 79.
28. Ibid., pp. 80–1.

Chapter 7

 1. For introductions to Marxism and Marxist literary criticism, see Terry Eagleton, *Marxism and Literary Criticism* (London: Methuen, 1976); David Forgacs, 'Marxist Literary Theories', in Jefferson and Robey (eds), *Modern Literary Theory*, pp. 166–203; Selden and Widdowson, *Reader's Guide to Contemporary Literary Theory*, pp. 70–102. For extended discussions of Marxist concepts of literature, language and culture, informed in different ways by modern theory, see Tony Bennett, *Formalism and Marxism* (London: Methuen, 1979); Terry Eagleton, *Criticism and Ideology* (London: New Left Books, 1976); Fredric Jameson, *The Political Unconscious* (London: Methuen, 1981); Pierre Macherey, *A Theory of Literary Production*, trans. G. Wall (London: Routledge and Kegan Paul, 1978); and Raymond Williams, *Marxism and Literature* (Oxford: Oxford University Press, 1977).
 2. Karl Marx, *Capital*, vol. 1, trans. Ben Fowkes (London: Pelican, 1976), p. 167.
 3. Ibid., p. 204.
 4. Karl Marx and Friedrich Engels, *The Communist Manifesto*, trans. Samuel Moore (Harmondsworth: Penguin, 1967), p. 105.
 5. Ibid., p. 98.
 6. Karl Marx and Friedrich Engels, *Collected Works*, vol. 5 (London: Lawrence and Wishart, 1976). See especially pp. 59–62.
 7. Ibid., p. 62.
 8. Eagleton, *Marxism and Literary Criticism*, p. 18.
 9. Georg Lukács, *The Meaning of Contemporary Realism*, trans. John and Necke Mander (London: Merlin, 1963), p. 19.
10. Ibid., p. 19.
11. Ibid., p. 24.
12. Theodor Adorno, 'Reconciliation under Duress', trans. Rodney Livingstone, in Ernst Bloch, Georg Lukács, Bertolt Brecht, Walter Benjamin and Theodor Adorno, *Aesthetics and Politics* (London: New Left Books, 1977), p. 175.
13. Theodor Adorno, *Minima Moralia*, trans. E. F. N. Jephcott (London: New Left Books, 1974), p. 65.
14. Adorno, 'Reconciliation under Duress', p. 160.

15. Ibid., p. 160.
16. Theodor Adorno, *Aesthetic Theory*, trans. Robert Hullot-Kentor (London: Athlone Press, 1997), p. 175.
17. Bertolt Brecht, 'A Short Organum for the Theatre', in *Brecht on Theatre*, 2nd ed., trans. John Willett (London: Methuen, 1974), p. 192.
18. Ibid., p. 193.
19. Ibid., p. 186.
20. Ibid., p. 188.
21. Ibid., p. 192.
22. Ibid., p. 193.
23. Terry Eagleton, *The Ideology of the Aesthetic* (Oxford: Blackwell, 1990), p. 4.
24. Ibid., p. 23.
25. David Scott Kastan, 'Workshop and/as Playhouse: Comedy and Commerce in *The Shoemaker's Holiday*', *Studies in Philology*, 84 (1987), 324–37 (328). I am generally indebted to Kastan's discussion of the play.
26. Thomas Dekker, *The Shoemakers' Holiday*, New Mermaids, ed. D. J. Palmer (London: Ernest Benn, 1975), II.ii.17. Further references to this edition are given within the text.
27. Kastan, 'Workshop and/as Playhouse', 328.
28. As Kastan, in ibid., likewise suggests of Rafe and Jane's eventual marriage, 'The reconfirmation of Rafe and Jane's marriage asserts the power of love over hostile social and economic forces that threaten to divide and degrade' (329).
29. William Shakespeare, *Macbeth*, The Arden Shakespeare, ed. Kenneth Muir (London: Methuen, 1951), I.ii.18. Further references to this edition are given within the text.
30. Peter Stallybrass, '*Macbeth* and Witchcraft', in Alan Sinfield (ed.), *New Casebooks: Macbeth* (Basingstoke: Macmillan, 1992), p. 36.
31. Malcolm Evans, 'Imperfect Speakers: the Tale Thickens', in Sinfield (ed.), *New Casebooks: Macbeth*, p. 72.
32. Alan Sinfield, 'Introduction', in Sinfield (ed.), *New Casebooks: Macbeth*, p. 6.
33. Georges Bataille, *Eroticism*, trans. Mary Dalwood (London: Calder and Boyars, 1962), p. 63.
34. Ibid., p. 68.
35. Ibid., pp. 38–9.

Conclusion

1. Gardner, in Lovelock (ed.), *Donne*, p. 242.
2. Jameson, *Ideologies of Theory*, p. 175.

Select Bibliography

Adorno, Theodore, *Minima Moralia*, trans. E. F. N. Jephcott (London: New Left Books, 1977).

—— 'Reconciliation under Duress', in Ernst Bloch, Georg Lukács, Bertolt Brecht, Walter Benjamin and Theodore Adorno, *Aesthetics and Politics* (London: New Left Books, 1977).

—— *Aesthetic Theory*, trans. Robert Hullot-Kentor (London: Athlone Press, 1997).

Aristotle, *The Poetics*, trans. Stephen Halliwell (London: Duckworth, 1987).

Armstrong, Isabel (ed.), *New Feminist Discourses* (London: Routledge, 1992).

Aston, Elaine and Savona, George, *Theatre as Sign-System* (London: Routledge, 1991).

Attridge, Derek, *Peculiar Language* (London: Methuen, 1988).

Bakhtin, Mikhail, *Rabelais and his World*, trans. Helene Iswolsky (Bloomington: Indiana University Press, 1984).

Barker, Francis, *The Tremulous Private Body* (London: Methuen, 1984).

Barthes, Roland, *Mythologies*, trans. Annette Lavers (London: Granada, 1973).

—— *Image–Music–Text*, trans. Stephen Heath (London: Fontana, 1977).

—— *The Pleasure of the Text*, trans. Richard Miller (Oxford: Blackwell, 1990).

Bataille, Georges, *Eroticism*, trans. Mary Dalwood (London: Calder and Boyars, 1962).

Baudrillard, Jean, *Simulations*, trans. Paul Foss, Paul Patton and Philip Beitchman (New York: Semiotext(e), 1983).

Beaumont, Francis, *The Knight of the Burning Pestle*, ed. John Doebler (London: Edward Arnold, 1967).

Belsey, Catherine, *Critical Practice* (London: Methuen, 1980).

—— *The Subject of Tragedy* (London: Methuen, 1985).

Belsey, Catherine and Moore, Jane (eds), *The Feminist Reader: Essays in Gender and the Politics of Literary Criticism* (Basingstoke: Macmillan, 1989).

Bennett, Tony, *Formalism and Marxism* (London: Methuen, 1979).

Bowie, Andrew, *From Romanticism to Critical Theory* (London: Routledge, 1997).

Braunmuller, A. R. and Hattaway, Michael (eds), *The Cambridge Companion to English Renaissance Drama* (Cambridge: Cambridge University Press, 1990).

Brecht, Bertolt, *Brecht on Theatre*, 2nd ed., trans. John Willett (London: Methuen, 1974).

Bristol, Michael, *Carnival and Theater* (New York: Methuen, 1985).

Bruster, Douglas, *Drama and the Market in the Age of Shakespeare* (Cambridge: Cambridge University Press, 1992).

Burns, Edward, *Character: Acting and Being on the Pre-Modern Stage* (Basingstoke: Macmillan, 1990).

Butler, Judith, *Gender Trouble* (New York: Routledge, 1990).

Carson, Neil, 'John Webster: The Apprentice Years', *Elizabethan Theatre*, 6 (1978), 76–87.

Cixous, Hélène, 'The Laugh of the Medusa', in Elaine Marks and Isabelle de Courtivron (eds), *New French Feminisms* (Brighton: Harvester, 1981), pp. 245–64.

—— 'Conversations with Hélène Cixous and members of the Centre d'Études Féminines', in Susan Sellers (ed.), *Writing Differences: Readings from the Seminar of Hélène Cixous* (New York: St. Martin's Press, 1988), pp. 141–54.

—— 'Castration or Decapitation?', in Mary Eagleton (ed.), *Feminist Literary Theory: A Reader*, 2nd ed. (Oxford: Blackwell, 1996), pp. 322–5.

—— *Rootprints*, trans. Eric Prenowitz (London: Routledge, 1997).

Coleman, Janet, 'Machiavelli's *via moderna*: medieval and Renaissance attitudes to history', in Martin Coyle (ed.), *Niccolò Machiavelli's The Prince: New Interdisciplinary Essays* (Manchester: Manchester University Press), pp. 40–64.

Cook, Albert, 'Historiography and/or Historicism: Context and Theoretical (De)-Integration of Renaissance Drama', *Centennial Review*, 40 (1996), 31–47.

Culler, Jonathan, *Structuralist Poetics* (London: Routledge and Kegan Paul, 1975).

Davies, Tony, *Humanism* (London: Routledge, 1997).

Derrida, Jacques, *Of Grammatology*, trans. Gayatri Spivak (Baltimore: Johns Hopkins University Press, 1976).

—— *Writing and Difference*, trans. Alan Bass (London: Routledge and Kegan Paul, 1978).

—— *Positions*, trans. Alan Bass (London: Athlone Press, 1987).

Drakakis, John (ed.), *Shakespearean Tragedy* (London: Longman, 1992).

Drakakis, John and Liebler, Naomi Conn (eds), *Tragedy* (London: Longman, 1998).

Eagleton, Mary (ed.), *Feminist Literary Criticism* (London: Longman, 1991).

—— (ed.), *Feminist Literary Theory: A Reader*, 2nd ed. (Oxford: Blackwell, 1996).

Eagleton, Terry, *Criticism and Ideology* (London: New Left Books, 1976).

—— *Marxism and Literary Criticism* (London: Methuen, 1976).

—— *Literary Theory: An Introduction* (Oxford: Blackwell, 1983).

—— *William Shakespeare* (Oxford: Blackwell, 1986).

—— *The Ideology of the Aesthetic* (Oxford: Blackwell, 1990).

Ellman, Maud (ed.), *Psychoanalytic Literary Criticism* (London: Longman, 1994).

Erasmus, Desiderius, *Praise of Folly*, trans. Betty Radice (Harmondsworth: Penguin, 1971).

Felman, Shoshana (ed.), *Literature and Psychoanalysis* (Baltimore: Johns Hopkins University Press).

Ford, John, *'Tis Pity She's a Whore*, New Mermaids, ed. Brian Morris (London: Ernest Benn, 1968).

Foucault, Michel, *The Order of Things*, trans. Alan Sheridan (London: Tavistock, 1970).
—— 'Nietzsche, Genealogy, History', in Paul Rabinow (ed.), *The Foucault Reader* (New York: Pantheon, 1984), pp. 76–100.
Freud, Sigmund, *The Interpretation of Dreams*, The Penguin Freud Library, vol. 4, trans. James Strachey (London: Penguin, 1976).
—— *On Sexuality*, The Penguin Freud Library, vol. 7, trans. James Strachey (London: Penguin, 1977).
Greenblatt, Stephen, *Renaissance Self-Fashioning* (Chicago: University of Chicago Press, 1980).
—— 'Invisible bullets: Renaissance authority and its subversion, *Henry IV* and *Henry V*', in Jonathan Dollimore and Alan Sinfield (eds), *Political Shakespeare* (Manchester: Manchester University Press, 1985).
—— *Shakespearean Negotiations* (Oxford: Clarendon, 1988).
Gurr, Andrew, *Playgoing in Shakespeare's London*, 2nd ed. (Cambridge: Cambridge University Press, 1987).
—— *The Shakespearean Stage 1574–1642*, 3rd ed. (Cambridge: Cambridge University Press, 1992).
Habermas, Jürgen, *The Structural Transformation of the Public Sphere*, trans. Thomas Burger (Cambridge: Polity Press, 1989).
Halpern, Richard, *Shakespeare Among the Moderns* (Ithaca: Cornell University Press, 1997).
Hamilton, Paul, *Historicism* (London: Routledge, 1996).
Harland, Richard, *Superstructuralism* (London: Methuen, 1987).
—— *Beyond Superstructuralism* (London: Routledge, 1993).
Hawkes, Terence, *Structuralism and Semiotics* (London: Methuen, 1977).
Haynes, Jonathan, 'Festivity and the Dramatic Economy of *Bartholomew Fair*', *English Literary History*, 51 (1984), 645–68.
Howard, Jean E., 'The New Historicism in Renaissance Studies', *English Literary Renaissance*, 16 (1986), 13–43.
Irigaray, Luce, 'This Sex Which is Not One', in Elaine Marks and Isabelle de Courtivron (eds), *New French Feminisms* (Brighton: Harvester, 1981), pp. 99–106.
Jameson, Fredric, *The Political Unconscious* (London: Methuen, 1981).
—— *The Ideologies of Theory: Essays 1971–1986* (London: Routledge, 1988).
—— *Late Marxism* (London: Verso, 1990).
Jardine, Lisa, 'Strains of Renaissance Reading', *English Literary Renaissance*, 25 (1995), 289–306.
Jefferson, Ann and Robey, David (eds), *Modern Literary Theory*, 2nd ed. (London: Batsford, 1986).
Jenkins, Keith (ed.), *The Postmodern History Reader* (London: Routledge, 1997).
Jonson, Ben, *Bartholmew Fair*, The New Mermaids, ed. G. R. Hibbard (London: Ernest Benn, 1977).
—— *The Alchemist*, Methuen English Texts, ed. Peter Bement (London: Methuen, 1987).
Kant, Immanuel, *The Critique of Judgement*, trans. James Creed Meredith (Oxford: Clarendon, 1952).
Kastan, David Scott, 'Workshop and/as Playhouse: Comedy and

Commerce in *The Shoemakers' Holiday'*, *Studies in Philology*, 84 (1987), 324–37.

Kastan, David Scott and Stallybrass, Peter (eds), *Staging the Renaissance* (New York: Routledge, 1991).

Kerrigan, John, *Revenge Tragedy* (Oxford: Clarendon, 1997).

Kristeva, Julia, 'Women's Time', *Signs*, 7 (1981), 13–35.

—— *Revolution in Poetic Language*, trans. Margaret Waller (New York: Columbia Univesity Press, 1984).

Kyd, Thomas, *The Spanish Tragedy*, New Mermaids, 2nd ed., ed. J. R. Mulryne (London: A. and C. Black, 1989).

Lacan, Jacques, *Écrits: A Selection*, trans. Alan Sheridan (London: Tavistock, 1977).

—— *The Four Fundamental Concepts of Psychoanalysis*, trans. Alan Sheridan (London: Hogarth Press, 1977).

Laplanche, Jean, *Life and Death in Psychoanalysis*, trans. Jeffrey Mehlman (Baltimore: Johns Hopkins University Press, 1976).

Leavis, F. R., *The Common Pursuit* (London: Chatto and Windus, 1952).

Leech, Clifford, *Tragedy* (London: Methuen, 1969).

Liebler, Naomi Conn, *Shakespeare's Festive Tragedy* (London: Routledge, 1995).

Lodge, David, *Nice Work* (London: Penguin, 1989).

Lucy, Niall, *Postmodern Literary Theory* (Oxford: Blackwell, 1997).

Lukács, Georg, *The Meaning of Contemporary Realism*, trans. John and Necke Mander (London: Merlin, 1963).

Lyotard, Jean-François, *The Postmodern Condition*, trans. G. Bennington and B. Massumi (Manchester: Manchester University Press).

Marlowe, Christopher, *The Complete Plays*, ed. J. B. Steane (Penguin: Harmondsworth, 1969).

Marks, Elaine, and Courtivron, Isabelle de, *New French Feminisms* (Brighton: Harvester, 1981).

Marx, Karl, *Capital*, vol. 1, trans. Ben Fowkes (London: Penguin, 1976).

Marx, Karl and Engels, Friedrich, *The Communist Manifesto*, trans. Samuel Moore (Harmondsworth: Penguin, 1967).

—— *Collected Works*, vol. 5 (London: Lawrence and Wishart, 1976).

Maus, Katharine Eisaman, *Inwardness and Theater in the English Renaissance* (Chicago: University of Chicago Press, 1995).

Middleton, Thomas and Dekker, Thomas, *The Roaring Girl*, The Revels Plays, ed. Paul Mulholland (Manchester: Manchester University Press, 1987).

Moi, Toril, *Sexual/Textual Politics: Feminist Literary Theory* (London: Methuen, 1985).

Montrose, Louis Adrian, 'The Purpose of Playing: Reflections on a Shakespearean Anthropology', *Helios*, n.s., 7 (1980), 51–74.

Moretti, Franco, *Signs Taken for Wonders*, trans. Susan Fischer, David Forgacs and David Miller (London: Verso, 1983).

Morris, Pam, 'Re-routing Kristeva: from pessimism to parody', *Textual Practice*, 6 (1992).

Mousley, Andrew, 'Renaissance Selves and Life Writing: *The Autobiography* of Thomas Whythorne', *Forum for Modern Language Studies*, 26 (1990), 222–30.

—— 'Self, State, and Seventeenth-Century News', *The Seventeenth Century*, 6 (1991), 149–68.

—— '*Hamlet* and the Politics of Individualism', in Mark Thornton Burnett and John Manning (eds), *New Essays on Hamlet* (New York: AMS Press, 1994), pp. 67–82.

Mullaney, Steven, *The Place of the Stage* (Chicago: University of Chicago Press, 1988).

Neill, Michael (ed.), *John Ford: Critical Re-Visions* (Cambridge: Cambridge University Press, 1988).

Nicholson, Linda (ed.), *Feminism/Postmodernism* (New York: Routledge, 1990).

Norris, Christopher, *Deconstruction: Theory and Practice*, 2nd ed. (London: Routledge, 1991).

Pechter, Edward, 'The New Historicism and its Discontents: Politicizing Renaissance Drama', *PMLA*, 102 (1987), 292–303.

Reiss, Timothy, *Tragedy and Truth* (New Haven: Yale University Press, 1980).

Robey, David (ed.), *Structuralism: An Introduction* (Oxford: Clarendon Press, 1973).

Rose, Mary Beth, *The Expense of Spirit: Love and Sexuality in English Renaissance Drama* (Ithaca: Cornell University Press, 1988).

Samuel, Raphael, *Theatres of Memory*, vol. 1 (London: Verso, 1994).

Saussure, Ferdinand de, *Course in General Linguistics*, trans. Roy Harris (London: Duckworth, 1983).

Scholes, Robert, *Structuralism in Literature* (New Haven: Yale University Press, 1974).

Selden, Raman and Widdowson, Peter, *A Reader's Guide to Contemporary Literary Theory*, 3rd ed. (New York: Harvester Wheatsheaf, 1993).

Sellers, Susan (ed.), *Writing Differences: Readings from the Seminar of Hélène Cixous* (New York: St. Martin's Press, 1988).

Shakespeare, William, *Macbeth*, The Arden Shakespeare, ed. Kenneth Muir (London: Methuen, 1951).

—— *Henry V*, The Arden Shakespeare, ed. J. H. Walter (London: Methuen, 1954).

—— *Othello*, The Arden Shakespeare, ed. M. R. Ridley (London: Methuen, 1958).

—— *King Lear*, The Arden Shakespeare, ed. Kenneth Muir (London: Methuen, 1972).

—— *As You Like It*, The Arden Shakespeare, ed. Agnes Latham (London: Methuen, 1975).

—— *Twelfth Night*, The Arden Shakespeare, ed. J. M. Lothian and T. W. Craik (London: Methuen, 1975).

—— *A Midsummer Night's Dream*, The Arden Shakespeare, ed. Harold F. Brooks (London: Methuen, 1979).

—— *Hamlet*, The Arden Shakespeare, ed. Harold Jenkins (London: Methuen, 1982).

Sharratt, Bernard, *Reading Relations* (Brighton: Harvester, 1982).

—— *The Literary Labyrinth* (Brighton: Harvester, 1984).

Shepherd, Simon and Womack, Peter, *English Drama: A Cultural History* (Oxford: Blackwell, 1996).

Showalter, Elaine (ed.), *The New Feminist Criticism* (New York: Pantheon, 1985).

Shuger, Debora, *Habits of Thought in the Renaissance* (Berkeley: University of California Press, 1990).

Sidney, Philip, *A Defence of Poetry*, ed. Jan Van Dorsten (Oxford: Oxford University Press, 1966).

Silk, M. S. (ed.), *Tragedy and the Tragic* (Oxford: Clarendon, 1996).

Simpson, David, 'Literary Criticism and the Return to "History"', *Critical Inquiry*, 14 (1988), 721–47.

Sinfield, Alan (ed.), *New Casebooks: Macbeth* (Basingstoke: Macmillan, 1992).

Soper, Kate, *Humanism and Anti-Humanism* (London: Hutchinson, 1986).

Steiner, George, *The Death of Tragedy* (London: Faber and Faber, 1961).

Strier, Richard, Leah Marcus, Richard Helgerson and James G. Turner, 'Historicism, New and Old: Excerpts from a Panel Discussion', in Claude J. Summers and Ted-Larry Pebworth (eds), *'The Muses Common-Weale': Poetry and Politics in the Seventeenth Century* (Columbia: University of Missouri Press, 1988), pp. 207–17.

Sturrock, John, *Structuralism* (London: Paladin, 1986).

Tennenhouse, Leonard, *Power on Display* (New York: Methuen, 1986).

Todorov, Tzvetan, *The Poetics of Prose*, trans. Richard Howard (Oxford: Blackwell, 1977).

Turner, Graeme, *British Cultural Studies* (London: Unwin Hyman, 1990).

Veeser, Harold (ed.), *The New Historicism* (New York: Routledge, 1994).

Vickers, Brian, *Appropriating Shakespeare* (New Haven: Yale University Press, 1993).

Wayne, Valerie (ed.), *The Matter of Difference: Materialist Feminist Criticism of Shakespeare* (Ithaca: Cornell University Press, 1991).

Webster, John, *The Duchess of Malfi*, The Revels Plays, ed. John Russell Brown (London: Methuen, 1960).

Weimann, Robert, *Shakespeare and the Popular Tradition in the Theater* (Baltimore: Johns Hopkins University Press, 1978).

Wells, Stanley (ed.), *The Cambridge Companion to Shakespeare Studies* (Cambridge: Cambridge University Press, 1986).

Wickham, Glynne, *Early English Stages, 1300–1600*, vol. 2 (London: Routledge and Kegan Paul, 1963).

Williams, Raymond, *Modern Tragedy* (London: Chatto and Windus, 1966).

—— *Marxism and Literature* (Oxford: Oxford University Press, 1977).

Wilson, Richard and Dutton, Richard (eds), *New Historicism and Renaissance Drama* (London: Longman, 1992)

Womack, Peter, *Ben Jonson* (Oxford: Blackwell, 1986).

Wright, Elizabeth, *Psychoanalytic Criticism* (London: Methuen, 1984).

Wymer, Rowland, *Webster and Ford* (Basingstoke: Macmillan, 1995).

Index